# Smart Parenting™

## An *Easy* Approach to Raising Happy, Well-Adjusted Kids

## DR. PETER FAVARO

CB
CONTEMPORARY
BOOKS
A TRIBUNE NEW MEDIA COMPANY

**Library of Congress Cataloging-in-Publication Data**

Favaro, Peter J.
    SmartParenting : an easy approach to raising
happy, well-adjusted kids / Peter Favaro.
    p.    cm.
    ISBN 0-8092-3431-9
    1. Child rearing—United States—Miscellanea.
2. Child psychology—Miscellanea. 3. Adolescent
psychology—Miscellanea.    I. Title.
HQ769.F279 1994
649'.1—dc20                          94-47985
                                          CIP

SmartParenting™ is a registered trademark of
SmartParenting, Inc.

Excerpts from SmartParenting audiocassette workbook
by Peter Favaro. Copyright © 1994 by Nightingale-
Conant Corporation. Reprinted by permission of
Nightingale-Conant Corporation.

Parents please note:
Wherever it is suggested that you consult a pediatrician
for further information, we also recommend that you
consult your family physician, who has expert knowledge
and professional experience, and provides competent
care in these areas as well.

Published by Contemporary Books, Inc.
Two Prudential Plaza, Chicago, Illinois 60601-6790
Manufactured in the United States of America
International Standard Book Number: 0-8092-3431-9
10  9  8  7  6  5  4  3  2  1

This book is dedicated to all the people who produce, manage, and maintain the world's most precious natural resource.

# CONTENTS

# ACKNOWLEDGMENTS

Although my fingers tapped out the words in this book, *SmartParenting* was a collaborative effort to which I owe many people thanks and appreciation.

First, I would like to thank all of the people who contributed the anecdotes that are liberally sprinkled throughout this book. My friends all know me as a person who never shrinks (no pun intended) away from giving advice; the only cost to them is to see their stories in print: Greg and Laurie Stemm, Scott Howard, Antoinette and Pete Miglionico, Joanne Zimmer, Rosanne Underberg, Ken Peres and Fran Swan, Michelle Peltzman, Liz Leight, Robin and John Koloski, Alyssa Mandaro, Lynn Rubin, and countless others.

Thanks to Mark Hershhorn and Rick Weyerman of National Media Inc. for their support. Thanks also to Lotus Development Corporation Inc. for providing us with an efficient office and document managing system.

I would also like to thank all of my new friends at Contemporary Books who have helped make *SmartParenting* look and read as well as it does. Thanks to the typesetter, Ellen Ferar, and project editor, Gerilee Hundt, for burning the midnight oil on tight deadlines and ambitious production goals. Special thanks to my publisher, Christine Albritton, my publicity wiz, Maureen Musker, and her intern, Tina Chapman, and my wonderful, patient, and talented editor, Linda Gray, who always works above and beyond the call of duty. Thanks also to Amy Kelley for her hard sales work.

Thanks to Maitreyee Angelo in Chicago and Maryanne Schalk in Middle Village, New York, for helping me edit the original *SmartParenting* audiotape scripts that ultimately led to a more polished and sensible book manuscript.

Finally, thanks to my tireless, supportive, and motivating colleagues at SmartParenting, Inc., to whom I owe the remainder of my sanity. Apart from dressing me in funny-looking sweaters for my television appearances, they always bring out the best in me in any kind of media. Thank you Greg, Laurie, Nicholas (four), and Adam (two) for providing up-to-the-minute examples of what this project is all about; John, Scott, Michael Mann, Jim Beggins, Mark and Carol Miller, and Jeff Herman; and last but not least, the person who coordinates the day-to-day activities of SmartParenting and looks after the thirty-eight-year-old baby who wrote this book, Theresa Favaro.

# INTRODUCTION

Welcome to *SmartParenting*! This book is written to help make the difficult job of parenting preteen children easier and more rewarding. I have tried to organize it in a way that makes it fast and practical to read, with important points, stories, anecdotes, and examples set apart in shaded boxes. At the end of each chapter you'll find a quick review of the major concepts covered, as well as a few exercises that will help you put those concepts into practice.

You will see that many of the points made in *SmartParenting* are illustrated with real stories from everyday life. As a clinical psychologist, I see hundreds of people in my private practice who are probably a lot like you—good parents who are concerned about their children and who want advice designed to help their kids grow up emotionally healthy. I believe that all parents benefit from learning how to become good teachers, because that is what raising kids is all about—teaching them how to survive and thrive in a difficult and demanding world. By coaching and educating parents, children become happier and better adjusted. This is how I approach my work, and it's what this book is all about as well.

In reading *SmartParenting*, you will see that I have covered many of the "usual" topics such as behavior management and time-out, but

I have also spent a considerable amount of time talking about topics that are not so typical of parenting books, including how to build your child's confidence, self-esteem, sense of responsibility, and social skills. I've also included techniques for helping your children become more successful and confident achievers.

I hope that *SmartParenting* is the book you reach for when you are in need of advice on how to solve a problem, and that the advice given works for you. I also hope that you will take the time to discuss what you have learned in this book with others who are providing care for your children. Even if you disagree with a particular technique or point of view, if it stimulates a discussion that puts you on a better path with your children I am happy to be a part of that process. Thanks for letting me become a part of your family.

# 1

# THE BASICS OF
# SMARTPARENTING  ◀

If you are like most parents, you probably sometimes feel as though you have a hard time controlling your child's behavior. All kids go through stages when they don't do what you tell them, or they behave in ways that disappoint you or fall short of your expectations. All kids act irresponsibly at times, by not taking care of their things or not keeping up with schoolwork. Just how do you teach kids to be responsible, thoughtful human beings, while at the same time understanding that they are "just kids"?

Think about it for a second. Kids, especially kids under five, don't really understand what it means to be responsible. Most of their day is planned for them. Their clothes are washed and picked out for them, and their meals are cooked for them. What a life! It's always you parents who are messing things up by asking them to turn off the television, to keep their rooms neat, to do homework, or, the ultimate insult, to go to bed. From a kid's point of view, having to behave always involves giving up something—whether it's giving up the joy of punching around a little brother or sister, giving up watching television or playing video games, or giving up a little bit of the freedom that comes with growing up and taking responsibility. Out of frustration, parents let themselves believe that kids don't behave because they enjoy seeing their parents become miserable. That's not true at all. What is true is that kids will resist any change that causes discomfort. But as kids grow older they all have to face the changes in their life that come with becoming mature and independent. That's what discipline is all about—teaching kids how to grow up to be responsible and independent.

## TEMPERAMENT: YOUR CHILD'S BASIC PERSONALITY

Good teaching requires technique, but before we get into technique we need to take a few minutes to discuss the importance of understanding your child's basic personality, or *temperament*. Knowing your child's basic style will help you adjust your technique to his unique personality. All children are not created equal, you know; some children are easy to manage and some are quite difficult, even if you do everything by the book. That's because each child has a unique temperament. *Temperament* is a word that describes those parts of a personality that are influenced more by genes than the environment.

### FOUR-YEAR-OLD KEVIN: A DIFFICULT TEMPERAMENT

Kevin's mom and dad describe their son as a "high maintenance" child. From the time he was born, Kevin was difficult to comfort. He was squirmy and irritable, and when he wasn't tended to in just the right way he let everyone know about it. Another word Kevin's parents use to describe him is "intense"; even his facial expressions are always serious. As a baby, Kevin had a difficult time sleeping at night. He was restless and irritable. Even now he is up two or more times during the night. As a toddler he was more defiant than most, easily frustrated, and prone to pushing other children. As a four-year-old, he is still very stubborn. He has to go to his room for a time-out when he misbehaves, which, according to his parents, is often.

Kevin's parents are normal and loving in every way. They read books and watch videos about parenting and take effective parenting classes. Yet they admit that Kevin's behavior is somewhat disappointing to them. They feel that he should listen more, be less aggressive, and play nicer with other children. They worry about his adjustment once he starts school full-time. Although Kevin is far from a "bad" kid, he tends to wear his parents down.

Actually Kevin couldn't care less about what the parenting books, tapes, videos, and seminars say. He was born with an intensity that can't always be moderated by time-out, positive reinforcement, or any of the other techniques that we psychologists recommend. In the end, however, he will do just fine. That's because he has loving, concerned parents who stick to a few very basic principles—such as picking and choosing their battles with Kevin carefully.

Everybody knows of one lucky set of parents who have a child who is blissfully easygoing and does most of what she is told. That's a function of temperament, just as much as the stubborn, irritating behaviors are.

Regardless of how easygoing your child is, all parents go through periods of testing with their child. Understanding where your child's temperament falls on the "easy" to "difficult" scale is very important. Children who require more attention and who are difficult to manage require more patience, more repetition to learn good behavior, and often times a bit more breathing room. You will find that kids who are stubborn or defiant by nature will often "dig in." They refuse to apologize for misbehavior, won't admit they are wrong about anything, and don't like to talk about or review their behavior. That's why parents need to trust that the simplest ways of correcting behavior are often the best. Kids don't have to apologize, confess, or make promises about changing their ways in order to learn to behave better. Sometimes all it takes is experiencing the natural consequences of their actions (something you will read a lot more about later). Knowing where your child fits on this easy- or difficult-to-manage scale will help you set reasonable goals for improving certain behavior, but more importantly it will also help you cope during those times when you might blame yourself for something that even the best child-care experts would have difficulty handling.

# A SIMPLE RATING EXERCISE

As a simple exercise, rate your child on a scale of one to ten on these behaviors. Use one as the lowest rating and ten as the highest.

1. *Does what he or she is told after only one or two times of reminding.* _____

2. *Shows responsibility about doing chores.* _____

3. *Is easy to get out of bed and ready for the day.* _____

4. *Is gentle/not aggressive with other children.* _____

5. *Is good at sharing/taking turns.* _____

6. *Learns from experience. (After he or she gets into trouble for something, will feel sorry and not repeat the same misbehavior over and over.)* _____

7. *Is respectful toward adults; will not talk back or use fresh language.* _____

8. *Is truthful.* _____

9. *Understands the relationship between what he or she does and the consequences of the behavior (e.g., knows he or she will get in trouble if he or she bothers or teases others).* _____

10. *Other adults find him or her pleasant to be around.* _____

While this list is far from comprehensive or scientific, it is a starting point for determining some basic elements of your child's personality. Most parents will rate their child between sixty-five and eighty-five on this scale, depending on what has been happening lately and what kind of mood the parents are in when answering the questions. If you find yourself rating your child at sixty or below on this scale, what you are saying is that you have a difficult time managing your child, and that your child is difficult to manage in general *and would be for anybody.*

## YOUR PERSONALITY AND PARENTING STYLE ◀

Now that you've taken a first look at your child's behavior style, what about your own? The apple doesn't fall far from the tree, you know, and I'm sure you have already seen how much your child learns by watching you. A lot of what we do as parents is the result of what our parents did to us. Many of you have made a conscious effort to be different parents than your parents were. Usually that means you want to give your children more freedom and more choices. Parents do want to give their children more freedom, but at the same time, they worry about overindulging them. Most parents want to know how strict to be, and whether giving a child choices can spoil them, so let's use those two concerns to focus in on your own parenting style.

On the one hand you want your children to be free to make choices for themselves, and you don't want to dictate to them. On the other hand, you don't want to give your kids too much control of their lives because you know they are not capable of making good judgments for themselves all the time. You would never want to give children the freedom to have bowls full of chocolate kisses for breakfast in the morning, but you would want them to have the freedom to choose between cornflakes and oatmeal. This is a simple illustration of how important it is for parents to find the right balance in giving their children certain freedoms and choices. Many of us grew up with parents who held the philosophy of "You will do it this way, and only this way, because I am the parent, and you will do what I say." Child behavior experts agree that there is no need for this kind of rigid approach. As a matter of fact, not giving a child any choices at all has a tendency to create a more defiant and rebellious attitude once a child reaches adolescence. That's when some real problems can begin. Research shows that children grow up best when parents let children speak their minds without being overly criticized, and when children are allowed some choice over the things that govern their lives. Now let me throw in a third thing about being an effective parent. Parents who have reasonably high expectations of their children produce children who are high achievers. All of this translates into three simple rules of developing an effective parenting style:

1. Let your children express their wishes. That doesn't mean you have to grant them all like a genie in a bottle—just let your kids talk without criticizing them.

2. Allow them to make choices. The choices come from you, not them, but allowing more than one choice offers children some sense of control over their lives.

3. Set high goals for your children. Have high expectations. This will help them set high goals for themselves and reach their potential.

## TOO STRICT, TOO LOOSE, OR "JUST RIGHT"?

Let's go back to the example of what to have for breakfast to show how parents can be too strict, too loose, or "just right" in their approach. Here is the too-strict parent. Six-year-old Joey has just requested a bowl of chocolate kisses for breakfast. The too-strict parent replies with criticism and no choices: "What are you, crazy? You know you can't have chocolate for breakfast. I'm ashamed of you. You will eat oatmeal or wait for lunch." The too-loose parent gives in or gives too many choices by saying, "I guess you're going to have to learn for yourself. Eat whatever you want. But if you choose not to have chocolate kisses I'll take you out for breakfast, and you can have anything you want." The "just right" parent says, "You know, that would be quite delicious, wouldn't it? Too bad chocolate kisses aren't on the breakfast menu this morning. You can have cornflakes and bananas, oatmeal, or some French toast." The "just right" parent doesn't care that the child made a silly request. This parent figures kids will be kids and will try to get away with whatever they can. There is no criticism, but no giving in either.

Now I can just imagine you are saying, "Oh yeah, I could give my kid those choices, and he would tell me he doesn't want any of them, that he still wants chocolate kisses. What do I do then?" What you do is *stick to your guns.* You prevent the situation from becoming an argument by saying, "Listen, we can't argue about this because those are your only choices. When you are ready to tell me what you want to eat I will get it for you, as long as it is oatmeal, cornflakes, or French toast." Many parents tend to engage their children in long, drawn-out negotiating sessions. This is a time-consuming and frustrating process. The conversation becomes an exercise in who is in control, and you don't need that, especially if you are trying to get some things done or get ready for work in the morning. The more you are willing to negotiate, the more your child will force you to give in to what he wants.

Remember, you provide the choices, and your child chooses between them and is not allowed to modify the list. From this you can see that giving a child choices doesn't mean you can't be strict. Limiting options is an OK kind of strictness. Criticizing or demeaning a child for expressing himself is not OK. The optimum parenting style allows for self-expression in the child but controls the options given to the child all the time.

## BASIC TECHNIQUES

Now let's talk about some specific techniques that help parents become better child managers or disciplinarians.

**Don't ask questions about things you already know the answers to.** This is one of the simplest and easy-to-follow techniques for everyday situations. The following story illustrates the problems that can occur when we ask kids questions about things we already know the answers to.

### JACK AND AMY

Mom has just observed Jack push Amy down during a squabble about a toy. Jack is clearly in the wrong, and Mom saw the whole incident.

Now, Jack is a child who doesn't like to admit when he is wrong. This tends to infuriate and frustrate his parents, who wonder whether he will ever take responsibility for anything he does. His mother and father are always trying to get him to own up to his behavior and promise not to repeat his actions. Usually this causes Jack to start making up stories about what happened.

Jack's mom and dad tend to make a very simple mistake whenever they confront him about his behavior—they ask him questions. In this case, Mom walks up to him and asks, "Did you just push your sister down?" Jack looks around nervously and blurts out, "I did not." This immediately causes Amy to start crying. (Even at the tender age of four she knows that her brother is on the hot seat, and the time is ripe for revenge.) Mom asks a second question, "Then why is she crying?" Jack's reply is, "I don't know." Here's Mom's third question: "Are you sure you don't know?" Jack's response is: "I don't know." By this time a number of interesting things have happened. Jack is moving deeper and deeper into his avoidance and lying pattern. His stress level is increasing because he knows that eventually he is going to be punished—he just doesn't know when. He refuses to give in to his mother and confess to what he has done because he knows she'll punish him anyway—probably twice, once for pushing his sister and once for lying about it. Why should he give her the satisfaction of an apology? Jack's mother is enraged. She knows he is lying, and she hates it when he does. Why won't he just tell the truth? Doesn't he see how much easier she would be on him?

Apparently not. The two have reached a standoff. The situation is already far removed from the original problem, which is "Jack shouldn't push his sister around." It has now become "Jack shouldn't lie about what he has done." Unfortunately, it doesn't end there. Jack and his mom continue arguing. Mom then asks another question. "Why don't you stop arguing with me and behave?" Now the issue grows into "Why does Jack argue with Mom?", "Why does Jack lie?", and "Why does Jack push his sister?" It is no surprise when Jack replies, "Why do you always take her side in everything? Can't you stop picking on me? I didn't do anything." Now Mom feels as though she must defend herself. Jack's comments cause her to feel guilty. Amy is a better behaved child and gets into less trouble, but does Mom pick on Jack? The issue grows even more complicated, and the situation gets worse. Mom tries to send Jack to his room, but he won't go. Mom now feels angry and guilty and has a splitting headache.

When parents fall into the trap of asking kids too many questions about their behavior they do three things:

1. They give kids the opportunity to lie or avoid what really happened.

2. They allow themselves to become frustrated, which can, in turn, cause them to give up before the situation is adequately resolved.

3. They allow the child to control the situation.

An alternative to this sequence of events involves not questioning Jack about his behavior. Instead, confront the behavior directly and take action. What Mom should say is, "I saw you push your sister down. Apologize to her and give back the toy, or go to your room now." This will not necessarily prevent Jack from denying what he did, but it will eliminate all of the subsequent sidetracks these situations usually take. If Jack says, "I didn't push her down," the reply should be, "I know what I saw. I guess you have made your choice. Go to your room." In this scenario, Mom is not going to give Jack a chance to avoid the consequences of his behavior, and Jack will be more likely to apologize to his sister and own up to his actions.

Please understand that this situation was based on Jack's mom observing something that she was absolutely sure happened. Many times, it is impossible to determine what the reality is when siblings fight and parents do not see it. When you haven't seen what has happened and one sibling complains about another's behavior the best way to handle it is to bring the children in front of you, ask for both sides of the story, and invite suggestions on how to handle it. After both have spoken their piece, separate them and tell them to play away from each other for an hour. Essentially, you are giving the children a time-out from each other. I'll explain more about this technique in a minute, but for now let's consider whether parents should avoid asking any other questions.

The same advice about not asking questions applies to any situation where you have prior knowledge of something, but feel the urge to have your child confess to it. Examples of these situations include:

- Knowing in advance from a teacher that your child is doing poorly in school or has failed a test, don't ask, "How did you do in school today?" or "Is there something you want to tell me about school?"

- Knowing in advance that your child has gotten into trouble for fighting, stealing, or lying, don't ask, "Is there anything you want to tell me about?" or "Do you want to tell me about what so-and-so's mother just said to me?"

- Knowing in advance that your child was someplace where she wasn't supposed to be, don't ask, "Would you like to tell me where you were this afternoon?"

If you want your children to tell the truth, don't give them the opportunity to lie. You may think your questions are giving your children the opportunity to *tell the truth*, but much of the time you ask these questions to make them squirm because you have found out information that they will probably try to hide from you. Confront your children openly, without criticism, and they will learn to tell you the truth and be more open in general.

## TIME-OUT: IT'S ONLY EFFECTIVE IF YOU KNOW HOW TO USE IT

Everyone uses a technique called "time-out" when their child gets out of hand. On the surface, "time-out" is a simple concept. A child misbehaves and, as a result, has to go to her room or sit in a corner for a while. Technically, time-out is a bit more complicated than that, and knowing a little more about it can make it much more effective.

Let's start with the expression "time-out"; this is a shortened form of the expression "time-out from reinforcement." The concept of time-out actually involves removing a child from a reinforcing situation so that he will be motivated to behave in order to get back into that situation. The notion that a child has to be given a time-out from something *positive* is very important, because it suggests that if an environment is hostile or chaotic, a place where there is hitting, yelling, screaming, and other undesirable behavior happening, a child doesn't have any motivation to return to that environment after a time-out. Instead time-out may represent a *relief* from that kind of environment. Effective use of time-out requires that your home or environment be a relatively pleasant place to begin with. This is the single most important aspect of using time-out to control behavior. In addition, there are several other things you might want to know about using time-out.

**The length of time a child spends in time-out is not really critical.** The important thing is that you have interrupted a negative behavior. This is especially important to know for younger children or children who have a difficult time staying in one place for any length of time. For kids under five a good rule of thumb is one or two minutes of time-out for every year. Ten to fifteen minutes, twenty minutes at the maximum, is all that is required for older children.

**It is not important for a child to emerge from time-out and offer a detailed explanation of why he did what he did and why he will never ever do it again.** Chances are he *will* do it again; you just hope that eventually he gets the message. Sometimes parents say, "You can come out when you are ready to apologize," or "You can come out when you are ready to tell me why what you did was wrong." I don't believe this is as important as feeling the consequence of misbehavior. Much of the time, children will apologize right away or quickly verbalize what it was they did wrong just to avoid being in time-out. It doesn't change their behavior, it just makes it easier to give an insincere apology or explanation. Parents must use their judgment in this area. If an apology or an explanation is sincere and it looks as though the child has learned a lesson by talking about it, then this is by far more important than "doing the time," as it were.

**Time-out is time for the parent to cool off, too.** You might want to use the time-out period to collect your thoughts and review your own behavior. There might be something you regret about the way you handled things yourself.

## WHAT IF I SEND MY CHILD TO HER ROOM AND SHE WON'T GO?

Whenever I talk about using time-out someone always tells me, "I try to use time-out, but my kid just won't go." A good example of this was nine-year-old Marissa. Marissa caught wise to the fact that if her mother told her to go to time-out and she flat out refused, there wasn't much her mother could do about it. Marissa's mother didn't want to drag her to her room, not at nine years old. What could she do? I advised that when Marissa refused to go to time-out her mother should say in a calm, even tone, "OK, Marissa, I'm going to ask you to go to your room one more time. You can either listen to me and go or I'll have to think about dealing with it another way." With that I told Marissa's mom to end the interaction by turning and walking away. The first time this happened Marissa was flabbergasted by the fear of the unknown. "What are you going to do, beat me?" Marissa yelled after her. The funny thing about Marissa's comment was that Marissa's mom had never once laid so much as a finger on her, even though she had always been a stubborn, difficult-to-manage child. It's just that not knowing what her mother was capable of shifted the balance of power. After several minutes of a tantrum Marissa turned on her heels, marched into her room, and started crying. When she came out, she apologized to her mom, something previously unheard of.

Marissa continued to test her mother's authority from time to time by not going to her room. The strategy I gave her mom called for waiting until Marissa wanted something from her later in the day. When Marissa approached her mom for a favor, say a ride over to a friend's house, her mom's reply was simply, "Look, we're not getting along very well today. Before when I asked you to go to your room you refused. It would have been all over if you had listened, but now I'm angry and I don't feel like taking you to your friend's house. Tomorrow is another day. You can try to be better behaved, and then I'll be more cooperative, too, but for today, no favors." In this little lecture Marissa's mom makes sure to do a few very important things. First, she makes sure to let Marissa know that there is a relationship between how Marissa behaves toward her and vice versa. If Marissa behaves, Mom is cooperative; if she misbehaves, Mom isn't cooperative. Second, Marissa's mom makes sure to explain that the situation is temporary and will change when Marissa's behavior changes. By saying, "Tomorrow is another day. You can try to be better behaved, and then I'll be more cooperative, too," Mom is letting Marissa know that her anger doesn't last forever.

In the heat of the moment it may be difficult to see this, but a child's use of sheer defiance as a way of gaining control is a weak strategy. Children rely on their parents for too many things. If a parent decides to withdraw from providing all the little favors and nice things that a good parent provides, kids feel it immediately. As soon as parents realize this, defiance becomes much less of a problem. Defiant behavior can only succeed when parents fuel a child's stubbornness by being equally stubborn, dragging out arguments, or giving in to defiant behavior. The key is to withdraw, calmly and neutrally, by giving the child a choice between time-out and whatever it is you will ultimately decide to do.

## WHAT ABOUT SPANKING?

What about hitting kids? There are plenty of parents who got a good sound spanking when they misbehaved and grew up just fine. Is there a limit to all this psychology, and an appropriate time to spank a child to deliver the message that negative behavior just won't be tolerated? The answer to these questions is that there is never an appropriate time to hit a child for any reason. We have at least fifteen years of solid research to back up the fact that spanking a child does nothing to improve her behavior in the short run, and in fact may cause psychological problems in the long run.

Spanking children delivers the message that hitting another person is an acceptable way of solving problems. When you spank your child for misbehaving, how can you explain that it is OK for *you* to do that but not OK for your older son to hit his younger brother when the little one annoys him? It's not. Children will imitate their parents behavior, and if your children see you hit, they will also hit.

Another reason to avoid spanking your children is that no matter how careful you are it is impossible to control what happens in a spanking situation.

## A STORY ABOUT SPANKING WITH A VERY UNHAPPY ENDING

Not too long ago I worked with a parent who went to spank a child for bringing a soda into the living room. As the parent reached out to grab the child, the child reeled back. He wobbled over on his ankle, losing his balance. By this time the parent wasn't looking to spank the child anymore, but to prevent him from falling backward. As she reached out for the child, it frightened him even more, causing him to fall back faster onto a thick glass coffee table. The child suffered thirty stitches in the head. This parent was not a child abuser—she just believed that whacking a child lightly on the butt was necessary to make a point. It was what her parents had done to her. Fortunately, the child recovered with no permanent injuries, but the mother suffered guilt, depression, embarrassment, and remorse for years.

The point of this story is obvious—don't spank your children. The SmartParenting techniques you are learning will be much more effective.

## REHEARSE FOR TOUGH SITUATIONS

Parents often tell me that they know when their children are heading for a rough time. For some parents and children, certain situations set off negative behavior. These situations might include shopping, riding in the car, or visiting certain friends or family members.

## TOMMY HATES TO GO SHOPPING

Tommy's mom knows that she will run into trouble whenever she takes her eight-year-old shopping in a mall or center where there is a toy store. As soon as he sees the store he starts whining for an expensive toy that Tommy's mom just can't afford. It's not as if Tommy doesn't have a room full of nice toys at home. Tommy's mom feels as though he doesn't appreciate the things he has and always wants more. Sound familiar? The problem is that Tommy doesn't really like shopping with his mother, and he feels as though there should be something in it for him. This idea was partially reinforced by Tommy's mom, who would often buy him toys to keep him quiet. When things got out of hand, though, Tommy's mom put her foot down—no more toys. She would break *that* pattern once and for all. This, of course, made Tommy angry. Indeed, he felt as though a toy was his "payoff" for accompanying her on her boring shopping trips, and if he didn't get the toy, he would dish out as much aggravation as possible. This way she would either go home as upset as he was or just give in and go back to buying toys for him. Shopping trips became nightmares. Tommy's mom would have loved to leave him home, but sitters were hard to find. What else could she do?

I advised Tommy's mom to rehearse shopping trips with him the night before. Right before bedtime Tommy's mom would prepare him for the experience by saying, "Tomorrow we are going shopping together. I realize you don't really want to go, but there's nothing we can do about that. And I know you are bored by shopping, but I'd like to try something that will make it better for both of us." At this point Tommy's curiosity was piqued. His mom continued, "You know I don't like it when you ask me to buy you things every time we go shopping. Actually, I wouldn't mind buying you a reward for keeping me company every once in a while, but sometimes you take advantage of that. I need to be sure that you will not give me a hard time so this is what will happen. If you come shopping with me and do not ask me for anything the whole time we are there I will let you pick from three pieces of paper. One piece of paper says that we will rent a movie before we go home; one piece of paper says I will buy you a pack of football cards; and one piece of paper says I will stop into the toy store and get you something small—five dollars or less. If you ask me for even one thing, I won't let you play the game. If you don't, we'll play just before we leave to go home." Tommy was very excited by his mom's imaginative game. They reviewed the rules of the game one more time, then Tommy's mom asked him what would happen if he forgot the rules and asked for something. Tommy quickly replied, "I don't get to play the game."

The next day they went shopping, and Tommy was like a new kid. He was helpful and cooperative the whole time. At the end of the day he chose the piece of paper that said rent a movie. They rented Tommy's favorite movie and had a great time watching it, too. Tommy's mom used more than just rehearsal to help him cooperate. She made up a little positive reinforcement game that gave him an incentive to behave. Together, these strategies worked wonders for Tommy.

Parents can use the time right before bedtime to rehearse for an upcoming difficult situation. Be sure that you present the situation positively, and try not to lecture. Here's another example: "Billy, tomorrow we are going over to Aunt Lucy's house. Your cousin Jimmy will be there, and you guys sometimes play a little too rough with each other. I want you to think about this conversation tomorrow so that if you think things are getting out of hand you will tell Jimmy to stop and break it up." In this instance, telling Billy to think about the conversation helps make him more aware of his behavior.

The same kind of rehearsal can be used to talk about an event that happened during the day that you don't want to see happen tomorrow.

## LETTING YOUR CHILD EXPERIENCE "NATURAL CONSEQUENCES"

Often, if you are patient enough, children will work themselves into a jam, and the difficulty they cause themselves is worse than any sanction you could deliver yourself. This is called letting children experience the "natural consequences" of their behavior. As an example, here is a very common problem that parents have with school-age kids:

how do I get my child to get ready for school in the morning without having a war?

Morning time is hectic, especially if Mom and Dad both work. There is usually far too little time for everyone to do what they need to do. Unfortunately, the last thing a kid wants to do in the morning is get ready for school. Watching TV or playing Nintendo would be much more desirable. Morning problems usually start with a simple request to get going. This is usually followed by a period of temporary hearing loss on the part of the child. The next reminder is usually more stern. The *next* one begins to sound like you are about to hit the panic button. The less time there is to get ready, the more everyone's stress and anxiety increases.

When does the system first break down? The first time the system breaks down is when parents do not give specific information as a first request. Instead of saying, "Get ready," parents need to say, "Come into the bathroom and start to wash up." At this point they may need to walk the child to the bathroom and get the whole process going. At every point in the process they may need to jump-start the behavior a little bit. Now parents will tell me, "If I do that I'll be spending my whole morning policing the situation." That may be true the first couple of times, but hang on and hear the rest of the strategy.

In very difficult situations the child's avoidance and stubbornness are just too much for parents to be able to handle effectively. No matter how much pushing and prodding a parent does, the child still manages to take too much time and make everyone else late. What are you supposed to do then? Well, one solution requires that you devote an entire morning to helping your child learn an object lesson about her behavior. I have often recommended that parents, just for one morning, not say anything at all to their child to help her get ready. After you wake her up, take the time to get yourself ready, and only yourself. Let her do whatever she wants. Do nothing to prod or push her to get ready. When your child is almost hopelessly late (let's say there are only about twenty minutes left to get dressed and out the door), and you are all ready for whatever it is you have to do, walk over and in a very calm tone say, "Can I talk to you for a second?" Wait for

> *Rehearse and role-play situations that you know are going to be difficult for your child to handle.*

a response and say, "How do you plan on getting to school today?" Explain that she is quite late because she didn't take the time she needed to get ready. If she misses the bus, how will she get to school? (Do not offer to drive.) If she misses school, how will she explain it to the teachers and principal? You can't write her a note, unless the note says, "Jane didn't feel like getting ready for school today, so she was very late and couldn't get a ride."

In most cases there is just enough time left to barely get it together and make the school bus, but in some cases I have actually recommended letting the child miss a portion of her day at school. Now I must caution you here. It is always best to get the cooperation of the school principal and teachers when you do this. They must be willing to take your child aside and talk to her about responsibility, too. The entire thing will backfire if the teachers or principal comes down hard on you because you let your child miss a few hours of school to teach her a lesson. The point is to let your child feel the "natural consequences" of her behavior. If you want your child to grow up to be responsible you cannot dress her every morning, or do school projects and book reports for her.

## PUTTING CHOICES, REHEARSAL, AND NATURAL CONSEQUENCES TOGETHER

We can combine a few of the things we have learned so far to develop a program for, say, getting your child prepared for school on time. The night before, around bedtime, it would be helpful to have a brief talk about tomorrow's schedule. Here is a typical bedtime chat—the purpose of which is to make things around the house go a bit more smoothly.

"Let's talk about something that is really important for tomorrow. We have been running late in the morning because you are busy watching television when you should be getting dressed. Tomorrow, you can either get up, wash up, brush your teeth, and get dressed without the TV on, or you can try it the way you did today. If you are late, or if I have to tell you to do anything twice, the TV will go off and you won't be allowed to watch it for the rest of the day and night. You can decide what to do."

In this little talk there are no threats, only choices. You are giving your child the opportunity to think about what might happen if he decides to try to get ready with the television on. You are also giving him fair warning of what might happen if he makes a choice that produces negative consequences.

## REWARDS, PRAISE, AND REINFORCEMENT ◀

An example I gave before showed how Tommy's mom made up a little game to help him behave better during shopping trips. That example is a great illustration of how it is so much better to motivate a child positively by praising, rewarding, and offering incentives than it is to do it negatively by taking things away, yelling, or punishing. Praise and kind words are the most important and easiest forms of reinforcement to deliver to children. Unfortunately, they are also the easiest things to forget. That's why I always recommend that parents follow this easy rule: *Try to make sure that the positive things that you say to a child outnumber the negative things by three to one.* For every one negative thing you say, try to find three positive things to say. Some parents tell me, "My child doesn't do three positive things in a day!" Well, you

> *For every negative thing you say to your child, try to make at least three positive comments.*

don't have to praise the outcome of what your child does. You can praise cooperation, effort, listening, helpfulness around the house, or even a few minutes of peace and quiet that your child doesn't even realize he's giving you!

Does praising a child or giving her a small reward mean that you have to bribe kids to get them to behave? Many parents resent the idea of having to "pay off" their children to do the things they should be responsible for on their own. There are two sides to this question, as well as a moderate, practical solution. First, of course it is unwise to bribe a child with outlandish gifts just to behave. If you start buying your kids expensive toys and rewards when they are in grade school, by the time they get to high school, you'll be buying them cars and trips to the Bahamas to do their homework or make curfew. It is also unrealistic to think that children should do everything out of the goodness of their hearts, with no praise or rewards. After all, people work for incentives for much of their adult lives. Salespeople work on commission, employees get raises for good performance, and most of us go to work every morning because we will be rewarded in the form of a paycheck. Why should children feel differently?

In technical terms we talk about motivation as being either "intrinsic," coming from within, or "extrinsic," coming from outside. Naturally, it is always better to have a child behave because it feels good, or because it is the right thing to do. But sometimes it is necessary to jump-start a behavior with an extrinsic incentive or reward. Rewards never have to be expensive; it is much more important that they be personal and special. That is why treats like going to a movie, staying up an extra half hour to watch a show on television, and having a special day doing something with Mom or Dad are more worthwhile rewards than expensive electronic games, or things like that.

As usual, your children will give you the best information on whether or not you have gone overboard rewarding them. If, for instance, you ask your child to set the table and his first response is, "What do I get for it?" then it's a safe bet that you have gone too far with the rewards.

Always remember, though, that you can *never* dish out too many kind words or pats on the back when it comes to influencing or motivating your child's behavior.

## TECHNIQUES OF LAST RESORT  ◀

The last thing I will relate to you regarding rewards is a system for modifying your child's behavior that works in the opposite way that most reward or behavior modification systems work. I will tell you now that I don't recommend parents try this first, and I only mention it because in cases where children have been extremely stubborn about changing a behavior, parents have reported some success with this. Rewards typically work to get a child motivated to do a task in order to earn something; this system works by letting a child know that if she doesn't do the task, something will be taken away.

▼

### WHEN ALL ELSE FAILS . . .

Nancy has a nine-year-old boy, Mark, who had a very fresh mouth. His way of communicating was nasty, rude, and just plain gruff. Nancy tried all of the traditional ways to get Mark to use better language and to be more polite but nothing worked. Finally, Nancy took a piece of cardboard and taped it onto the kitchen wall. On the cardboard she taped four dollars in quarters. This was Mark's allowance for the next week. Every time Mark was fresh, Nancy would walk up to the cardboard and rip off a quarter, making next week's allowance a quarter less for every infraction. The first week Mark lost $3.25, the next week he lost $1.75, and in subsequent weeks he lost nothing. If children are particularly stubborn and do not respond to rewards, behavioral incentives, or praise, you might try a system like this.

Another application of this principle utilizes something called a "Sunday box" or a "Sunday closet." A Sunday box works well with children who are very careless about leaving their toys on the floor. The system is simple: Mom warns that if toys are not picked up by the end of the day, everything left on the floor will go into a box or closet and stay there until Sunday. Obviously the consequence seems much more severe if the infraction happens on Monday, but a more standardized system would require complicated bookkeeping. In any case, the length of time the toy is removed is not really as important as showing the child that there is a consequence for the behavior.

Please remember that the examples of the Sunday box and the allowance system are given primarily as methods of last resort. Negative methods of motivating children are, on the whole, never as effective as those that utilize praise and positive reinforcement. Just think of adult behavior. For example, society has put into place methods to support the practice of safe driving. Most of those methods involve punishment for driving mistakes. Take speeding. We are given speeding tickets and fines to prevent us from exceeding the speed limit. The more we speed, the more severe the consequences—we are forced to pay stiffer fines, suffer insurance consequences, and eventually, if we speed too often, society sends us straight to our rooms by taking away our driving privileges altogether. Now with that progression of consequences, it should follow that every reasonable adult should never speed. It makes even more sense that if we make a mistake, and we are caught speeding during a moment of poor attention to our driving habits, we should never do it again, right? After all, getting the ticket should teach us a lesson, shouldn't it? In reality, getting a speeding ticket teaches many lessons.

> *Praise and kind words are often the best tools to use to improve your child's behavior.*

It teaches the lesson of where there are speed traps. It teaches the lesson of what an unmarked police cruiser looks like. It teaches the lessons about what it takes to avoid getting caught the next time. You might even go so far as to say that it teaches us how to be better, more devious speeders. Well, why should it be any different for children? If we try to motivate children by taking things away or fining them or punishing them, they will not necessarily learn to behave any better; instead they will learn how to avoid being caught the next time.

A very important key to all of this is understanding what side of behavior to work on. Every behavior has a negative side and a positive side. Let's take the case of siblings who fight with each other. The negative side of the behavior is all of the things that the siblings do to annoy or abuse each other. The positive side of the behavior is all of the things they should be doing instead, like cooperating, sharing, and speaking politely. If parents spend more time punishing siblings for abusing each other, they will learn how to be more sneaky and better at ambushing each other. They will develop new and devious ways of tormenting each other. They will reduce the whole procedure to a single look or glance that will send the other flying into a rage. Where else but in a household with two siblings close in age can you hear a parent yell at kids because of a fight that started when one of them *looked* at the other?

If you get to the point where the only way you can influence your children is by taking everything they own away from them, your home is more likely to take on the feel of a penitentiary rather than a place where people feel comfortable living and interacting. These last few tactics I described should not be the everyday tools you rely on to influence your child's behavior. If things get too rough and you feel as though things are out of control, consult a professional who can give you some good coaching.

## WHAT DOES IT REALLY TAKE TO BE A SMART PARENT?

Developing a good parenting style requires that you stick to just a few basic principles. These principles will help you maintain a more peaceful household with better behaved kids and a less stressful environment for you. Will it make things perfect? Not at all. Kids aren't nearly as interested in keeping law and order around the house as you are, and, being kids, they will always test the limits of what they can get away with. At the same time, there are days when *you* won't be acting your best, and you will lose your temper and just want to close yourself in behind a locked door. These ups and downs are part and parcel of what it takes to be a parent. Believe it or not, though, and you won't believe it until it happens, the day your children leave for college or go off and get married, you will probably wish for some of the noise you want to get away from now.

In the following chapters we will cover what I feel are the most important everyday issues, events, and behaviors involving parents and kids. I've tried to identify the most important aspects of a child's social, emotional, and educational growth and development, and I've developed strategies for helping you guide your children through these areas of life successfully.

1. Because every child is different and every parent has his or her own unique style, parenting is a difficult task. Children do not develop good behavior unless they are taught to, and since they don't come with an "owner's manual," parents need practical information to solve everyday parenting problems. Discipline means teaching kids about positive, successful, and healthy ways of behaving.

2. Children are born with unique temperaments that can make them easy or difficult to manage. It is important to know where your child fits on the easy- or difficult-to-manage spectrum.

3. A parent's natural style is equally important. Parents who are warm and democratic and who keep high expectations for their children's behavior and performance raise kids who tend to be happy and goal-oriented.

4. Don't ask a child questions about things you already know the answers to. It gives the child the opportunity to avoid what's going on by saying "I don't know," it makes you frustrated, and it brings you both away from the topic at hand.

5. The purpose of time-out is to interrupt undesirable behavior. In order for time-out to work, the environment you move a child out of has to be desirable enough for him to want to go back to it. If you give a child a time-out from a chaotic or negative environment, the strategy won't work.

6. Spanking a child has not been shown to produce good changes in behavior and teaches a child that violence is an acceptable way of solving problems.

7. Always reward the positive side of a behavior (e.g., playing nicely with your little sister) as opposed to punishing the negative side (e.g., fighting with your sister).

8. You don't always have to reward a behavior with material things (toys, money, etc.). Reward with praise, privileges, and support. Reward effort, cooperation, and attitude, not just the end result.

**EXERCISES FOR PARENTS**

## BRINGING OUT THE BEST IN YOUR CHILD

It is easier to concentrate on negatives rather than positives in children because it is the negatives that increase stress. Take a few minutes to list the five best qualities and characteristics of your child.

1. _____

2. _____

3. _____

4. _____

5. _____

Now take the time to notice and point out these things at least three times a day.

## COPING WITH ROUGH TIMES

What you think about and tell yourself during difficult times can keep you from losing your cool and burning out. Write down some things to remind yourself when you are having "one of those days." Here are some examples to get you started:

"I did the same things when I was a child, and I still turned out OK."

"My children give me some of the most aggravating times of my life, but they also give me some of the best fun and good times, too."

"Eventually, my child will come around. As long as I keep my cool things will be all right."

## EXERCISES FOR PARENTS

Your own coping response:

_____

_____

_____

_____

# 2

# AM I SPOILING MY CHILD?

◀

While parents struggle to achieve just the right balance between loving and nurturing children and disciplining them, there is often a concern about whether or not it's possible to spoil a child, even as an infant.

Because the word *discipline* is often associated with a "spare the rod and spoil the child" attitude, discipline has come to be understood in negative terms. Thus, we feel badly about having to teach our children to control the things they would like to do that would most certainly get them into trouble if done outside the house. At the same time, we feel guilty about showing too much appreciation, attention, or concern for fear that they will get too used to this "special" treatment.

In truth, you can never love a child too much, nor can you have expectations for appropriate behavior that are too high. To love a child as best you can and to communicate a high standard for excellence and personal growth are the two essential goals of parenting.

In this chapter, I'll talk about both of these goals as they relate to what most people mean when they talk about "spoiling" a child. I'll cover issues that come up during infancy first, then finish up with issues that apply to kids who are a bit older.

## I'D NEVER LET MY CHILD
## GET AWAY WITH THAT . . .

On a bright summer day, you arrive at the park to meet the crew of "regulars" who convene there. You are part of an informal group of mothers of newborns, all between the ages of three months and a year. Suddenly, your six-month-old begins to wail. She wants to be picked up. Instinctively, you put your conversation on hold, reach down, and lift the baby up for a little attention. Just off your left shoulder you hear another mother pronounce glibly, "If I did that for my Sarah, I'd be holding her all day. She'd be so," and then you hear her lips curl around the word "*spoiled.*"

This is precisely the type of dilemma that makes parents question their basic instincts about loving and caring for their children.

**Can a child be spoiled during the first year of life?** Some child-care experts say it is impossible to spoil a child in the first year of life, and others say it is best to allow children to manage their own needs as soon as possible because it teaches them to be independent. I will tell you that we would be much better off if we agreed never to apply the term *spoiled* to a child for *any* reason at *any* age. Milk gets "spoiled" when it is left unattended—it gets sour, curdles, and becomes useless. When something is spoiled it is generally hopeless—ruined beyond redemption or repair. Furthermore, when something is spoiled we usually have to throw it out! Do we really want this term applied to something as precious as a child? Going a bit further, consider what else the term *spoiled* implies about parents and kids. A child becomes "spoiled" because he is so *selfish* that he will not allow his caregiver a moment of peace without having to tend to his every need and whim. It also implies that the caregiver is spineless and wimpy because he cannot stand to see the baby fuss without tending to him.

It has become popular to characterize the interactions between a parent and child in negative terms and metaphors. I have been guilty of this myself. We refer to these interactions as "battles," "struggles," or "power plays," but this language complicates something that is really quite straightforward. Children, from the first day they are born, are negotiating the task of figuring out how the world works. They pick up their first and most important lessons on how to do this from their caregivers. It's no wonder that children act as though the world should cater to them—it should! The parents' task is to teach children to seek and respect limits that are ultimately placed on everyone. When a parent has difficulty doing this, a child grows up thinking that *everyone* will treat her like her parent who has taken an "anything goes for my baby" approach to child rearing.

## IS HE <u>SPOILED</u> OR JUST <u>CREATIVE</u>?

Josh's mom believes that her three-year-old son should have the freedom to explore everything. Lately he's been collecting bugs in the backyard and bringing them in the house to show his mom and anyone else present. One day, Josh and his mom went on a visit to a friend's house. Josh's mom saw nothing wrong with Josh bringing a half dozen or so wiggling, moist specimens in a dubiously sealed plastic container. When Josh pranced into the living room with his six-legged friends, he was promptly asked to deposit them outside. Josh was offended and threw a tantrum. Josh's mom was also offended. Josh's mom's friend was—you guessed it, also offended and promptly labeled Josh "spoiled."

Mom's desire to allow Josh to explore the world was an excellent parenting strategy. Unfortunately, she neglected to teach Josh that her friend's living room does not make an appropriate field laboratory. Josh had no basis for understanding the limits of his exploratory behavior, so he was just going about his normal business and was put off because someone was interrupting it.

## EVEN ONE-YEAR-OLDS CAN UNDERSTAND LIMITS

It's easy to see we should set limits on a three-year-old's behavior, but can we expect a child who is under one year to begin understanding concepts like *limits* and *self control*? Surprisingly, yes, we can expect infants to *begin* this process—but we should never believe that love and attention should be withheld in the first year under any circumstances. Love, attention, and support are as critical to your infant as food and water—maybe more so because, while a child can get too chubby from being overfed, she can never be loved too much.

## TEMPERAMENT PLAYS A ROLE

Your child's temperament—the genetic contribution to behavior, personality, or style—will show itself in your child's "neediness" in the first year of life. Some children require more contact, more holding, and more tending to than others. Raising children who need a bit more attention is harder work, but giving them the attention that they need is by no means spoiling them. Here's an example. Antoinette is the mother of three-month-old Gina. Gina is a happy baby, but she has learned to communicate through a cry that is already instantly recognizable by her mother that Gina needs to be picked up and held. Antoinette wonders whether she should always "give in" to Gina, fearing that if she does the child will become dependent on her. The answer to this question is that Gina *is* dependent on her. At this age that is precisely how things should be. As Gina and all children grow up, they will learn to comfort themselves. The way they learn is to have all of those great experiences in the first year of life when someone comes and does it for them. When children become old enough to understand the words, "I'm here now, everything is all right," they will already have a reference through being touched, cuddled, and held, that you will back up your words with your physical presence and support.

Today's parents can be so confused by "advice from the experts" that they sometimes question what feels natural and right. If your child needs a bit of extra attention to be soothed, by all means give it to him. It won't be long before life becomes so complicated that it will take much more than being held for just a few more minutes to make everything good again. Remember, you are the one who spends the most time with your child, and children vary widely as to what they require in terms of holding and attention. Give your child the holding and tending to that you have learned he needs.

# AGE MILESTONES

There are cycles and rhythms to the biological events that govern a child's waking and sleeping states. These cycles become fine-tuned during the first year of life through the interactions that you have with your baby. Again, some babies fall into regular, predictable patterns faster than others. Parents who are having a difficult time establishing regular sleeping and feeding times can get very stressed out. During the first three to six months an infant's outward behavior is strongly influenced by what's happening inside of her—gas, colic, hunger pains, fatigue, sensitivities to environmental conditions, and dozens of other things. During at least the first six months be extra attentive to behavior that indicates discomfort. Fussing over your baby is not only normal, but part of what is required to keep your baby happy.

You will notice that as your child passes the six-month mark, several things happen. His movements are no longer as random or jerky, but more controlled and deliberate. Instead of just operating in response to the environment he is actually making his mark on the environment. As the sensory systems become more acute, and the motor systems become more precise, you can see him developing into more of an autonomous person. During the second half of the first year your baby's relationship with his primary caregiver

> *Children don't become "spoiled." Some, however, simply never learn to manage their own needs.*

strengthens. Play takes on a more give-and-take quality. Recognition of his "favorite person" is quicker and defined by fits of absolute joy. You can have your first "conversations."

As the relationship intensifies, you will observe more anxiety over separations. This is when parents begin to feel guilty about going out without baby, and sometimes equally guilty about devoting all available time to keeping him occupied. What should you do? First, realize that the bond that is developing between you and your child is necessary for her healthy growth and development. You will never go through this period again with your child, so while it's here make the most of it. Does this mean that you have to exclude everything else so that you can give your baby completely undivided attention? Of course not. You are entitled to a breather whenever you feel you need it. Just don't let yourself believe that it is "better" for the baby to mind herself at this age. It is at this point that kids benefit most from having two parents who share in the child rearing. When Mom gets fatigued, Dad can step in and provide the attention and stimulation necessary. If the person who minds the baby most during the day (yes, this is sometimes Dad) needs to run out, it's always great to have a "second shift" standing by to relieve him.

During the first half of the second year you will begin to see signs that your child is becoming comfortable managing herself. This can only happen after you have convinced her that you and the other one or two most significant people in her life are constant and reliable. If a child is not comforted during her separation-anxiety time, it will take much longer for her to feel comfortable with herself.

## THREE AREAS THAT PARENTS WORRY ABOUT MOST IN INFANCY: SLEEPING, FEEDING, AND HOLDING

Sleeping, feeding, and holding are the three things parents worry about most in the first year. How to put a child to sleep has been the subject of intense debate for years now. I am of the opinion that children are not really *designed* to sleep apart from their parents, and if you want them to sleep away from you, they need to be taught. Because children are so helpless and dependent, it doesn't make sense that they should feel comfortable sleeping in a place where they will be outside the safety of their caregivers. This was certainly the case hundreds of years ago when the environment was much more dangerous. Today's parents feel very guilty when they can't get their children to sleep independently. They are often advised to let their children cry until they put themselves down. I have never felt completely comfortable with this advice, and certainly I don't feel that it applies during the first year of life. There is simply too much to check on. Toward the latter half of your baby's first year you can begin helping him to develop the behavioral pattern of going to sleep on his own by spending some time with him before he goes to sleep, then leaving while he is still awake but groggy. This way he will feel comfortable nodding off without you being there all of the time. In general I believe people have made too much of a fuss over sleeping. Poorly established sleep routines can certainly make your life miserable, but I believe that an extreme emphasis on maintaining schedules increases anxiety and stress in everyone and makes the whole process that much more difficult. If you are having trouble getting your child to sleep, please take a look at Chapter 11, where it's covered in much greater detail.

Feeding and sleeping are somewhat related because they both have to do with habits and schedules. Feeding is also a time of intimacy and sharing, so it touches upon the emotional needs as well as the physical needs of the child. Your pediatrician will help you determine the best feeding pattern for you and your child, but here's a word of caution. If your child is more than a few months old and you are feeding her "on demand," with some of those feedings taking place in the middle of the night, you will be helping your child develop internal cues for hunger in the middle of the night and you will be conditioning that pattern of behavior.

> *Children who are cuddled often during the first year of life tend to grow up more secure and independent.*

Some children have a very strong need to suck, so it can be hard to tell the difference between the urge to feed and the urge to suck. Trust that eventually you will be able to differentiate between the two. Gently guide your baby's hand toward her mouth to help soothe the urge to suck. Pacifiers have their pros and cons, but many people believe that fingers and hands are more sanitary. The most important thing you can give your baby during feeding is a calm, relaxing environment with plenty of cuddles, eye contact, and conversation. You may find that this is what she was really after in the first place!

Most infants love being cuddled and held. As they pass through the six-month period, your infant's needs for all types of attention increase and intensify. You will feel like you are the only person in the world who can make him feel comfortable and happy—and you are! Is it unreasonable to assume that a child can learn to be patient and wait for attention during the first year of life? No, it's not unreasonable, but the emphasis should be on what children are *beginning* to learn. Most children don't enjoy having to be patient for your attention, and they will let you know it. Don't let this aggravate you. When was the last time someone couldn't live without your company! A recent University of Virginia study suggests that children who are held and cuddled during their first year of life tend to grow up to be more secure and independent, so rest assured that you can cuddle your child to your heart's content without fear of spoiling him.

You can also help your child adjust to your not being around by making good-byes and hellos as pleasant as possible. If you are anxiety-ridden and guilty when it is time to say good-bye, your baby will pick it up and respond negatively. Leave after giving her a smile and a pat on the tummy. Over time your nonverbal behavior and your words will provide the reassurance needed for your baby to begin to comfort herself in your absence.

# IS QUALITY TIME ENOUGH IN THE FIRST YEAR?

As a way of helping ease some of the guilt experienced by working parents, psychologists and the media have come up with the notion of "quality time." The idea is that if you spend brief but "good" time with your child, his emotional needs will be met. This is simply not true. In the first year children need "quantity" as well as "quality." Does that mean that it is impossible to work and raise a newborn? No! What it does mean is that it is a difficult task that will require some sacrifices in your work schedule during the first year. Unfortunately, the idea of quality time is to force the baby to accommodate the parents' schedule. In the first year, Mom and Dad have to be available to form the kind of bond necessary to create feelings of trust and security in the child—and that requires being on the *baby's* schedule.

Careful coordination between Mom and Dad is critical. It is easy to fall into the supermom trap of working a full day and taking care of baby and Dad at night, just because that's what society says mothers are *supposed* to do. Keep an open line of communication between you and your spouse and discuss a reasonable split of baby-related chores. The ideal situation is having some time where Mom and Dad switch off, one spending time alone with the baby while the other catches up on household tasks, as well as a period where Mom and Dad spend time with the baby as a family—playing, strolling, and just enjoying each other's company.

## CAN GRANDPARENTS SPOIL YOUR BABY?

During the first year of your baby's life, rest assured that no matter how hard they try, grandparents will never be able to take your place. Many grandparents will indulge kids and encourage them to break the rules parents have set. Some are even so bold as to claim it is their "right" as a grandparent to "spoil" a grandchild. In most cases the love and attention that kind, caring grandparents provide are worth whatever disruption they cause. But when there are tensions between parents and grandparents, an unhealthy competition over "who loves the kids most" can result. These kinds of conflicts often require, at the least, a sit-down talk where feelings can be aired, and if things have moved beyond that a counseling intervention may be necessary. If you do need to approach your parents about the way they interact with your baby, be gentle but direct. Start by acknowledging something positive, like the fact that you appreciate how much they love the baby, and that you can see the baby loves them, too. It's hard to stroke someone's ego when they are doing something that annoys you, but it will make your criticism a little easier to swallow. Follow these comments by using simple and neutral requests. For instance, "I know you love Jimmy and want to make him feel special when you visit, but he's been getting very used to the sugary treats you bring him, and now he wants them all the time. We're trying to cut back on sugar in the house in general, so it would help us if you brought something else instead." If your parents belittle your request, don't engage them in an argument. Instead, wait and see what happens. Your parents may feel the need to gloss over your advice, because no one likes to be reprimanded by their kids (you'll see soon enough), but they will more than likely heed it anyway.

## GETTING YOUR BABY READY FOR INDEPENDENCE

The key to setting the stage for healthy independence and separation in toddlerhood is to indulge your baby during the *early* part of her development. Heaping lots of love and attention on your newborn provides the emotional foundation necessary for coping with the separations, frustrations, and new experiences of the second and third years. As life goes on, your baby will learn to share you with others and to manage and fend for herself. This happens gradually with brief periods of separation or time alone to manage and comfort herself and with constant reassurance that you are right behind her. You can experiment with these periods of separation during the later part of the first year, but remember that each child is different; some take to separations easier than others. Don't rush it. The basis for feeling secure at any age is knowing that there is someone close by who loves you and wants to take care of you. If you are ever at a loss for understanding how your baby feels, simply sit down, close your eyes, and examine all the things that you require from the people who love you—a warm hand to hold, a kiss and a cuddle, a feeling of safety and security, and most of all, a person who gives these things generously. Why should your infant want anything less?

## WHAT MAKES AN OLDER CHILD TOO DEPENDENT?

Parents sometimes react very negatively when I suggest they use prizes or privileges (or even money) to motivate their children to behave. "If I pay him for things he should be doing anyway, he'll get spoiled." On the surface, this seems like a very reasonable concern. But think about it. You have a job, and you get paid to do things that are part of your job description, right? You also probably do things, such as volunteer work, that you do not receive money for. Why do you do that? The answer is that people, including children, *are* motivated by tangible things like money and prizes, but they are *also* motivated by things like the need for attention and recognition. Of course, if every interaction you have with your child amounts to some form of bribery, then you will be setting up a situation where your child might expect to be paid off for everything. But kids won't get spoiled by earning rewards for good behavior as long as you make things like verbal praise, appreciation, and plenty of hugs and kisses available to them while they are growing up. It's only when parents use tangible items like toys and money to *replace* genuine love and affection that children become "spoiled."

# VISITATION WEEKENDS THAT LEAD TO OVERINDULGENCE

When parents have limited visiting time as a result of divorce, they sometimes try a bit too hard to create an atmosphere that revolves around fun, good times, and no limits. This is hard on the custodial parent, the kids, and, eventually, the noncustodial parent as well.

For the first year after his divorce Mark filled his visitation weekends with one nonstop good time after another. He made sure the kids were always occupied, and when all else failed, a trip to the toy store usually kept smiles on the kids' faces. Mark took a great deal of pride in the fact that the children always loved visiting him, until one day when he had to tell his eight-year-old daughter, Melanie, that he couldn't take her shopping because relatives were coming in, and he wanted her and her brother to spend some time with them. Melanie threw a fit and refused to settle down. The weekend was a nightmare, and it wasn't until a few hours after the kids had left that Mark realized he had contributed to Melanie's behavior. From that point on special occasions were just that, but it took quite some time for Melanie to adjust to "a regular life" over at her dad's house.

1.  Parents often worry that if they show too much love for their children they will grow up spoiled and unable to handle the demands and challenges of life. You can never love a child too much or have expectations that are too high. Always encourage your child to strive for excellence, but do it in a way that conveys warmth, not criticism.

2.  It's not really possible to spoil an infant during the first year of life, but you can and should begin to set limits, so that children can learn to regulate their needs.

3.  Understand that your child's natural personality style or "temperament" will help determine how needy your child is for support and attention.

4.  Regulating sleep and feeding patterns during infancy will depend in part on your infant's temperament and in part on how *you* set the pace.

5.  "Quality time" with parents just isn't enough during the first year of life. In order to insure a strong bond there has to be quantity time, too. This goes for both parents.

6.  One key to helping your child become independent is indulging her with love and attention during the first year. Independence cannot develop unless the child feels that she has been supported and nurtured by you.

## UNDERSTANDING YOUR INFANT'S TEMPERAMENT

Observe the following behaviors in your child and rate them
accordingly:

1. *When it comes to soothing my infant, he or she is:*

Easy ☐

Moderately Easy ☐

Moderately Difficult ☐

Difficult ☐

2. *When it comes to the amount of time my baby needs to be held,
he or she requires this amount of attention:*

Relatively Little ☐

About Average ☐

A Little More than Average ☐

A Lot More than Average ☐

3. *My baby seems to respond to other people:*

Very Hesitantly ☐

Hesitantly ☐

Pretty Easily ☐

Very Easily ☐

4. *I would describe my baby as:*

High Maintenance ☐

Medium Maintenance ☐

Low Maintenance ☐

## EXERCISES FOR PARENTS

The way you rate your child on these characteristics should give you some idea of how much your child needs your supervision and direct support. Tune in to your baby's needs early, and you will encourage independence later on.

# 3

# AGES AND STAGES

▶

Human beings are very complex creatures. No two people are exactly alike (even identical twins). That's because behavior is always the result of a number of different forces that act on us—genetics, the environment, the events of a particular day, and countless other influences that affect us at any given time. Whenever we assume that a behavior is part of a phase, we suggest that it is something that "just happens" or something that will "come and go with time." This kind of thinking further suggests that the behavior operating is beyond anyone's control. If, for instance, during the toddler phase of development you find your child getting into things, touching and pulling on whatever, should you just let the child be until the "phase" passes, or should you begin setting limits so the child will learn to discriminate dangerous situations from those that aren't?

In this chapter the concept of age-related phases, or stages, is used to identify some of the behavioral and emotional keyholes that children pass through during their development. However, always remember that humans are actively engaged in their environment, not just passively driven through a stage of development.

As a preface to talking about some of my favorite ages and stages of childhood, let me point out that there is a tremendous amount of variation in children. If I say a behavior tends to occur around a certain time, understand that some children pass through this phase a bit sooner and some a bit later.

# FOUR TO SIX WEEKS: BECOMING SOCIAL

Six weeks is an interesting age for infants. About this time parents will notice that their children smile in response to seeing them. Prior to this time the smile that parents think they see may just be wishful thinking or gas! Infants this young also show very clear preferences for faces and for lines that are curved as opposed to straight. At about this time parents will also see a clear synchrony between themselves and their infants. *Synchrony* refers to that kind of unspoken communication between a parent and newborn that involves patterning, imitating, and reacting and adjusting to the caregiver's behavior.

# NINE TO TWELVE MONTHS: LEARNING TO TALK

Lots of behavior develops between six weeks and nine months. Most of it is motor behavior, such as lifting the head or transferring an object from one hand to the other, but nothing is as exciting as when a child begins to say his first few words. Babbling begins at about six months, and children tend to repeat sound patterns over and over, like "ba-ba-ba," or even "da-da-da." Between nine and twelve months children will make purposeful attempts to mimic familiar words like *mommy*, *light*, or *doggy*. Infants seem to be emotionally, physically, and psychologically ready to develop language between now and the end of the third year. By the time a child is about eighteen months, she will begin putting a few words together. By the beginning of preschool, a child will have acquired about *fourteen thousand* words! During the period from nine months or so to four years, children's language is stimulated by the adults around them. That's why it is so important for adults to engage children in as many "talking games" (e.g., "What's this?" "Who is that?") as possible.

## THE TERRIBLE TWOS

Why are the toddler years often called "terrible"? Think about it for a second, and imagine you are a two-year-old. After two years of lying around on your back, staring at the ceiling, you have finally figured out how to move around on your own two feet. There are places to go, things to do, VCRs to disassemble. And there are any number of holes, closets, refrigerators, and garbage disposals to explore. But can you get a moment's peace? No! Look! A delicious-looking bottle of red hot sauce has just found its way into your chubby little fingers. The bright yellow cap is hardly a challenge; it twists off without protest. Just as you raise up the bottle for a nice healthy slug, Mom swoops in, closes the refrigerator, scares the heck out of you with a thundering "No!" and scoots you off to another part of the house. From there it's, "Get down from there," "Don't put that in your mouth," "Don't touch that," and "Put that down." It should be no surprise that all of that negativity has you saying "No!" whenever anyone asks you to do something.

## THREE TO FIVE: BECOMING INDEPENDENT

Three years old is a big transition age. Children learn to use rapidly developing language skills to gain access to things in their environment and to express their will. Pretty cool stuff. From the child's point of view you simply say "milk" (she might actually say "muk") and you get milk. You can get "more" of just about anything, or you can demonstrate your newfound sense of mastery simply by pointing to and naming everything.

Children also learn that there are boundaries and limits to what they can have, even if they've learned how to ask for it. Since children are self-centered, and since they have been catered to for the first few years of life, understanding the meaning of the word *no* can be frustrating. This can set the stage for power struggles and control issues, which can be especially trying if your child is strong-minded by nature.

At about three years of age children are faced with the challenge of learning how to regulate themselves. This challenge is manifested in such activities as sleeping, eating, toilet training, being responsible for picking up toys, and minding one's manners.

Physical development also proceeds at a hectic pace and places an additional amount of strain on the child. Now add to that increased social demands such as learning to share, taking turns, or giving up an object that belongs to someone else.

All of these changes together result in your child's life being both exciting and tumultuous. In many ways it is a period of greater self-definition and independence than adolescence is. It is during this phase that parents need to be mindful of the things that are worth making an issue of and those that aren't. Picking and choosing your battles carefully can mean the difference between an enjoyable day with your child versus one that is peppered with fights and squabbles.

## JENNIFER: STUBBORN LIKE HER MOM

At four years old, Jennifer is a very independent young lady. Mom says that Jennifer likes to have everything her own way. The situation is tough because Mom also likes things to run with order and predictability. There are some days when everything seems like a battle. Here's a typical interaction.

"Jennifer, sweetheart, come here and put on this pretty dress."

"I want to wear this." (Points to her favorite jumper.)

"You can wear that some other day, honey. Come get this on."

"No." (Whines.)

"Let's go, Jennifer. We have to get moving."

"No!" (Stomps foot.)

"Right now, young lady."

(Jennifer runs out of the room.)

Mom begins to think that it's going to be another one of those days, and she is probably right.

Whenever you are engaged in a power play with your child, ask yourself whether the situation is really worth taking a stand over.

If Mom and Jennifer were on their way to someplace where Jennifer absolutely had to wear a dress, then this would have been a time to take a stand. But if the issue boils down to "I want you to wear what *I* want," you must decide if it is really worth the aggravation.

## FIVE TO SEVEN: THE DEMANDS OF LEARNING

Five- to seven-year-old children are heavily influenced by the demands of the learning environment. Homework, play dates, and preparation for spelling tests, science projects, and school plays require a new appreciation of structure, order, and, most important, self-control during situations that create frustration.

During this phase of life parents must tune in to their child's learning style and teach positive ways of managing the structure and frustration that is part of every child's early school experience. If you find your child turning off to reading or avoiding homework early in her school career, it is time to get help. Start by consulting her teacher, and stay in contact with the teacher until a plan to get your child on the right track is worked out.

## EIGHT AND NINE: THE AGE OF ANXIETY

Around the third grade some children appear to go through a phase of anxiety and self-doubt. It is at this age that children can develop a number of peculiar behaviors that telegraph this anxiety. These can include tics (throat clearing, head jerking, eye blinking), nail biting, stuttering, sleep problems, or psychosomatic complaints (tummy aches, headaches).

In many cases these behaviors coincide with increased academic and social demands. After all, the typical schedule of an eight- or nine-year-old child includes school, several types of lessons (dance, music, karate, etc.), sports, play dates, parties, and other engagements. Many of these activities have a social component to them, and acceptance or rejection by a peer group (especially the "right" peer group) can contribute to anxiety.

It is at this age that children begin to form closer one-to-one attachments with other children (this is especially true for girls). The emotional advantages of this are obvious—it is great to have a "best friend" to pal around with—but at the same time it's also upsetting to lose your "best friend" to someone who has a pool in his backyard or the newest toy. Hence, social relationships tend to take on a soap-opera-like feel, and if you are close to your child you will have to listen to report after report of this social injustice or that disloyal friend. During these times you will be tempted to jump in with sage advice and a wealth of your own life experiences. Unless your child solicits your philosophy on human relationships, skip this lecture until he is about twenty-five. Young children respond much better to a sympathetic ear, encouragement to tell the whole story with all its grisly details, and a glass of milk and some cookies.

By the way, this is also the age when children develop a keen interest in the gross, the horrific, and anything that pertains to bodily functions and fluids. This is especially true of little boys, who can sit around for hours describing in great detail and with utter glee the various forms, sounds, and methods of imitating the expulsion of gas from the human digestive system. I don't think there has ever been a scientific study that has determined how this interest develops, but it is interesting to note that it tends to occur at precisely the same age when children's own bodies are starting to prepare for some pretty big changes.

## ELEVEN TO THIRTEEN: HORMONE CITY

What could possibly be more important to an eleven-year-old girl than what happened to her favorite character on the most popular teen-hunks-on-the-beach television drama? The answer to this question is, of course, "nothing," except whatever else is going on in her life. *Everything* is important, *very important*, from the way she fusses with her hair to the amount of time she *needs* to spend on the phone, the type of sneakers and clothes she wears, the music she listens to, the words she uses to express herself, and the people she hangs out with.

I often refer to these preteen years as "the frantic phase" of child development. The eleven- to thirteen-year-old child tends to see every-thing as larger than life, with little differentiation between the big picture and tiny details. During this phase children learn to sort through complicated emotions and more complex and abstract ways of thinking. It is around this age when children discover sarcasm, and they do not hesitate to point their curled lips at whatever target seems hypocritical, unjust, or just plain open for a dig. Those things that often make kids this age seem intolerable to other people fascinate me, because instead of attributing their behavior to a need to be smart-mouthed, I look at it as evidence of the evolution of an incredible mental process. This process involves abstract reasoning, learning to use language in different (and sometimes unbelievably gross) ways, and developing a new set of thinking skills geared to solve problems and explore the environment in a more scientific and precise way.

*Good discipline is a matter of teaching your child the skills needed to survive in a complex world.*

Socially, this age also represents something of a "coming out." We used to think of sixteen years old as being associated with this kind of social development, but the fact is that it happens much sooner. Most eleven- to thirteen-year-old kids are already thinking about dating, kissing, and being popular with the opposite sex. That is why it is essential for parents to be frank and honest with their children about how their changing and developing bodies work.

Because children's bodies develop quickly at this age, it is also important to realize how the onset of puberty, the interaction of hormones, and the different rates at which children's body parts grow influence their perceptions of themselves. Junior-high-school-age kids often feel very out of place in their own bodies. As the shape of their faces and bodies change they can feel awkward, uncomfortable, and very self-conscious. It is vital for parents to be sympathetic and supportive about such things as body perception, weight, pimples, and the myriad other things children this age focus on. Even a playful tease can cut pretty deeply.

1. Children do not grow at the same pace. There is always a danger in assuming that all kids pass through certain milestones at a given time. When you make this assumption, you can lose track of the individual style and nature of the child. On the other hand, certain phases of life bring fairly typical problems and situations, and knowing about them in advance can be helpful.

2. During the first two months of life parents watch their infants become social creatures. Children learn to smile at and recognize their caregivers. And they react to the stimulation of sights, sounds, and sensations.

3. During the period between nine and twelve months, infants become wide open to learning language, which begins first with babbling and cooing sounds and continues with the rapid acquisition of new vocabulary. Part of the reason why the twos are so "terrible" is because children become mobile and are interested in exploring the environment, but as yet have no idea about dangers in that environment or appropriate limits for behavior. Limit setting becomes a parent's number one child-rearing task.

4. Between three and five years, children struggle to become independent. As language develops, preschoolers develop more mastery of their environment. Children at this age are very self-centered; that is, they tend to see themselves at the center of all the action around them. As a result they can often seem demanding and physically and emotionally draining.

5. Between five and seven years of age, children have to adjust to the demands of learning. Learning to read, write, sit still in class, socialize, share, wait on line, do homework, and be on someone else's schedule is stressful, but most kids seem to handle it very well. Parents need to be on guard for signs that all this new activity might be frustrating their child and stressing him beyond what is normal. If the demands of school

seem to be placing too much stress on your child, please see your pediatrician so that she can help direct you appropriately.

6. Ages eight and nine (or thereabouts) can be a time when children experience a lot of anxiety that can come out in the form of tics, stuttering, sleep problems, or bodily complaints. These bouts with anxiety usually come and go, but if they seem to be interfering with your child's day-to-day functioning for longer than a few weeks, see your child's pediatrician.

7. The preteen years are marked by a change in a child's thinking style from concrete to abstract. Children show their growing sophistication by being more sensitive to criticism, prejudice, and sarcasm. This period is also marked by physical changes that signal the onset of puberty. These changes can cause anxiety over body perception and social acceptance. This is one time of life when parents have to be extra-sensitive about teasing and negative criticism.

# 4

# TEACHING YOUR CHILD
# TO HAVE SELF-ESTEEM

Self-esteem can help you weather life's stormiest crises. When we try hard at something and fail, self-esteem is what helps us pick ourselves up and try again. When relationships turn sour, self-esteem is what helps us evaluate what went wrong, own up to our contribution to it, and move on. Self-esteem prevents us from punishing ourselves unnecessarily, and it keeps us from tolerating unfair treatment from others. Self-esteem keeps us from continuing patterns of behavior that are self-defeating or destructive.

It's impossible to overemphasize the importance of helping your child develop a good self-image. Research indicates that a foundation of self-esteem is essential for creating a need to achieve in children, as well as for preventing circumstances like drug and alcohol abuse and teenage pregnancy.

## EXAMINE YOUR OWN
## FEELINGS ABOUT FAILURE

The first step in understanding how to create confidence and self-esteem in children is to understand your own thoughts, feelings, and attitudes about failure. Our reactions to failure cause us to program ourselves with certain thoughts and attitudes about our worth as people. The person with low self-esteem fails at something and concludes, "I can't do this because I'm stupid," or "I can't do this because I'm incompetent." That person also closes the door to future success by adding, "I'll *never* be able to do that." The person with high self-esteem evaluates the situation by saying, "I wonder what went wrong *this time*," or "I wonder if there is anything I could do to improve my performance." The person with high self-esteem copes by saying, "I know if I try hard enough I can accomplish this."

## HOW FAILURE HELPS US ADAPT ◀

Every single person that walks around on the face of this planet is programmed to fail. That's right. Whatever force in the universe created us obviously thought that failure was an extremely important part of the learning process. There are failures and mistakes in every aspect of nature. Failure provides us with important feedback that helps us fine-tune our behavior and learn better ways to adapt to our surroundings.

You might remember from a biology course you took in school that animals evolved according to their ability to adapt to their surroundings. Animals that could adjust to the demands of their environments survived, while those that couldn't perished. We don't have to worry about hunting for food anymore, but we still live in an environment that is stressful, challenging, and at times difficult to cope with. As adults we experience the challenges of having to earn a living, pay bills, and survive during times when economic resources are scarce. Children face the prospect of having to grow up and prepare to face these same challenges. Their stress includes going to school, making friends, and learning about the world around them. Successes and failures are measured on an almost constant basis in children's lives, whether it's how they performed on today's spelling or social studies test, how they did in this afternoon's soccer match, how many points they scored on a Nintendo game, or how they succeeded in any one of the many competitions, tests, or games they face every day.

Children are *constantly* being evaluated. In school, children are evaluated by how they do on tests, how they behave, how much effort they show, how neatly they write. Could you imagine reporting to a boss who was in contact with you all day long, criticizing you on the neatness of your desk, the effort you show, and the quality of your penmanship? Children must cope with this all day long at school. Then they come home. As soon as they walk through the door they are faced with homework responsibilities, chores, and getting along with siblings, all of which are more opportunities for evaluation. Over the course of twelve or thirteen years, the messages that kids get during the day at school and at home from Mom and Dad play a major role in defining the kinds of attitudes and beliefs children have about themselves. When these attitudes are positive, self-esteem develops; when they are negative, children suffer.

## JAMES: THE YOUNGEST OF FOUR BROTHERS

James is eight years old and has three older brothers aged eleven, thirteen, and fifteen. The family is extremely competitive. Dad makes sure that all of the kids are involved in sports, so every year all four boys play soccer, lacrosse, and baseball. Dad is competitive with the boys, and the boys are competitive with each other. Because James is the youngest, the smallest, and the most sensitive by nature, he takes the most ribbing from his brothers and from his dad. Mom worries about this. Whenever James does poorly in school or in sports, he cries and says very negative things about himself. It is clear that being in an environment where he is overshadowed by his brothers is taking its toll on James's self-esteem. The funny thing is that James's brothers would do anything for him. They are very protective of their little brother, but that doesn't come through to James as much as the name-calling and the kidding about him being smaller, weaker, or "the baby."

It is vital to James's development of self-esteem that his parents teach him that failure is not a terrible thing. When failure causes new learning to take place, it is actually a step forward toward some final goal, but when failure causes self-punishment it stamps in feelings of self-doubt and a belief system that says, "I am a worthless person."

## SHOULD I LET MY CHILD EXPERIENCE FAILURE?

The parent of a child who has learning difficulties, and who must work many times harder than most children just to achieve passing grades, recently called me. She was very worried. "Steven just came home and told me he is going to run for class president." "Oh," I said. Based on the tone of her voice I added, "It sounds like you don't think that's a very good idea." "It's not that I don't think it's a good idea," she said. "It's just that he has such a hard time simply getting by, and he already has to deal with so much frustration. What if nobody votes for him? Is he just setting himself up for failure?" I thought about it for a minute. Nobody wants to help someone walk into a situation where it is clear that he is going to get clobbered. Was it a bad idea to encourage Steven to run for class president if it was likely that he would lose?

Then I began thinking about whether the end goal of becoming class president was the most important part of the whole experience. It wasn't. Steven was, on his own, approaching the situation with a great attitude. I explained to his mother that the fact that Steven wanted to take the risk was a good sign, and as long as he was prepared for the experience Steven's choice to run for class president could be a win-win situation. We explained to Steven that everyone who participates in an election hopes to win, but that only one person can. We also explained that it would be great to talk to new people, make new friends, and be part of an important event. We also tried to prepare Steven for people who might be insensitive or rude to him while the election was going on. The day of the election came. Steven won a commendable share of votes and was absolutely thrilled. It turned out to be a great experience for him. In the end, his mother and I wondered why we ever even considered preventing him from having an experience as rich as this.

## REDIRECTING NEGATIVE COMMENTS

Sometimes, even when you prepare your children for negative outcomes, they are very hard on themselves. That's when it is necessary for parents to provide support and redirect any negative things kids say about themselves. When a child is moping and saying things like: "I stink, nobody likes me," or "I'm no good at anything," it's important to acknowledge the feeling. You might begin by saying, "I know that it can really hurt when things don't turn out the way you want them to." Next disagree with the part that is a put-down by saying, "I can't agree with you when you say you are no good. When you say that it makes it sound like you are no good in general. I think you are a great person. You might need a little more practice in baseball (or whatever it is the complaint is about), but as a person you are just fine." There is no need to turn the conversation into a long philosophical lecture. The effect of what you are saying might not be absorbed immediately, but saying the words "You are a good person" is important.

Unfortunately, we don't live in a society that teaches us to be proud of the good, loving parts of our personalities. We are taught that pride is a mystical quality that somehow develops within ourselves. We value modesty, which is also a good thing, because no one wants to be around a person who gloats over his accomplishments or makes himself sound godlike so other people will feel inferior. In order to develop a sense of pride, however, we must be near people who are willing to be supportive and "talk up" our good side. This is a very important role that parents play in the lives of their children, and it requires a special skill. It isn't necessary to hang every piece of artwork your child creates on the refrigerator door; doing so might lead the child to believe that everything she does is a nugget of gold. Then later on when other people don't acknowledge everything she does as positive, she will become upset. On the other hand, praising effort, motivation, and hard work will never cause anyone to develop unrealistic ideas about herself. Talking up these qualities will make a child who fails at something still feel good about the fact that she knows she gave it the best effort possible.

> *Keep the development of your child's self-esteem on your mental list of daily parenting responsibilities.*

## ALWAYS PRAISE EFFORT OVER OUTCOME ◀

Keep in mind that you should always praise effort over outcome. The outcome of an event, such as winning or losing something or getting a high mark or a failing grade, is always secondary to the path taken to get there. There is always an opportunity to praise a child for trying hard, doing his best, improving his performance, or having a great attitude or "team spirit."

# WHAT IF YOUR CHILD HAS EXPECTATIONS THAT ARE TOO HIGH?

What happens when your child chooses a path that is clearly out of line with her abilities? This is a very difficult question. Parents often worry when their children set their goals or expectations too high. What message should you give a child who wants to do something that you know she cannot do? Should you gently try to modify her expectations and help her to set more reasonable goals? Or should you let her forge ahead into a situation where failure is certain? The answer is that it depends on your child and how she has handled failure in the past. Some people react well to failure by restructuring their own expectations and trying again.

## SHARON'S SCIENCE PROJECT

It was twelve-year-old Sharon's goal to enter a school science contest. Unfortunately, the genetics project she chose was way over her head—she just didn't have enough of a grasp on genetics to master the complicated undertaking. She tried and tried, but she was very frustrated. As the science contest drew closer, she had to abandon her genetics project in favor of a demonstration on how to make a homemade fire extinguisher. Her presentation was clever and one of the most popular exhibits at the contest, but she did not win. When the contest was over, she resolved to learn more about genetics and make next year's entry a success.

In Sharon's case, there was no harm in exploring something that was way over her head. Her failure only strengthened her resolve to do better next year. Another child, with a different kind of personality or reaction to failure, might have shut down and pulled out of the contest altogether. It is difficult to know why some kids react like Sharon and others shut down and turn off. Certainly Sharon's past experience with success and failure had something to do with it, and the fact that Sharon has loving, supportive parents also contributed to the outcome. But a third factor, Sharon's inborn or natural tendency to stick with things and absorb frustration, also figured heavily into the mix. Children differ in temperament, and resistance to frustration does seem to be a trait that is influenced by genetics. Sharon might simply have a higher tolerance for frustration than other kids.

## KNOW YOUR CHILD'S STRENGTHS AND LIMITATIONS

Clearly, it is up to parents to know their child's own strengths and weaknesses. If your child is particularly vulnerable to frustration, and situations arise when there is a large gap between what your child has taken on and what he can actually do, it might be wise to suggest more reasonable goals. But don't hesitate to let your child take "smart risks." Smart risks are risks that don't necessarily guarantee success, but do guarantee a worthwhile learning experience regardless of the outcome.

## SELF-ESTEEM DEVELOPS THROUGHOUT CHILDHOOD AND ADOLESCENCE

The development of confidence and self-esteem is a cumulative process. It happens a little every day. If a child is nurtured and supported, a single bad experience does little to influence a child's feelings about herself. On the other hand, if a child is put down every day, one really great experience—even several great experiences—is not enough to turn that child's perceptions around for the better. That is why parents have to make contributions to their children's confidence and self-esteem every day. This can be hard if you are tied down to the tasks of daily living, or if your children are going through a period of testing the limits of what you will tolerate. Take the time to comment on your child's appearance or work habits. If your child is having a rough day and doesn't seem to be listening, turn his behavior in a more positive direction. Give him a small task that you know he will accomplish and then praise him for doing that. A good example has to do with keeping a room or play area tidy. If you start out by saying, "I want this room spotless in ten minutes," you are increasing the chance that he will not meet your expectations, and then you will have to deliver a reprimand and a criticism. Instead choose one task, like picking up his clothes from the floor, praise his completion of the smaller task, and then move on. Every time the child hears something positive, not only will another part of the room be clean, but you are also allowing your child to feel as though he has done something to please you. Both of you will feel better, and you can avoid an entire lecture that involves saying things like, "You never do anything I ask you to," "You're disappointing me," or "I don't know why I bother asking you to do things." All of these stamp in the perception that the child is incompetent, a disappointment, and a failure. A constant diet of these lectures can erode confidence and self-esteem and allow the child to develop negative rather than positive expectations.

## WHO DETERMINES HOW YOUR CHILD FEELS ABOUT HERSELF?

Let's talk about the people who determine how a child feels about herself. There are three categories of people who influence a child's self-esteem: parents, other relatives and important adults, and peers. Let's talk about parents first.

## PARENTS

Parents send messages relating to how competent and worthwhile their children are every day. Parents' opinions about their children influence their feelings and behavior even into adulthood. Because parents have the biggest impact on how kids feel about themselves, they should try to understand how their style affects their children. One aspect of a parent's style that is extremely important is something psychologists call "warmth." Warmth is a characteristic that is often equated with friendliness, openness, or just plain niceness. The opposite of warmth is coldness. People who are cold appear critical, unfriendly, and unapproachable. Individuals who are warm have good people skills. They are comfortable around others, enjoy giving compliments, and are forgiving and understanding. The funny thing is that some who *appear* cold often do not *feel* that way, and they can't understand why others do not get close to them. It is hard for people who are cold to understand that when others are around them they feel unappreciated, belittled, and put down. Our own upbringing has a lot to do with how warm or cold we are as adults. If we grow up in an environment where there is little tenderness, emotional support, or sharing, or if there is meanness, criticism, or hostility, we tend to absorb that style. Sometimes, even if we fight to develop differently, the tendency still exists and will come out from time to time, often during critical points in relationships.

Parents influence their children's self-esteem by their style of communication. Think about your own style for a moment. When you want your child to get something for you, do you say, "Bring the vacuum in," in a tone that sounds more like a command than a request? Focusing on such mundane forms of communication might seem petty or insignificant, but it is not. Kids react very strongly to feeling as though they are being dictated to. In the end, it really boils down to a simple matter of etiquette. Do the people in your home com-

> *Body language is as important as words. Really listen to your child, and make eye contact when you speak.*

municate to one another in a nice way? Surprisingly, many families admit that their home is simply not a place where people respond nicely toward one another. The everyday courtesies of "please" and "thank you" are often ignored, as well as the praise and supportive comments that acknowledge success and appreciation in general. In order for a child to develop self-esteem, the number of positive things she hears must outweigh the negatives. If you really want to shock yourself, just for a day, or even a half day, count how many positive things are said as opposed to negative things. Also, take note of the volume at which things are spoken. Some families develop a yelling style that makes ordinary communication virtually impossible. If you come from a family of screamers, try this simple exercise. Whenever you have the urge to yell, lower your voice to just above a whisper. You may find that conversations, as well as your blood pressure, stay much more in control.

## BLAME DESTROYS SELF-ESTEEM  ◀

Another family style that breaks down self-esteem is the tendency for some family members to blame others. "It's your fault that nothing ever gets done around here." "If it wasn't for your messiness and inconsideration your father and I wouldn't fight so much." Messages that imply that a child is the cause of family trouble are very damaging to self-esteem. Children tend to feel responsible for family troubles. This is often the case when parents are divorcing. Many children from divorced homes say that if they had only behaved better, their mom and dad probably wouldn't have gotten a divorce. When children see parents fighting over how a child is being raised they feel responsible for the break-up of the family, and this can leave serious emotional scars for a lifetime.

An alternative to focusing on blame is focusing on responsibility. The idea of constructive criticism leaves plenty of room for talking to a child about maintaining responsibility for chores and other cooperative efforts around the house. When parents focus on what a child's responsibilities are, it becomes much easier to reinforce the positive instead of criticizing the negative.

## RELATIVES AND OTHER IMPORTANT ADULTS  ◀

Relatives and other important adults also influence a child's self-esteem. Siblings, especially older siblings, can have a powerful impact on a child's self-esteem in a positive or negative direction. Big brothers or sisters can sometimes tease in a way that amounts to emotional abuse. In one family I know, a six-year-old boy was stressed to the point of developing a stomach ulcer by his older brother telling him that his parents were going to put him in a foster home because he was such a pain in the neck. The younger child was too terrified to ask his parents about it for fear of finding out it might be true. When one sibling seems to be taking abuse or is being scapegoated by another sibling, parents must step in to support the child who is being teased. Parents should never, even as a joke, tease the child in the same way as the older sibling. Constant teasing, even if it is done in a presumably good-natured way, can be very damaging to confidence and self-esteem.

## TEACHERS INFLUENCE SELF-ESTEEM, TOO

Teachers are another group of important adults that help determine a child's self-esteem. Teachers spend as much or more time tending to children than parents do. While there are many excellent teachers who make a positive difference in children's lives, there are also teachers who are mean and who can damage a child's self-esteem.

## A BAD SITUATION IN SCHOOL

Just recently a parent told me that her nine-year-old son's teacher gave him back a test and in front of the entire class belittled him because he had failed the test, while a non-English-speaking Japanese classmate had been able to pass. The child was crushed by the fact that the comments were made for the whole class to hear, and that the teacher said it in such a disapproving tone. The child developed such bad feelings from the incident that he had bad dreams at night and refused to go to school. The outcome was that the parents had to change teachers midyear. The teacher was never even admonished by the principal for her behavior. I've heard many other stories of teachers calling children names, publicly humiliating them, or behaving in ways that are not child-centered. Of course, teachers are human and, like anyone else, can have a bad day. Parents do, however, need to investigate their children's complaints about teachers and talk to other parents whose children have had experiences with those teachers. By all means parents should be strong advocates of their children's welfare and do their best to make sure that they avoid placing their children with teachers that have a reputation for belittling students. I have found that parents are much too willing to tolerate inappropriate behavior by teachers. We have all grown up to believe that teachers know better, but some, unfortunately, do not. On the other hand, some teachers are truly remarkable human beings. A kind, concerned teacher can literally make the difference between a child becoming motivated to succeed and do well, versus burning out, becoming frustrated, and losing interest in school altogether.

## COACHES

Coaches are another example of adults who can make or break a child's self-esteem. Involving a child in organized sports with the right kind of coach can be a wonderful experience. With the wrong kind of coach, it can be a disaster. If you can, be sure to observe a coach in action before signing your child up for a sports team. The best coaches offer a balance between fostering the competitive spirit and allowing each child to have a chance to play. Look for a coach who praises sportsmanship and effort. Remove your child immediately from any team where you observe a coach calling a player stupid or using any derogatory language. Any coach who would do this is more concerned with his own ego than with your child's experience.

## PEERS

Peers constitute the third group of individuals that have a profound impact on your child's esteem. A good solid friendship can help any child, any person for that matter, weather the toughest emotional crisis. But peers can be one of the toughest problems parents have to deal with as well. So often a parent can see that a person who their child calls a friend is, in reality, bad news. Kind, sensitive children often wind up becoming friends with kids who take advantage of them. It's almost as if opposites attract in some cases. Children can be so caught up with wanting acceptance from another child that they let themselves be compromised. Parents hate to see this, but often when they try to give advice or intervene, their child protects the friend and gets upset with the parent. In cases such as these parents can do little more than sit back and help their child pick up the pieces when things fall apart.

> *You can't protect your child from every bad relationship, but your support and sympathy are always valued.*

Parents need to avoid telling their kids things like, "Oh, you know Mary is not really a good friend to you. She takes advantage of you and never calls you back when you leave phone messages for her." Instead be sympathetic and supportive. Ask if there is anything your child would like to talk about. Remark that so-and-so must feel very lucky to have a friend as nice as your child. Continue by saying that you have learned to appreciate friends like that, and that's why you always treat those kinds of friends with love and respect. In other words, instead of focusing on how rotten and mean the other child is being toward your child, praise and acknowledge the way your child behaves. By doing this you can hope that your child says, "You know, Mom (or Dad) is right. I am a good friend, and I should be treated a lot better than I am."

## FOUR PRACTICAL GUIDELINES TO BUILD SELF-ESTEEM ◀

**One: Accentuate the positive.** It is always more effective to praise the positive aspects of behavior than it is to punish the negative aspects. Look for reasons to praise your child's skills, talents, and abilities. Praise good effort, cooperation, good sportsmanship, and sticking with something until it is done. When your child does something negative, screen or censor your impulse to use a name like "brat" or "baby" to describe him. Counting to ten really does help you cool off in situations like this.

Avoid giving praise in negative ways. For instance, don't praise a child for good behavior by saying, "Finally, a day where I had ten minutes of peace and quiet," or "Well, look at the way you are dressed today. It's so nice to see you looking like a human being instead of like a street beggar," or "It looks like you still managed to do a good job on your homework, even though you waited much too long to do it." When you have to correct something negative, be supportive while you are doing it. For instance, say, "I know you can do a better job keeping your room neat if you put your mind to it." Help your child improve her behavior by setting a goal you know she can attain. You might say, "I want you to make sure that you pick up everything that can be thrown away and then empty the garbage. Next we can figure out what to do with all of these clothes that are lying around. I'll be back in a few minutes to check on how things are going."

## YOU CAN GIVE A CHILD TOO MUCH PRAISE

It is possible to praise a child too much. There is some very interesting research that indicates that when children are overpraised it makes them feel uncomfortable. This is especially true of children who have low self-esteem to begin with. If you praise a child for something that is not really outstanding they become mistrustful and wary. Focus your praise on specific behaviors and attitudes. Acknowledge the positive aspects of the behavior without laying it on too thick.

**Two: Be a good listener.** The way you listen is just as important as the way you talk. Be a patient listener. Try not to dispute what your child is saying. Reflect the feelings that your child is trying to communicate. For instance, if your child tells you that his feelings were upset by a friend who left him to go play with someone else, don't say, "Oh he's so mean, you can find better friends than that." Instead say, "Tell me all about it. It sounds like your feelings are hurt." Most parents want to make bad feelings go away as quickly as possible. They don't like to see their children hurt or upset. It's not always that important to "fix" bad feelings; just listening is often more desirable than long lectures or advice-giving sessions.

**Three: Show that you are listening with body language.** Be sure that you are giving your child nonverbal cues that indicate you are listening to what she is saying. If your child is telling you something and you have your back to her and are washing dishes, it is hard for her to tell that you are interested in what she has to say. If you are distracted by something that is more pressing, make plans to talk later, when you can give your complete attention.

Sometimes parents become frightened or put off when their child expresses something very negative. Children, especially younger children, can be very graphic when they are angry. Seven-year-old Christopher said he wanted to "break his brother's bones" when he teased him about something. Kids will often say they wished their teachers or friends or siblings would die or disappear and never come back. Don't be overly concerned by this. When children do this they're just venting their feelings. Children under twelve have not yet mastered abstract thinking, so they are much more likely to express their anger in more concrete terms.

**Four: Foster independence.** From the time children are old enough to button clothes and tie shoelaces, parents have to decide how much independence and autonomy their children should have. Some children are, by nature, very independent and demand autonomy at an early age. Other children need to be coaxed and cajoled into doing things on their own. Independence is a critical component of self-esteem. As we get older we must learn to fend for ourselves, manage ourselves, and, when necessary, spend time alone. Parents can sometimes express their *own* need to be needed by fostering dependence in their children. This can sometimes happen when a marriage is strained and a spouse is feeling unloved or neglected.

The issues of autonomy and independence express themselves in many ways, shapes, and forms throughout the growing-up years—from when to give up the bottle or pacifier in toddlerhood, to encouraging a child to pick out her own clothes and get dressed by herself in early childhood, to trusting a child to play safely outside of your supervision, to sitting down independently to study and do homework. If you teach your children to constantly rely on you they will never develop problem-solving or coping strategies for themselves. This will put them at a tremendous disadvantage later on. As a rule, encourage your child to brainstorm about a particular project or situation. Encourage him to examine all of the possible steps and evaluate each one to see if it will get him any closer to solving the problem. Reinforce good judgment, and gently question strategies that do not seem appropriate. Allow your child to learn from his mistakes without criticizing, and be sure to acknowledge the fact that he tried to solve the problem on his own.

## GIRLS AND SELF-ESTEEM

Research shows that we still live in a society that makes it more difficult for girls to develop self-esteem than boys. Although things have begun to change, girls are still treated much differently than boys. They are expected to be more passive and more dependent. Many teachers still assume that boys should excel in science, computers, and mathematics, but that these might not be worthwhile pursuits for girls. If you are raising a girl, you will need to be sensitive to people evaluating your child on the basis of her gender rather than on her interest patterns or abilities.

## QUICK REVIEW

1.  A good foundation of self-esteem in children is essential in creating the need to achieve and is an excellent hedge against drug and alcohol abuse.

2.  People with low self-esteem react to failure by blaming themselves and concluding that they will never be able to perform adequately. Parents need to teach children that failure is a step (it may be an unpleasant step) toward reaching a goal.

3.  Parents should take the time to praise effort and motivation (how hard someone tries) instead of simply the outcome of something (whether or not the child succeeds).

4.  Teach your child how to take "smart risks." A smart risk is an experience that challenges a person and may create a situation where the person fails, but, regardless of which way it turns out, something valuable is gained.

5.  Carefully examine the social situations your child is in. Note the people around her. Besides you, teachers, siblings, friends, coaches, and other relatives (Grandma, Grandpa, aunts, and uncles) all have an impact on a child's self-esteem. Who are the positive influences, and who are the negative ones?

6.  Blaming a child for problems in the family can destroy his self-esteem. What kinds of messages do you give when things aren't going well?

7.  If your child's teacher is giving negative messages to your child on a daily basis, you have a responsibility to intervene. Although many teachers are positive and supportive, some teachers destroy children's self-esteem.

8.  Always accentuate the positive in your child. Learn how to control your anger so you don't say things that you will regret later on. Be a good listener. Let your child know that what she is saying is important.

9.  Remember that girls need as much attention to their self-esteem as possible. We still live in a society that favors "masculine" characteristics.

## TURNING NEGATIVE MESSAGES INTO CONSTRUCTIVE FEEDBACK

When children misbehave or fall short of your expectations, it is easy to blurt out something you later wish you hadn't said. How would you rephrase the following negative messages into messages that do not destroy self-esteem? In each of these messages, eliminate the parts that are critical, demeaning, or negative. Replace them with a simple, neutral phrase or request for change. I'll start you off with some examples that preserve self-esteem.

### Messages That Preserve Esteem

"I'd like you to stop what you're doing and clean your room. I'll check back with you in ten minutes to make sure you've started."

"Please be more careful around those things. They break easily."

"The food you're eating is unhealthy. From now on it's off-limits unless you ask me first."

### Messages That Damage Esteem

"I can't believe you let yourself live like such a slob."
Better way of saying this:


"Why are you so lazy whenever it is time to do your homework?"
Better way of saying this:


"Why do you have to break everything you touch?"
Better way of saying this:

## EXERCISES FOR PARENTS

"I can't stand seeing you fight with your brother. You're like animals. Now both of you get out of my sight."
Better way of saying this:



"Put on a clean shirt. That one looks disgusting."
Better way of saying this:

# 5

# TEACHING YOUR
# CHILD SOCIAL SKILLS

All you need to do is spend an hour observing children interacting
with one another in any park or playground to see that some children
command a lot of attention and social power in a group, while others
are shy, passive, or withdrawn. Some children seem absolutely fearless
when it comes to introducing themselves to someone new, while others
sit and worry about whether they will be liked or accepted.

## PEOPLE SKILLS

Good social or "people" skills are very important for success in life. A
person can be very book smart and have impressive knowledge, but he
probably will not get as far as someone with average intelligence but
a keen sense of how to interact positively with people. Knowing how
to interact with people probably constitutes a type of intelligence all its
own. Dr. Howard Gardner, one of Harvard's most well-respected contemporary psychologists, has been working to redefine our notions about
intelligence. In his work he identifies something he calls the "social
intelligences" to describe the cluster of skills and abilities essential to
making positive and effective contact with people.

# IS YOUR CHILD A "PEOPLE" PERSON?

Review these skills and qualities to see if your child has good social skills. Although you can usually see these qualities a bit earlier, the descriptions I'll present here fit children who are five years and older. The child with good social skills:

- Doesn't mind sharing.
- Can wait his turn or even give up his turn in a game.
- Is sensitive to other children. The child with good social skills can often be seen comforting a crying child in a schoolyard, or sticking up for someone who is being taken advantage of.
- Keeps good eye contact and open body language when communicating.
- Is not afraid of new kids or new situations, and actually seems to thrive in those conditions.
- Is usually a natural leader. She wants to take charge, and other kids want her to take charge, too.
- Is often sought out as company for play dates and after-school activities.
- Smiles and laughs a lot, and knows how to give compliments. In general, kids with good social skills know how to make people feel good.
- Has a good image of himself.

On the opposite end of the "people skills" scale are children who are shy, withdrawn, and almost afraid of people. That is not to say that they always have poor social skills. Sometimes children can be very polite but are just very shy. Some children, however, do seem to have poor social skills and, without wanting to or realizing it, rub other children the wrong way.

## ZACH HAS PROBLEMS PLAYING WITH FRIENDS

Seven-year-old Zach has always had a difficult time with other kids. From the time his parents could remember, he preferred playing by himself. When he was a toddler, he was very aggressive and tended to push or hit the other children he played with. As he got older, his mom and dad saw that he didn't seem to know what to do when a friend came over. Once, last year, he had a play date with a child that he idolized and spoke about all the time. When the friend came over to play, Zach insisted on choosing all of the games they played. The other child became frustrated when Zach took all the turns and made him watch for practically the whole time. The two boys wound up arguing. One thing led to another, and Zach punched the other little boy. It was almost impossible for his parents to explain to Zach why the boy wouldn't return to play again. Zach insisted he did nothing wrong.

This was one of the most frustrating aspects of Zach's behavior—the fact that he could never figure out why he produced such a negative response from friends. Zach's parents realized that it wasn't that Zach would never learn how to make friends, but that it would take a lot longer for them to teach Zach about this area of life because he wasn't naturally skilled at it.

Parents often wonder what makes some children so naturally social while others have so much difficulty in this area. The answer to this question might very well lie in the genes. Shyness, for example, appears to be a trait that is very much influenced by temperament, the genetic contribution to behavior. People who are very shy feel almost as if it is a handicap because they have so much trouble speaking up in groups or overcoming fears, anxieties, and embarrassments about social situations. If shyness is genetically influenced, does it mean that a shy person will be controlled by their shyness forever? Of course not. It just means that a shy person will have to work harder and overcome more to be more outgoing. Or, with children who just don't seem to understand the rules of good social behavior, it is a case of teaching them a more desirable way of interacting with others. Just about anything is possible with the right kind of support and motivation. The job of the parent in either of these situations is to be a good role model and teacher, and to avoid the use of harsh criticism.

# WHAT PARENTS CAN DO TO HELP

What can parents do to enhance their child's social skills and provide the foundation for good interpersonal relationships? Plenty. I've outlined some of the most important skills you can teach your child in this nine-point list. Let's see what they are and how to teach them.

**Skill one: teaching children how to say "hello."** Start by teaching children that it is OK to approach someone and introduce yourself. This skill, which is as simple as walking over to someone and saying, "Hello, my name is Peter," is one of the biggest stumbling blocks for all people who feel uncomfortable in social situations. Introducing oneself creates anxiety and tension because people worry that they will be rejected or thought of as odd or crazy for just walking up to someone and talking to them. To adults with this fear I always say, "Well, it's your choice. If you don't try, you'll never risk being thought of as odd or pushy, but then again, you'll also never know how many great relationships you've let yourself miss out on, either." Children can't really relate to this point of view, but they have an advantage over adults in this area. Although children can be mean and rejecting, most times they aren't nearly as judgmental or standoffish as adults are and tend to be more open to friendship. When a child is mean, it is usually because he perceives a difference between himself and a child who wants to be part of the group. The key to minimizing the risk of this happening is to give your child a chance to make new friends in an atmosphere where there is a "common ground." For example, you might bring your child to a place where other children are interacting for the first time. It would be a bit more risky to bring your child to a place where there is an established group of children who have been playing together for a long time.

> *Not all children are born communicators. Some must be taught even simple skills such as introducing themselves.*

Teaching children this skill can be especially difficult if you are afraid of approaching people, too. An excellent way to begin teaching this skill to younger children is by role-playing with dolls or toys. Be sure to let your child play the role of the person being approached as well as the one doing the approaching. This way she will recognize that it can be flattering when someone wants to meet you. With older children, say seven or older, you will have more to rehearse. The older children get, the more they tend to break off into cliques or groups, shunning newcomers or "outsiders." You will have to prepare your child for the possibility that she might be rejected. Do this by explaining that people in cliques are sometimes unfair when they're approached. It is always best to try to approach someone you want to make friends with away from his group.

While you are teaching your child to introduce himself you must also teach him to ask permission to join the other child in whatever situation he is in. When this is done politely, it greatly reduces the chance that the other child will feel forced or pressured to let the child doing the asking join in. Here are some examples: "Hi, my name is Peter. What's yours? If you're not doing anything, would you like to play together?" or "Hi, my name is Peter, would you like to play catch with me?" or, for older kids, "Hi, my name is Peter.

> *Children with good social skills have a warm personal style and know how to put people at ease.*

I recognize you from school. I was wondering about whether you'd like to hang out after school one day." or "Hi, my name is Peter. Would you mind if I sat with you during lunch today?"

There is no real formula other than introducing yourself, smiling politely, and asking if it would be OK to join in whatever the other person is doing. Acknowledge that introducing yourself is a very difficult thing to do, but also point out that once you get up the nerve and actually meet some people, you will be very happy that you are not feeling alone or left out anymore.

## Skill two: learning how to put people at ease. After introducing yourself to someone, it is important to let them know that you are friendly. Communicating this requires sensitivity to what is appropriate and what is not in social situations. For instance, right after his parents got a divorce, seven-year-old Brian moved to a new neighborhood. He didn't have any trouble introducing himself to people but tended to say things like, "I'm Brian. I just moved here because my parents got divorced. Are *your* parents divorced?" Brian didn't really understand that talking about very personal information can be seen as negative in the beginning of a

relationship. What people look for in the beginning of a relationship is warmth. The child who greets his friends with a smile on his face and who is not quick to broadcast bad news or complaints to everyone is a child who will be welcomed.

There are many ways to communicate that you are happy to see someone. Some involve nonverbal gestures such as a handshake, a smile, a pat on the arm, or a hug. Others involve questions that show you are interested in the general well-being of the other person. "How's it goin'?" "How's life treatin' you?" "What's up?" These are all common everyday examples. People who feel uncomfortable in social situations sometimes say that these things sound corny or stupid to them. As corny and stupid as they might sound, these are things that most people consider signs of warmth and interest. One of the most common things that people say about friendly people is "He always says 'Hello.'" It's remarkable how that one little word can help enhance a person's popularity.

### Skill three: showing empathy.
Empathy is something psychologists spend an awful lot of time thinking and writing about. Empathy describes our ability to communicate to people that we understand their point of view. It goes far beyond just being able to say, "I know how you feel." As a matter of fact, some people really hate it when that is said in an attempt to comfort them. Having empathy means telling a person that you understand their point of view and showing them through your actions as a friend that you can appreciate what they feel. Empathy is the most necessary ingredient to forgiving someone who has made you angry or upset, and forgiveness is one of the most essential ingredients in close relationships. True friends never plan to hurt the people they are close to. Circumstances, imperfections, and sometimes even fears of losing friends can cause people to do foolish things and inadvertantly hurt someone's feelings. Empathy allows us to acknowledge that the closer we become to someone, the more we are allowed to see that they're imperfect. Empathy permits us to forgive someone for being imperfect. It doesn't take away the sting of the hurt as much as it paves the way for the relationship to continue without resentment.

> *Saying "I'm sorry" when we're wrong is one of the most important people skills anyone can learn.*

Teaching children to become empathetic can only be done by example. Your child will learn empathy if you are sensitive and demonstrate the quality yourself. It used to be thought that children under the age of five could not learn empathy, but recent research seems to suggest that even toddlers can learn a very rudimentary kind of sensitivity and empathy. One of the greatest ways to enhance your child's social skills, therefore, is to demonstrate a warm, sensitive, empathetic style yourself.

### Skill four: understanding the importance of loyalty. Kids
between the ages of, say, five and eleven tend to base friendships on utility. It is not unusual to hear of one friend dumping another because a third child has better toys or promises something more interesting to do. Children frequently complain about someone stealing a friend away from them. As kids grow older, however, loyalty and trustworthiness become the cornerstones of good relationships. The time for impressing these values on children is as early as possible. Gently question your child if you notice that she is gravitating toward a child because of material things or promises, or if you know she is hurting someone's feelings by leaving them to play with someone else. For example,

> *As kids get older, loyalty and trustworthiness become the cornerstones of their relationships.*

"I notice that you have been spending a lot of time at Billy's house since he got his new computer. Do you think Mark is upset that you don't seem to call him as much anymore?" It is almost impossible to make a young child own up to responsibility in relationships—indeed, it is much better to let a child see the consequences of her own actions in relationships. But from time to time it is good to plant the seed by gently asking about or reflecting back on the situation you have observed.

### Skill five: tuning in to body language. Children who are socially
successful show confidence in their walk, their smile, and their gestures. They understand the rules of personal space. They are physically close when appropriate, and they back off when appropriate. Children who have difficulty with social skills crowd other children, use inappropriate body contact, and have a difficult time modulating the tone of their voice or their gestures. Kids who have a hard time with their gestures

and body language can appear rude, overbearing, or nerdy. The type of behavior I am talking about is very easy for many parents to observe, but they often don't have the slightest idea of what to do about it.

## "KEISHA ALWAYS LOOKS OUT OF PLACE"

One mom recently told me, "Keisha always looks out of place in a group of children. She seems uncomfortable in her own body. She never knows where to sit or stand or even where to look. I know the other children make fun of her. They call her 'geek' or 'nerd.' I just don't know what to do. Can you coach a child to be 'cool'"? Keisha's mom makes some keen observations and excellent points. Even if you can identify behavior that makes a child appear gawky or uncomfortable, can you do anything about it?

Actually, there's a lot you can do about it. The first thing to do is to make your child more comfortable in her own territory. Offer your child the opportunity to use your home as a place for entertaining other children. In her own territory your child will feel more comfortable and familiar. As a host she will have more control and social power. Another thing you can do is some role-playing exercises. Many children who have social difficulties are overly "touchy." They are too quick to put their arms around someone or get too physically close. While children are growing up they go through different stages and can be very embarrassed about being touched. This is especially so of boys approaching the age of seven or eight, who are usually oversensitized to the issue of homosexuality and will repel another little boy who tries to get too close. It is unfortunate that this is the case, but it is a fact of growing up. Parents are the best people to gently encourage their children to use an appropriate physical distance. Teach your child how to recognize appropriate behavior by pointing it out when you are walking past a park or school. It might not be possible to teach your child how to be "cool," but you can help her develop a finer sense for which kinds of behavior are acceptable and which are not.

Skill six: understanding the value of compromise. Children, like all people, engage in power struggles in their relationships. What toys to play with, who to invite over, what activity to do next—all are items that are negotiated during almost every play session. The child who is rigid and must control every aspect of the relationship will often find himself out of favor with friends. So, by the way, will kids who are very passive and agree to everything. Children who understand the value of compromise will do best and will be sought out by other children.

The other day I watched two children try to make a play decision at the park. One child wanted to practice pitching, while the other wanted to play basketball. The child who wanted to practice pitching was whining to the other child. It was annoying even for *me* to listen to. Finally, the child who wanted to play basketball said very matter-of-factly, "OK, look, I don't really want to sit there and catch balls for you all day. I'll give you sixty pitches, and then we'll stop and play basketball for a while." The other child perked right up. Now, I don't know whether sixty pitches was a good compromise or a bad compromise or where the number even came from. In their ten-year-old world, however, the number seemed very adequate. I did notice the two of them playing basketball by the end of the afternoon, so it seemed like they worked it out. This problem was resolved because one of the boys rose above the selfishness of insisting on doing what he wanted to do to offer a solution to the problem. Children will learn this skill if they come from an environment that allows them to make choices and suggest reasonable compromises.

> *The child who understands the value of compromise will be sought out as a friend by other children.*

Skill seven: learning how to say you're sorry. A bit earlier I said that forgiveness and empathy are vital to successful relationships. Well, empathy and forgiveness are delivered a lot more easily when apologies come from the other side. Admitting that you have behaved in a mean or inconsiderate way is difficult. Doing so is a direct statement that the relationship is important enough to rise above that difficulty. It is hard to apologize to your children, but sometimes parents do make mistakes. I'm probably beginning to sound monotonous by now, but the only way you can teach the importance of apologizing to your child is by example. Parents truly are the models for all of the most necessary ingredients of successful relationships of all types. If you treat your children with respect, warmth, and love, they will have firsthand experience in what it means to be a good partner in a relationship.

**Skill eight: being a "team player."** Children need to learn to be team players. It is true that children respect leadership qualities, and those qualities are important to value and reinforce. By the same token, however, even the best leaders understand the value of working as a team. Leaders direct the team, but they are also a part of it. Being bossy or pushy does not equal good leadership.

## HARRY: A BIT TOO BOSSY

Being a good leader and being bossy are two very different things. Nine-year-old Harry found this out the hard way. Harry has a very aggressive personality. When he moved to a new school he wanted to make sure everyone knew he was there. Because he is so persuasive, Harry convinced four or five children he knew to be part of a game he made up called "basic training." Every day he would lead the group of kids he assembled in exercises, karate fights, and other activities. After a few weeks there was a mutiny. The kids didn't like being told what to do by Harry anymore, and they told him that they would prefer it if he returned to his old school.

This story is a good example of how possible it is to turn other kids off even if you are relatively outgoing. Harry is certainly outgoing, but he has too much of a need to control what's going on, and that is what has created difficulty with his friends.

**Skill nine: successfully negotiating conflict resolution.** Parents can help kids be socially successful by teaching them not to use aggression to solve problems. Kids who are bullies command attention in social settings through fear and intimidation—not unlike some adults. Bullies usually learn their style very early on. Contrary to popular belief, a bully is not always a physically superior child. Sometimes it is the smaller kids who have learned that they can quickly take control of a group of children by being aggressive. Either way, parents have to be honest with themselves about what they observe. If your child tends to intimidate other children, it is time to intervene. First, look at your own style. Children who hit might be aggressive because they live in a house where hitting, pushing, and spanking are acceptable ways of expressing anger. Kids who are spanked are frequently the most aggressive kids in a group. If your child is heavily involved in sports, examine the way you or your spouse has reinforced competitiveness. Have you stressed that "winning is everything," or that you must "crush" anyone who opposes you? Competitiveness can be a very positive trait when it is tempered by sensitivity, but it can also be very destructive.

## TEACH BY EXAMPLE

The very best way to teach your child social skills is to use them yourself. This can be done in a number of important ways. Here are just a few.

1. Be a good listener. Show your child that you want to hear what she has to say. Let her express her feelings. Try not to criticize or interrupt. Maintain eye contact when your child addresses you.

2. Let your child see you treating your own friends well. Your child will notice how you treat other people. Do you give your friends a smile and a warm greeting? Do you compliment them? Do you tend to gossip about them when they are not around, or talk down about them? Kids will pick up on the negative things you say about people when they are not around.

3. Show your child how people respond to his behavior. Let your child know when he's made a friend feel comfortable

and welcome. When he's rude or rough, gently point out to him that his behavior made someone else uncomfortable or upset. Praise and reinforce your child for following simple but necessary rules of etiquette like saying, "please," "thank you," and "you're welcome."

4. Teach your child how to give genuine compliments by giving them yourself. Try not to give "backhanded" compliments such as, "You dressed yourself in colors that match for a change." Let your child know that her opinion is important. This will help build self-esteem, and self-esteem is very important to making friends. Let your child know that her opinion counts for something even if you don't agree with it, and that her opinions are an important part of the family decision-making process.

5. Resolve family conflicts in healthy ways. If your child sees you resolve conflicts by yelling, hitting, or putting down another person, chances are he will imitate that style. Teach the values of forgiveness, empathy, and compromise. When you lose your temper, apologize. This shows your child that it is OK to say you're sorry. Saying you're sorry can repair hurt feelings in a relationship.

6. Respect your child's preferences when it comes to friends. Some children prefer the company of one or two close friends; others are more comfortable in a large group. Girls, on the whole, tend to have closer one-to-one relationships, while boys tend to play more in groups. Whichever your child's preference, try to respect it. Try to prevent yourself from meddling in your child's friendships although the temptation will be very hard to resist, especially when you feel as though your child isn't being treated nicely by a friend. When you see that your child is being mistreated by a friend it is always better to focus on your child's behavior by saying, "Gee, Betty must feel very lucky to have someone who is as good a friend as you." This way, if your child ever feels put off by that person, she will have that as a reference for saying, "You know I've treated her very nicely. This isn't fair."

From time to time you will see your child become frustrated, upset, disappointed, or hurt by something that has happened between him and a friend. These are difficult times. Parents feel naturally protective and don't want their children to be hurt by others. Sometimes the tendency is to say something like, "Oh, she wasn't a good friend anyway. You'll find a better friend and be much happier." In our haste to soothe the wound, we don't realize that this approach almost never works. Instead, listen quietly, encourage your child to tell you the details of whatever situation caused her to feel upset and respond to the feelings by saying, "Oh, that must have really hurt your feelings." Resist the urge to say things like, "Well what did you do to make Betty not want to play with you in the first place?" Human relationships are difficult to manage at any age. You will have much more influence as a supportive listener who can give gentle advice in very small quantities.

## SOCIAL-SKILLS GROUPS

If your child has a lot of social difficulties it might be helpful to try to locate a social-skills training group in your area. These groups are run by psychologists, social workers, or other professionals and can be very helpful. Speak with your pediatrician or with your child's teacher or guidance counselor to get feedback from other people who know your child. Watching a child grow up can be a very difficult thing for parents. There is so much to try to protect children from, yet at the same time, you want to make sure that kids have the skills they need to handle themselves without your intervention, and ultimately to be successful human beings.

Good "people sense" is as important as anything kids will ever learn in school. Teaching positive ways of socializing begins in infancy, when parents first notice at around six weeks of age that children will smile when they recognize their caregivers. It is at this point that the child begins to make the connection that his actions generate responses from other people. From here, parents need to help children become aware of the connection between their behavior and the behavior of the people around them.

1. Children vary in how comfortable they are with and around other people. Some children are naturals when it comes to socializing and interacting; other children are fearful and hesitant about social situations. Some people believe that this is an inborn tendency, but *anyone* can learn how to be more social and comfortable around people.

2. Do not hesitate to teach your child how to introduce herself to others. A simple introduction is best. "Hello, my name is so-and-so. Would you like to play?" Good eye contact and open body language are also essential elements in this situation.

3. Cultivate warmth and empathy in your children by encouraging them to understand what it is like to be "in another person's shoes."

4. Your child will develop good social interaction skills if you treat him with kindness and respect. Always remember that how you treat your child forms the basis for how he will treat others.

5. Teach your child the value of compromise. It is better to be with someone you like and do what they would like to do, than do what you like but do it alone. When you play with friends, you have to compromise on the things you would like to do.

6. Teach your child the importance of apologizing for doing something that hurt someone else's feelings. Many people feel as though it is a sign of weakness to apologize. Good friends know how to resolve conflicts and move on.

7. Leadership is a great trait and one that should be reinforced. Being a team player is also important. Try to help your child understand the importance of things like group support, sportsmanship, and modesty—especially if she is aggressive or somewhat overbearing.

**EXERCISES FOR PARENTS**

These exercises are most appropriate for children who are between four and seven years old. Use them to stimulate discussion about friends and social issues.

## ROLE PLAYING WITH DOLLS, PUPPETS, AND TOYS

Using dolls or sock puppets, engage your child in a fantasy story about making friends. Use the puppets to practice saying "hello" or to work through difficult situations. Be sure to respond to all of the emotions of the story. Try not to interfere with the fantasy during the playtime by asking direct questions like, "Were you feeling angry at Lisa the way the puppet was feeling angry about her friend?" Later on in the day or at night before bedtime you may carefully broach the subject. Above all, never interrogate. If you are patient, children will open up and tell you what's on their mind.

## THE "GUESS WHY" GAME

This game represents a variation of the fantasy role-playing game. You simply ask a question and then tell the child to "guess why." Never prod or push for an answer, and if the child is not interested in playing, don't force him to continue.

1. *A little girl (or boy) named (make up a name but don't use your child's name) doesn't think anyone wants to play with her. Can you guess why?*

2. *(Name) wants to make friends with someone he likes, but is afraid to do it. Can you guess why?*

3. *(Name) was playing with a friend, and another little girl (or boy) came over and started to play. (Name) and the new friend left the first friend behind and that made her very sad. Can you guess why?*

4. *(Name) wouldn't let any of his (or her) friends play with his new toy, and then everyone was sad and angry. Can you guess why?*

5. *(Name) doesn't want to play at her friend's house anymore. Can you guess why?*

# 6

# TEACHING YOUR
# CHILD RESPONSIBILITY

All parents want their children to grow up to be responsible, but how often do we ask ourselves what we mean by that? There are different kinds of responsibility. One type of responsibility relates to everyday things like doing chores around the house, getting ready for school in the morning, and doing homework. These responsibilities come from developing certain habits. Forming these habits makes us productive, reliable workers. A second type of responsibility is related more to attitudes and beliefs. It is the type of responsibility that goes with admitting mistakes, being unselfish, and caring for another individual's health or feelings. Developing these types of responsibilities makes us more than reliable workers—it makes us special people.

Most of the parents I speak to want their children to grow up to be good people. They want their toddlers to learn to share, they want their three- to five-year-olds to learn how to play nicely with other children, they want their eight- to twelve-year-olds to develop good manners and do their homework, and they want their thirteen- to eighteen-year-olds to develop the skills necessary to become successful, independently functioning human beings. All of these things require a sense of responsibility.

## CHILDREN AREN'T BORN BEING RESPONSIBLE

How do you teach children to be responsible? Well, the first important thing to consider is the word *teach*. Kids are not born with an overwhelming desire to be responsible. Maybe that's because being responsible requires a certain level of giving, and young children are more likely to look for things that others will give *them*, such as nurturance, food, and support. Some of the hardest adjustments a child has to make are the adjustments that go along with becoming independent, and responsibility and independence go hand in hand.

You can see how hard this adjustment is when you observe a three- or four-year-old child learn to adjust to the presence of a new baby brother or sister. All of a sudden life becomes a lot more difficult. Getting Mom or Dad's attention isn't such a sure thing anymore, and horror of all horrors, they even ask you to help *do* things for that little pain in the neck. Sometimes the reaction is to want to become more childlike and go back to drinking from a bottle and wearing diapers. After all, life was much simpler then. Mom and Dad showed how much they loved you by doing stuff for you.

## RESPONSIBILITY AT THREE YEARS

Some of the classic ideas and theories about psychology and human behavior placed a great deal of emphasis on the period of life between two and four years old because the whole experience of toilet training was supposed to predict a lot about how responsible and well-controlled a person would turn out. While I don't believe that the toilet-training experience has to have a profound influence on the rest of your life or personality development, I will say that it does highlight a kind of transitional period in a person's life.

> *In order to develop responsibility, children must be allowed the opportunity to be responsible.*

Learning how to take responsibility for yourself does begin happening at about three or four years of age, and it doesn't only involve toilet training. Most three-year-old children can begin learning simple responsibilities that include picking up toys, dusting off a tabletop, or washing a bunch of carrots.

Many kids this age take a great deal of joy and delight in doing simple tasks like these, especially if they find that it brings them a new kind of attention from Mom and Dad. And that's where it all starts. You see, a moment ago I spoke about the difference between responsibility that develops out of good habits and responsibility that develops from having certain attitudes and beliefs. At three or four years old the process is very simple—you ask your three-year-old son to help wash the carrots for dinner. He does it, and you make a big fuss over him for being such a big boy and so helpful. It's the praise and support that you give him that begins to lay the foundation not only for the habit, but for the idea that being helpful to another human being is a rewarding, satisfying experience. As long as both of these things are happening, whether the child is three or sixteen, he will grow up to be responsible and also have the internal sense of responsibility that is so important.

## KEYS TO TEACHING CHILDREN RESPONSIBILITY

Teaching children how to be responsible is not as difficult as it seems, and there are a few key steps you can take that make the job a lot easier. I'd like to share these with you now.

**Responsibility involves moving a child away from a natural tendency.** Remember that when you are teaching a child about responsibility you are moving the child away from his natural tendency to be more interested in himself and his needs than in others and their needs. If children seem selfish or self-centered, please understand that they are designed to be that way. Our biology forces us to have a strong need for self-preservation so that we can survive. That's one reason why kids are so demanding, and it's why they are always behaving in ways that say, "Take care of me" and "Make sure I get what I want." It is a kind of survival insurance. One of the beautiful parts about how parenting works is that through interaction with their parents, children learn how to become *less* dependent and *more* self-reliant, and in the end it is this interaction that contributes most to healthy survival. But all of this is a process that happens over time.

**Give plenty of opportunity to be responsible.** A child will only learn to be responsible if he is given the opportunity to be responsible.

The hectic two-working-parents family lifestyle and the difficult single-parent lifestyle have given us the opportunity to see what happens to children when they are given a lot of responsibility at an early age. We call kids who take care of themselves after school "latchkey" kids. Kids as young as nine or ten years old are taking care of themselves after school, starting dinner, cleaning the house, and minding siblings. Research shows us that although it may be difficult and far from an ideal childhood, most latchkey kids do handle the responsibility, and they handle it well. This shows us something about the capacity of kids to learn responsibility. Now, please understand that I am not in favor of having a child manage his whole life or be responsible for the running of a household at nine years of age, but if a child has the capacity to take on that much, then you should certainly help encourage responsible attitudes by developing a set of reasonable expectations about responsibility.

**Develop a set of reasonable expectations for your child.** At every stage of a child's life, parents need to sit down and formally develop a set of reasonable expectations of responsibility. Parents should begin when a child is three or four years old and revise the expectations as the child grows and matures. Simple tasks around the house are appropriate for three- to five-year-olds. These include putting toys away, shutting off the television when it is time to stop watching, settling into bedtime and bathroom routines, helping set the table by putting napkins out, and taking her own dish away from the table. During this period of life, parents have to make a conscious effort to be aware that children are already developing a sense of independence. At this age children are no longer helpless infants; they can do things! Praise effort and reward your child when he does things without having to be reminded.

## HOMEWORK RESPONSIBILITY

Expectations increase when a child enters school and homework becomes a responsibility. As early as possible, parents need to evaluate their child's work habits. Children who are "turned off" to school usually turn off very early. From kindergarten or first grade, parents should be aware if sitting still to do homework is frustrating and causes major problems. Look for signs that your child is avoiding homework tasks. These signs include not writing down assignments, not bringing home books, and "forgetting" that there is a test or report due the next day. Quite often these behaviors are associated with learning difficulties or attention and concentration problems. Please don't assume that your child is lazy or unmotivated. If your child is having trouble sitting still to do homework, have a competent professional rule out the existence of any learning problems.

Record keeping for homework assignments and tests and quizzes is a good way to start developing responsible habits. Most second graders should be able to keep a written homework-assignment record. By the time children reach fourth grade they should be able to do most schoolwork independently. That means they shouldn't be relying on you to write or type reports for them or do other projects. But that doesn't mean you can't be helpful. If your child is having a hard time getting organized for these tasks, help by making an outline or a time line and breaking large complicated tasks into smaller ones. A typical outline for a book report might consist of going to the library, reading a third of the book by a certain date, the second third of the book by another date, and the last third by another date. Set a date for writing an outline for the book report and a date for the actual writing of the book report.

By ten or eleven years old your child should begin having some experience managing money. Managing money is one of the most difficult and stress-inducing aspects of adult life. If kids learn how to be responsible with money early on, it will be of great benefit later. Some parents choose to give an allowance. Although everyone has different views on allowance, I think it is important for children to learn that financial rewards come with work. The notion of allowance without work seems like a missed opportunity to me. When you give a child an allowance that is tied into doing chores or work, it becomes much more meaningful and begins teaching children about the rewards and frustrations of having to "earn a living." Parents should be very clear about what allowance money is used for, and at what point children become responsible for buying their own sneakers, clothes, and things like that. As children get older, they might be able to secure a little income from babysitting, delivering the paper, or doing other odd jobs.

At this point, and there are a number of opinions on this issue as well, parents have to decide whether they will ask their children to contribute a portion of their earnings to help run the house. Parents are often reluctant to ask their children for a portion of their hard-earned money, but one day, when life is more than just an exercise, your children will need to budget for life's necessities. If children give 10 percent of their earnings back to "the house" as it were, you can trade off that 10 percent for privileges. This way the child gets the satisfaction of knowing and feeling that he is a contributing member of the family and also receives the reward of added freedom in the form of privileges earned from being a responsible person.

## WHEN KIDS DON'T MEET THEIR RESPONSIBILITIES

Now go a little further and consider what happens when kids are given responsibility but don't own up to it. Invariably, children will reach a point where they fall short of your expectations for responsibility. Chores might go undone, their room might be a mess, or a note home from a teacher saying that homework or a project hasn't been handed in might be sent home. There are several pitfalls that parents fall into when dealing with situations like these.

## AVOIDANCE

Sometimes it is easiest to avoid dealing with tough situations altogether. Parents tend to do this when frustration is high. Have you ever let yourself avoid dealing with a situation by saying things like, "Oh, you'll never learn to clean your room, you'll always be a slob," or "I can see I'm not going to get any help around here today, so I might as well set the table myself," or "It's so much trouble to get her to do things. She fights me every step of the way. I'd rather just back off and avoid a war. She'll never learn, and I only get aggravated." When you use logic like this you have basically given up your responsibility as a parent. It's not hard to get to this point when you have tried your best to encourage a certain pattern of behavior and things are not working out as you had planned.

The main drawback of falling into this pattern is that your child will live up to the expectations you have set for him—the child who is not motivated to clean his room will grow up to be sloppy about how he keeps his things. The child who is let off the hook for not setting the table will never offer to help around the house because she will feel she doesn't have to. The child who bullies you by fussing, complaining, or having temper tantrums over responsibilities will learn that this is an effective way of avoiding the discomfort of having to do work. He will develop an attitude that is based on the idea

> *When a child behaves irresponsibly, it's up to the parent to confront the child and correct the behavior.*

that when anyone asks him to become responsible, it is an insult. The prevailing attitude will become, "How dare anyone tell me to do something I don't feel like doing."

It should be clear that doing nothing or avoiding confrontation with a child who is not living up to her responsibilities creates serious problems in the long run. If you are the type of person who grew up shying away from difficult confrontations, understand that unless kids are directed and given structure they will usually choose the mode of behavior that makes life easier for them. They will care less about their work and will behave in ways that make them dependent on others. They will appear selfish rather than independent. Confronting children in a situation where they have avoided responsibility doesn't have to turn into a battle. A simple and effective strategy in these situations is to stay focused on the behavior.

## HE'D RATHER PLAY VIDEO GAMES THAN COME FOR DINNER

Let's take the case of a child who has been told to set the table for dinner, but is more interested in playing video games. The first time Mom asks for help setting the table the response is "in a minute." Mom doesn't want a confrontation so she waits. In ten minutes she has to ask again. Now the response is, "I just want to finish this one game." Another few minutes goes by. Mom asks again. This time the response is "OK," but there is no action, he just keeps on playing. Does this sound like a familiar story? What's causing the problem in this situation? Would you say the problem is being caused by the child who is being lazy? Or by the parent who doesn't want to behave assertively by stepping in and requiring the child to stop playing? What's the alternative in this situation?

Here is how it could have happened a different way. Mom makes the request for help setting the table. The response is "in a minute." Even if you want to give in a little to the child's desire to play his game you can say, "OK, finish up. But in a few minutes I'm going to ask you again, and if you don't shut it off and give me a hand I'm going to have to shut it off myself." You see in this situation, you remain in charge, and you decide when the game playing stops. You don't have to be mean or aggressive about it. You don't even have to say, "Shut that game off this minute and get in here and help," which would be too aggressive. The key in this situation, and many others, is to make sure that you are calling the shots and are remaining focused. Now is not the time to launch into a speech about how he never does anything the first time you ask, or how inconsiderate he is about doing chores or whatever it is you argue about in these situations. Remember, stay focused on the behavior.

Now I can hear some of you asking what happens when you say you are coming over to turn off the video game and your child whines, complains, or starts a fight when you do? What happens then is you briefly review the situation, again staying focused on the behavior, and say, "I need you to help me with the table. In order to do that you have to stop playing for now." That's all you need to say, keep it very plain and simple and stick to the situation. Now give your child a choice, again, using a firm and assertive tone. "You can help me set the table now, or you can disconnect the video game and put it away for a few days so that it doesn't prevent you from doing your chores. It's up to you." Most kids won't push it past this point. You have stood your ground and have also shown them that there are worse things that can happen than just temporarily stopping play.

## TOO MANY WARNINGS ◀

In a perfect world, all people would ever need after behaving selfishly is a warning not to let it happen again. In reality, this style isn't too different from avoidance. The way I recommended that Mom resolve the problem of her child not wanting to leave the game to set the table was to provide a consequence, which was to lose video-game-playing privileges altogether. The consequence was explained in the form of a choice. Giving a choice is crucial to motivating the proper behavior. It helps the child put the situation into perspective and forces the reasoning, in this case, that setting the table isn't so bad compared to losing the privilege for a few days. When parents give warnings about behavior they are allowing the opportunity for the behavior to happen again. They are putting off having to confront the behavior until the next time. Talking about a behavior without acting on it sets up a pattern where kids will learn that they will always have a few free chances at avoiding responsibility before they have to give in and accept it. Ultimately this will create a barrier to learning how to be responsible.

## CREATING GUILT OR SHAME ◀

Creating guilt as a means of coercing responsibility can have bad side effects. While all parents want their children to be responsible, I can't think of anyone who wants her children to feel so responsible that they interpret everything as their fault. Have you ever spent time around someone who apologizes for everything, even when they have nothing to do with what is going on? People like this can make you feel very uncomfortable simply because they always act as if they have disappointed you.

> *Creating guilt or shame as a means of coercing responsibility in your child can have negative consequences.*

When children are controlled by guilt they often resent living up to their responsibilities, even though they do. Guilt forces someone to behave in a certain way because there is an outside influence compelling it to happen. Parents want responsibility to develop from the *inside*. The only way this can happen is by placing your child in situations where responsibility is valued and appreciated. Even if you have to give your child the choice between setting the table or losing video-game privileges, after he sets the table you must be sure to acknowledge the responsible behavior in a positive way. The parent who uses guilt will say, "I can't believe that I had to threaten you with taking your game away before you would help me. After all, I do so much for you, you really disappoint me." The parent who encourages responsibility from within will say, "I know it was hard for you to leave your game to help me. Thanks for helping me." Teaching responsibility to children means that you have to understand that accepting responsibility means accepting discomfort. Parents can teach this lesson by appreciating the times a child does step away from that comfortable situation to accept the responsibility. Taking on the responsibility might be uncomfortable, but the new reward is the sense of satisfaction and the praise received for doing it.

# PUNISHMENT

Another style parents use to produce responsible behavior is punishing kids when they don't live up to their responsibilities. Now here I have to make a distinction between punishment and consequences. Punishment is a response parents make after something happens.

> *Punishment usually does not increase a child's motivation to behave responsibly.*

The intent of punishment is to "teach a lesson," although punishment very rarely works to stop behavior. A typical example of punishment might result when you walk into your child's room after you have told her a hundred times to clean it up and it still looks like a mess. This time you can no longer contain yourself. You call her in from playing outside and announce that she is to go to her room and stay there until it is spotlessly clean—no dinner, no television, all privileges are suspended until she can get her act together.

Now many parents would say, "What's wrong with that? She should have listened to her father when he asked her nicely the first hundred times." If the strategy is to get the child to clean her room, there's nothing wrong with it. No one likes to be banished to her room, so she'll probably clean it up very nicely and be done with it. The question is, does it really have any effect on the next time? Probably not. In this case the child will always rely on her father getting to that point before she thinks about cleaning her room. The responsibility will always be on her father's shoulders, because he will decide when the room gets cleaned.

How can we alter this situation so that the chore becomes *her* responsibility? The best way to do this is to set up a situation that helps her develop the habit, then praise good performance so that she develops the attitude. One good way to do this is to tie another privilege to whether or not the room is cleaned. If Dad knows that his daughter enjoys time playing outside he can set up a simple program that works like this. He can break up the task of cleaning her room so that each item is worth a certain number of minutes. The items on the list could include keeping clothes off the floor, putting away toys, and making the bed. Dad can set it up so that each of these items is worth fifteen minutes, and there is a fifteen-minute bonus for having all three done. The rule is that before the child goes out to play Dad has to check the status of the room. The amount of time spent playing depends on what responsibilities are accomplished.

There are many variations on systems like this, but the key is to tie the privilege to the responsibility. This way the child is always responsible for how much of the privilege she earns for herself. Of course, it is also up to Dad to praise performance, effort, and improvement. Setting up a system like this is far more desirable than punishing the behavior. When you reward responsible habits with privileges, you are working on the positive side of the behavior. When you punish a behavior, you are working on the negative side. In other words, it is better to reward a child for taking good care of her room than it is to punish a child for being sloppy.

## CONNECTING RESPONSIBILITY TO PRIVILEGE

The idea of putting together responsibility and privilege works well throughout childhood. As children grow older they want to extend their curfew time and have more independence. Of course, that requires responsibility. Parents worry that if they let their children stay out longer they will lose track of time and come home late. Most parents want to know that their children will return home reliably at a given time. Take the case of eleven-year-old Judy who wanted to be able to stay out with her friends until 9:30 at night in the summertime. Her usual curfew was 8:30. Judy presented her case maturely, and she even offered that the extended curfew could apply only to those nights when she and her friends were at a given location like the pizza place or the ice cream parlor in town. Judy's parents worked out a plan. They said that they would be willing to let her earn that extra hour by proving she could be responsible. They agreed to bump Judy's curfew up by twenty minutes each week she came home on time. So the first week she had to be home at 8:50, the second week 9:10, and the third week 9:30. By the end of three weeks, if Judy proved she could be home on time, 9:30 would be her new curfew time. By the end of the third week Judy missed curfew only once, by ten minutes, and she had called to say she would be late. Her parents concluded that she was responsible enough to handle the extra hour, and everyone was happy. This is another example where the parents chose to work on building responsibility as opposed to punishing irresponsibility.

Sometimes a parent needs to step away from a situation and allow the natural consequences of a behavior to provide the learning experience. When your child becomes lazy with homework, do you step in and help him finish up? Parents are reluctant to let their children go to school with unfinished homework because they are afraid the teacher will judge them as bad parents. Good teachers prefer it when parents let children do their own homework. If you get into the habit of doing your child's homework, you are taking responsibility for his work habits. That's not to say that you should ignore poor or sloppy homework habits. If you are concerned about homework speak directly to the teacher about it and if possible schedule a conference that your child can also attend. Let your child answer directly to the consequences of not getting the job done.

## CHARACTER BUILDING

So far four styles that have been covered—ignoring the behavior, giving a warning, inducing guilt, and punishing—all have drawbacks. The advice I've given is to reward responsible behavior, set reasonably high expectations, and let children earn privileges by behaving responsibly.

The best way to encourage responsibility involves all of these things, but it also involves a bit more. Encouraging responsible behavior involves developing a style that works even when you encounter a gray area. For instance, what happens when you tell your child to sweep the floor in the kitchen, and he tells you he feels tired and just wants to rest? It can break a parent's heart to force a child to do something when he's feeling uncomfortable, but is it really the right thing to do to let the child off the hook? What about when you tell your child to clean the toys off the floor, and she follows the request by shoveling everything on the floor into the bottom of her closet? She is quick to remind you that she did do what you told her to. What about the child who tries to negotiate a "better deal" every time you ask him to do something? If his request is reasonable do you reduce your expectations?

> *Letting your child feel the natural consequences of irresponsible behavior can be very effective.*

As children get older, they will be quick to point out that you don't practice what you preach all the time. Is your room always neat? Do you always do your chores? The best parenting style for teaching responsibility requires that you maintain high expectations. Just think about what you are preparing your children for. I've had to go to work when I don't feel 100 percent fine. I've done sloppy work that I have had to redo a second or third time because I needed to get it right. I've been in situations where a lot has been expected of me, and there is no chance of getting away with doing less because I was responsible for the whole load of work that was given to me. What I am trying to explain is that you must be confident that allowing your children to step up to responsibility even in difficult circumstances will never do them wrong. In the old days experiences like this were called "character building." There is a great deal of virtue still left in that concept. The best way to teach responsibility is to let kids have the opportunity to develop responsible habits, then step in and praise responsible attitudes. The ability to admit making mistakes and the ability to take responsibility for causing hurt feelings and making an effort to make amends are two more hallmarks of responsible behavior. There is only one way to teach these two important things, and that is you must model them yourself. Nobody's perfect, and children need to learn that very few mistakes are fatal. Even if you make a terrible mistake it is better to own up to it and accept the consequences. Children who learn this will be less likely to avoid responsibility and more likely to develop the traits of honesty and reliability.

# GUIDELINES

These guidelines show examples of what kinds of things kids can be responsible for at different ages and stages.

| **Three-Year-Olds Can:** | **Fours and Fives Can:** |
|---|---|
| help put napkins on table | wipe off table |
| help wash vegetables | put away dishes |
| put away toys | dust things that won't break |

| **Six to Eights Can:** | **Nine to Twelves Can:** |
|---|---|
| take out garbage | manage pet responsibilities (feed fish, clean gerbil cage) |
| vacuum | |
| set the table | warm up dinner in microwave (after being supervised several times) |
| help make a salad/sandwich | |
| straighten room | take reliable phone messages |
| manage homework tasks | |

## QUICK REVIEW

1. Responsible behavior has to be actively taught to kids. By nature, children tend to be self-centered. They are used to having parents do things for them. As they get older, responsibility taking is tied to the development of independence.

2. Teaching children to be responsible is a two-step process. The first step is to teach the habit (e.g., keep your room neat). The second step is to praise the performance, attitude, and effort (e.g., "Thank you for keeping your room neat. Knowing I can rely on you makes my life so much easier.").

3. Kids need the opportunity to be responsible, and it should be given to them as early as possible. Children as young as three can take on simple responsibilities, with adults watching and, of course, praising performance.

4. You will never hurt your children by having high expectations about responsibilities.

5. You can teach children how to be more responsible about schoolwork by stepping in to help organize or outline. Never do homework for your child just to get it done or because you feel sorry about how frustrating it is.

6. When children avoid responsibility parents can deal with it in a number of ways. Ineffective ways of dealing with it are to let the incident pass or pass with just a warning, make the child feel guilty, or punish the child. More effective ways include pairing responsibilities with privileges, so that if the responsibilities aren't taken care of, the privileges aren't earned; and keeping expectations for responsibility high.

## EXERCISES FOR PARENTS

## IDENTIFY EXPECTATIONS

Use the boxes below to develop reasonable expectations for responsibility taking.

**Child's Name:** _____

**Responsibilities:**

_____

_____

_____

_____

_____

**Child's Name:** _____

**Responsibilities:**

_____

_____

_____

_____

_____

## EXERCISES FOR PARENTS

## WEEKLY RESPONSIBILITY CHART

You might find it helpful to list daily responsibilities in this weekly chart. Photocopy this sheet so you can reuse it.

| | |
|---|---|
| Monday | Chores: |
| Tuesday | Chores: |
| Wednesday | Chores: |
| Thursday | Chores: |
| Friday | Chores: |
| Saturday | Chores: |
| Sunday | Chores: |

# 7

# TEACHING YOUR
# CHILD COPING SKILLS
◀

Jared and Maria, both six, are sitting side by side, drawing cars. Neither one is happy with the results, but they express their disappointment in different ways. Jared's brow is deeply furrowed, and his tension and frustration show in firm pencil strokes that tear the paper. When this happens, he crumples his drawing up and tosses it onto a large pile of other failed attempts. Maria, on the other hand, talks as she draws. "Well, this doesn't look much like a car," she says. "I'll put wings on it and make it a rocket ship."

In Jared's mind there is no alternative to drawing a car exactly as he sees it. He is angry when he isn't able to do this. Maria is much more forgiving of herself. She sees no great loss in not being able to draw exactly what she sees in her head. She improvises. In short, she copes.

## WHAT IS COPING?
◀

Coping is the set of thoughts, ideas, and behaviors that we use to manage difficult circumstances in life: frustration, disappointment, loss, irritation, and anger, to name a few. Actually, the circumstances don't always have to be difficult. There is even a kind of coping that we need to handle positive things like success, new opportunities, and just about every significant life change.

Some parents notice that their children have difficulty coping from infancy. These children often reacted negatively to changes in feeding schedules, traveling, new tastes or sensations, and variations in their sleeping and waking schedules. Other parents say their children were always easygoing. Research shows some children may indeed be genetically predisposed to adapting easily.

Few of us, however, were born with the ability to cope with everything. We need to learn how. Most times we do it simply by trial and error, which is not always the best way to learn an important skill like coping. Learning to cope can be especially difficult if your child is stubborn and tends to take a little longer to learn from experience. Even a child with the most rigid behavioral style, however, can learn coping skills in an environment that encourages adaptability.

## HOW TO TEACH YOUR CHILD GOOD COPING SKILLS

Teaching your child how to cope with the stresses and strains of everyday life will not only make her happy and successful, it will also keep her healthier. Good coping skills, a positive attitude, and a flexible behavioral style have all been found to be good predictors of physical and mental health. Use these techniques to teach your child how to cope with difficult situations:

**Set a good example for coping.** We live in a stressful world, and it's hard not to react to the pressures we face every day. We can, however, moderate *how* we react to things. This can be done by paying attention to how we communicate anger, disappointment, hurt feelings, sadness, and other negative emotions.

Family counselors see many families that are "screamers." These families resolve tension with loud arguments, yelling matches, and other communication styles that reflect poor coping. Not long ago while I was working with a family, the father criticized his nine-year-old daughter in a loud, stern voice. This prompted a chorus of angry yelling from the mother and daughter. The girl's two-year-old sister reacted by joining in at a higher volume. She had already begun to learn her family's poor coping skills.

**Teach your child problem-solving skills.** You can do this by helping her see that there might be more than one solution to a problem and helping her make good choices.

## HELPING CHRISSY MODERATE ANXIETY

This was the lesson nine-year-old Chrissy learned the day she forgot to take her homework sheet home from school. Chrissy was frantic, and she began to cry. Chrissy's mother helped her cope by offering a solution. "I have your classmate Julie's number right here on the wall," she said. "Why don't you give her a call and see if she will read the homework sheet to you over the phone?"

Later that evening Chrissy's mom explained what happened in terms that Chrissy could learn from. "Today you forgot to take a deep breath and say to yourself, 'There must be some other way I could find out what tonight's homework is.' I'm glad you asked for my help, and I'm glad we came up with a good idea. The next time, just say, 'Before I get so upset, let me try to think of a good way to handle this.'"

**Don't give in to your child every time she wants something.** Ten-year-old Melissa has learned to cope with not always getting what she wants. She couldn't convince her parents to raise her allowance. Two weeks later Melissa announced that she had found a job helping a neighbor after school to supplement her allowance. Her parents' refusal to raise her allowance motivated Melissa to develop a more positive strategy.

**Teach your child that he is competent and capable.** That way he'll have the confidence needed to cope. You can help your child develop confidence by:

- Setting reasonable expectations so that your child has the chance to feel successful.
- Praising her for efforts as well as results.
- Giving support in the form of statements such as, "I know you can do it."
- Encouraging your child to finish school projects on her own.
- Resisting the impulse to say hurtful or derogatory things such as, "You can't do anything right."
- Teaching your child that failure can be an important learning experience. Don't be too critical of his mistakes. Instead help him view failure as feedback that indicates more learning is needed to accomplish the desired goal. Remember that the personal history of almost every great woman or man is marked by some kind of failure.
- Teaching your child the value of persevering and learning from her mistakes. Let your child know she will almost always get a second chance.

## STAGE FRIGHT

When Jessica, age nine, muffed her lines at the school play, her father found her crying backstage. Jessica's dad helped her cope by saying, "Well, I did hear when you got some of your words confused, but it didn't seem to make any difference to the people around me. Did you know that even the best actors and actresses on TV sometimes forget their lines? Since these shows are videotaped, we don't see that because they repeat it again and again until they get it exactly right. I think you are a good actress. Every time you practice, you'll get better and better."

## HELP YOUR CHILD COPE
## IN SPECIFIC SITUATIONS

Some situations are difficult for almost all children. Here are some tips you can use to help your child manage some of the most common ones.

**Friendship problems.** Friendship problems abound during the four-to-ten age span, when children are looking for peer acceptance. If your child feels rejected by his peers, help him understand that there may be a number of reasons why his feelings were hurt. Offer a few different ways of handling the situation.

When eight-year-old Jeremy was left out of the playground football game, he felt hurt and rejected. Jeremy's mom explained that people can and do act in insensitive ways, but that doesn't have to stop Jeremy from having a good time. "You know, Jeremy, I'll bet that if *you* were making up the sides for a football game, you would include everyone and try not to hurt anybody else's feelings," she said. "I don't blame you for feeling left out." Jeremy's mother told him that he could have tried to be more assertive about being included or even started up a game of his own. Jeremy did start another playground football team and had great social success with it.

**Coping with frustration and disappointment.** Have you ever promised your child that you would go to the toy store to pick out a special reward or surprise, only to find that there are none left? This situation is usually difficult for children to handle but can serve as a powerful lesson. Everyone must cope with disappointing news, broken promises and engagements, and circumstances beyond their control. But how can you teach your child that there are certain things outside of even Mom's or Dad's vast sphere of influence? It's better to help your child cope with disappointment from time to time rather than let her believe that if she wants something badly enough, it will magically appear.

At times like this, try saying, "I know that I promised to get you a toy. I was just as disappointed as you that we couldn't find it. Sometimes no matter how hard you try, things don't work out the way you wish they would. We'll have to try to find the toy again another day."

**Coping with loss, separation, or moving.** This includes friends moving away or your own family's move; the death of a family member, friend, or pet; family separation; and many other situations that involve some type of loss. Coping with these strong emotional issues is difficult even for adults. You can help prepare your child to cope with loss by talking about it beforehand when possible. This, of course, is easier to do when your neighbors are planning a move across the state than when a grandparent is gravely ill and may die. In this instance all the preparation in the world will not prevent strong negative emotions, confusion, anger, and all of the psychological hurt that such a loss causes. That is why it's important to accept these reactions in your child, answer questions, and help him cope by acknowledging that these are normal ways of feeling.

> *Acknowledge your child's negative feelings and let him know that you can see his point of view.*

**Coping with frightening situations.** When seven-year-old Benjamin had to go to the hospital for an operation, I spoke to his surgeon about the procedures he would be using and then explained them to Benjamin in his own terms. We also visited the hospital and answered Benjamin's questions. This took some of the fear of the unknown out of the process and set Benjamin up to cope with what would be happening at the hospital.

Telling children what kinds of fearful things might happen beforehand (and making sure they understand the explanation) is important, particularly with children who are naturally shy or fearful of new situations.

## THE MOST IMPORTANT COPING DEVICE ◀

There is one coping aid that can make all the difference in the world to children who are feeling upset, frustrated, disappointed, or rejected. It's a simple two-step technique that almost always brings good results. Step one is to place your arms securely around your child and squeeze lightly. Step two is to say the magic coping words, "I love you," to let your child know that no matter how difficult life gets you will always be there.

# HEALTHY SELF-TALK HELPS CHILDREN COPE

When things are going badly for me, I usually say, "Maybe tomorrow will be a better day." Research tells us that positive self-statements like that help people handle stress. Children need to learn the words to say to themselves when things are going poorly. Here are some examples of things you can teach your child to say to herself when coping with a difficult situation:

- "I don't understand this homework, but that doesn't mean I'm stupid. It just means I have to ask my parents or teacher for help."
- "If the store doesn't have what I want today, it doesn't mean I won't get it, it just means I have to wait."
- "Just because my friend canceled our plans doesn't mean I have to sit alone and do nothing. I can call another friend or find something fun to do myself."
- "If my friend is angry with me today and doesn't want to play with me, that doesn't mean he will hate me forever. Tomorrow I can talk to him and we will probably be able to work it out."

Whenever it's possible to prepare your child for a situation that might have a negative outcome, it's helpful to explain what she can tell herself. For instance, if you know that a friend who has promised to come over frequently forgets or cancels at the last minute, you could say: "You know that Tommy sometimes forgets to come over when he says he will. If that happens, try not to take it personally. You can make sure that you keep your appointments, but sometimes there isn't much you can do when someone doesn't keep his." This is a good way to take the edge off of any frustration your child may feel if she's disappointed.

## QUICK REVIEW

1. Coping is the set of thoughts, ideas, and behaviors that we use to manage difficult circumstances in life. These circumstances include frustration, disappointment, loss, irritation, and anger. Besides negative feelings we also need to learn to cope with positive change like promotion, winning, and success.

2. Two essential ingredients of coping are a positive mental attitude and a willingness to be flexible. An important skill that parents can teach is solving problems by coming up with an alternative plan.

3. You can help a child learn to cope by making suggestions that require her to act independently. In other words, don't solve your child's problems for her. Instead, present a list of suitable options, then let her try whichever one she thinks will work best.

4. Parents can enhance coping by building their children's confidence and self-esteem. Avoid sarcastic or critical comments. Instead, suggest an alternative to whatever behavior was inappropriate or ineffective.

5. Teach your children how to look forward to better times. Support a sense of hopefulness that implies, "Tomorrow I will look for one thing that will make what is happening today seem more positive."

## EXERCISES FOR PARENTS

### COMING UP WITH PLAN "B"

Oftentimes, when things don't go as well as you would like them to, you stop and say, "OK, what's Plan 'B'?" Use the situations below to help your child develop a flexible attitude and a positive problem-solving style.

1. *Today everyone was supposed to go swimming, but the weather turned bad, and we couldn't go. What would make a good Plan "B"?*

2. *Mommy promised that she would take her daughter to buy a toy at the store, but she had to take care of some things at home, and it got late so they couldn't go. What would make a good Plan "B"?*

3. *You came home from school today and realized that you left your assignments in your desk at school. The school is locked, and you can't get back to your desk. What would make a good Plan "B"?*

4. *Your best friend was supposed to come to your house after school, but she just called you and told you she couldn't come. What would make a good Plan "B"?*

5. *You wanted to go outside and ride your bicycle, but it took you longer than you thought to do your homework, and now it is dark outside. What would make a good Plan "B"?*

### MAKING LEMONS INTO LEMONADE WITH SELF-TALK

Sometimes people let annoying situations become catastrophic situations because of the way they talk to themselves. Cognitive psychologists point out that when we exaggerate events around us, we teach ourselves to respond as though we are in a constant state of emergency. Talking to ourselves and putting things into a rational perspective can help transform those "catastrophes" back into "nuisances." In the following examples, find a way to make the catastrophic self-talk into more reasonable and less irritating self-talk. I'll start you off:

*Situation: While I was riding my bicycle today, I got a flat tire and had to come home.*

*What I said to myself: "I can't believe this stupid bicycle. It's such a piece of junk. I never want to ride it again. I hate not being out there with my friends."*

What I could have said to myself: "This wasn't such a good day. I got a flat tire. Oh, well, at least I have a bike to ride, and it won't be long before it is fixed and I am back on the road."

*Situation: Billy wants to go to Burger Heaven for dinner, but his two brothers have convinced their mom to go to Captain Jack's Seafood Shack.*

*What Billy said: "I can't believe this. Mom loves those two jerks more than she loves me. I hate Captain Jack's Seafood Shack. The french fries taste like they were dragged across a plate of sand before they serve them. I hate those cruddy fish filet sandwiches. They probably don't even make 'em out of real fish. I never get what I want."*

What Billy could have said to himself:

*Situation: Mary wanted to be good at soccer. In today's game she tried very hard but didn't score any goals and didn't feel like she helped the team.*

## EXERCISES FOR PARENTS

*What Mary said to herself: "I stink at soccer. I'll bet the coach hates me and doesn't want me to play anymore. Everybody on my team hates me. Maybe I should just quit."*

What Mary could have said to herself:

# 8

# TEACHING YOUR
# CHILD THINKING SKILLS

Eight-year-old Kim is standing over a broken action figure. Her six-year-old brother is on the floor howling, and her mother is trying in vain to intervene.

"What do you mean you don't know why you did it? Didn't you think you were doing something wrong when you ripped the arms off that toy?"

"No. I was just playing with it."

"Would you like it if someone played with your toys like that?"

"I guess not."

"Did you think about that while you were breaking your brother's toy?"

"No."

"Do you have anything to say for yourself?"

"I'm sorry."

"'I'm sorry' is not good enough. I want you to think before you do things like this."

# IMAGINING THE
# CONSEQUENCES OF OUR ACTIONS ◀

Almost all parents struggling to raise thoughtful, responsible children go through periods when they feel as though their kids don't think before they act. One of the things that separates immature, childish behavior from mature, adult behavior is the ability to think through your actions before you make them and decide whether or not they are a good idea. This process involves imagining the consequences of your actions. It's something that most of us do every day, as we make decisions on what we should do or say in any given situation. Let's say your boss is giving you a hard time about something insignificant. You've just done a tremendous job on something else, something that makes both you and her look good, but nothing's good enough by her standards. Now you're steaming. Could you imagine letting yourself say or do all the things that had come into your head while she was acting like a jerk? If you are imagining honestly, you are probably picturing yourself right out of a job. When your patience is being tried in this manner, what happens inside your head is a lot different from what you let come out of your mouth. How did you learn this? If you are like almost everyone else, you learned from experience. You said or did things in the past that you regretted, and now you have figured that it is better to hold on to certain thoughts and actions rather than let them out.

## MY NEIGHBOR'S DOG

When I was about nine years old, there was a very mean dog that was attached to a rope in the front yard of a house three doors down from mine. I had to pass that dog to get to my friend's house. Every time I'd pass the dog it would growl at me—not ferociously, but just mean enough to let me know that I should pass by the house as quickly as possible. Every time it happened it made my heart beat faster from fear. I really grew to have an intense dislike for this dog. Then one day I woke up a bit braver than usual. I passed by the dog, and when it growled I barked back. In an instant the dog was up on its feet and charging. I had never realized that the dog had more than enough rope to grab me by the pants even though I was on the sidewalk. That was the first and last time I messed with that or any other dog that way. From that point on I thought twice about it.

Experiencing the consequences of my behavior allowed me to censor or control the urge to do other things like it that might put me in a similar predicament.

## LEARNING FROM EXPERIENCE

Psychologists sometimes use words like "conditioning" to describe the process of learning by experiencing the consequences of our actions. I prefer to just call it an example of learning from experience. One reason why adults can control their behavior better than children is because, presumably, they've had more experiences to learn from. That's one reason why we shouldn't be so hard on kids when they use poor judgment. After all, they haven't had the opportunity to mess up as many times as we have.

Another thing we should realize about kids is it usually takes more repetition to get them to make that connection between what they want to do versus what they should do. Kids are used to being taken care of— they grow up with the idea that comfort will be provided to them from people like Mom and Dad. When we are more independent, there is a lot more on the line, a lot more to risk. For kids, using poor judgment might result in being sent to their room, a bawling out from the teacher or principal, or a couple of bruises from being too much of a daredevil on the bicycle. For adults, the consequences of poor judgment could mean losing a career, destroying a marriage, or going to jail. Learning to use good judgment or thinking before we act is not an easy skill to learn. Human beings of all ages seem to need to make a lot of mistakes before they can start learning from them.

One key to learning how to think before we act is being able to tune into the little voice inside our head that talks to us. This inner voice has been referred to as many things, but I think most people probably call it a *conscience*. I don't like the word *conscience* very much because it always conjures up the picture of the devil who sits on one shoulder and the angel who sits on the other. Perhaps a better analogy would be a "gatekeeper" or "security guard." When we learn from experience, we sharpen the skills of that security guard, who will prevent us from doing the kinds of things that deliver negative consequences. When we behave impulsively or act before thinking, we send that security guard out on a break.

## PLAYING WITH FIRE

Jimmy is eleven years old and has always been a "good kid." At school today he was able to somehow acquire a book of matches. After school he took the matches up to his room. As he held the matches in his hand his heart started to pound. This was the first signal that helped him identify that he was dealing with something that could have some negative consequences associated with it. He lit one match, then quickly blew it out. It made him feel very powerful and strangely brave for some reason. For a second, he smelled the sulfur and wondered whether anyone downstairs could smell it. He quickly pushed that thought out of his mind. He lit another match, and this time he watched it burn a little longer. For a second, he reminded himself that playing with fire was very dangerous. Then right after that he thought, I don't know what these adults are fussing about all of the time. As long as you keep the match in your hand, and blow it out before it can burn you or fall on something it seems pretty safe.

Jimmy tested this hypothesis a few more times, but then the exercise became boring, so he spent some time putting together a little pit that he made from some old fish-tank rocks. In the center of the pit, he put a piece of plastic and some paper, and then he lit a small fire. The outcome was that the fire, much quicker than he expected, burned a hole right through the plastic and made a nasty black mark on his dresser. It also created enough smoke to arouse the attention of his mother downstairs who quickly called up to him, "Do you smell smoke upstairs?" Not in a million years did she suspect Jimmy was up there playing with fire. He just wasn't that type of kid. As a matter of fact he was usually very responsible. "No, Mom," he called down.

Now, in a total panic, Jimmy tried to clean the black mark from his dresser, and to his surprise a lot of it came off, but there was still a dime-sized black mark in the center where the wood was actually burned. About a week later, his mother questioned him about the mark. With some relief he finally told the story of how it got there. He had been waiting for his mother to discover the mark and the anxiety of waiting was killing him. When his mother spoke to him about it, she told him that if he was curious about lighting matches, she or his father could have supervised him outdoors. "The problem," she explained, "wasn't the matches as much as it was a lack of judgment. Accidents happen when you don't think far enough ahead, or you don't consider all of the possibilities." She explained to Jimmy that he hadn't considered all of the possibilities, such as how flammable the objects around him were, how easy it would have been to drop a lit match on the floor, or how quickly the fire he lit could burn.

Jimmy's mom didn't punish him. She knew that the only purpose punishing him would serve would be to humiliate him out of doing it another time. Instead, she made Jimmy accompany her to the library, and they got out some books on fire safety. She reasoned that Jimmy had a curiosity about fires, and that he was trying to satisfy that curiosity in a dangerous way. He needed information on how potentially damaging a fire can be, so that he would think differently about it in the future. By doing this Jimmy's mother chose not to concentrate on creating a feeling of shame, guilt, or disapproval. Instead, she chose to try to influence how he was thinking.

## SHOULD KIDS BE PUNISHED FOR USING POOR JUDGMENT?

There is a basic flaw in the kind of reasoning that goes along with punishment. I've already said that adults should be better at thinking before they act, but the fact of the matter is that some adults are not. When they use poor judgment and break the law, they go to jail, presumably to be punished into learning a lesson. The unfortunate thing is that being in jail doesn't really teach a lesson at all. We know this because the tendency for people to repeat criminal behavior after they get out of jail is quite high. Why should it be any different for kids? The lesson you want to teach kids is to follow the progression of thought to action to consequence. Jimmy thought it would be interesting to light those matches. He acted on the thought before considering the consequences. He couldn't consider the consequences because he wasn't motivated to collect all the information he needed. If he had considered all of the information, he might not have chosen to do the action.

## PHILIP: CAUGHT SMOKING

Eleven-year-old Philip came home with a pack of cigarettes in his jacket pocket, which his mother discovered when she picked up the jacket from the floor to hang it in his closet. When the cigarettes fell out she panicked. She called Philip downstairs to confront him. As Philip saw the cigarettes he, too, panicked, especially after seeing the look in his mother's eye. Both reactions were strong. Philip's first impulse was to dodge the situation by saying he was just holding the cigarettes for a friend. Mom flew into a rage, "Do you think I was never young? That's the oldest excuse in the book. Are you going to lie to me on top of everything else?" After fifteen minutes of accusations and arguing Philip finally admitted to buying the cigarettes from an eighth grader and smoking them with his friends. Mom and Dad held a family conference. Several sanctions were put in place. Philip was to come directly home from school every day. He was not allowed to play with his friends except for two hours on Saturday, and his allowance was restricted for a month. Philip's mom and dad decided that this is what would be necessary to teach him a lesson about smoking. There was no discussing it.

On the surface, many parents would agree that a harsh punishment was necessary in this case. The question is, does a harsh punishment prevent the behavior from happening again? In this case, the answer was no. Philip simply became more careful about hiding cigarettes, and continued smoking all throughout his childhood and adolescence. A better strategy might have been to take some time to try to figure out *why* Philip became interested in smoking, and what he was getting out of it. Maybe he was trying to impress his friends. This is a tough example because things like smoking cigarettes and drinking are strongly influenced by peers. The fact is that if parents cut themselves off from the reasons why something is happening, they lose whatever influence they have. Instead of punishing Philip they could have made him sign a contract that he agreed not to smoke cigarettes for health reasons. Would this have worked any better than punishing him? It's hard to say. Many parents would consider having Philip sign a contract a wimpy strategy. Maybe so, but it would not create the need for Philip to be defiant.

## A THREE-STEP STRATEGY

Teaching children to think before they act requires that you teach them to understand a three-step process.

1. Identify the impulse or urge to do something.
2. Consider the action.
3. Think through the consequences of the action.

Now, it's all well and good to make a nice neat list of steps, but how does a parent actually go about teaching these things? Believe it or not, teaching children to tune in to this three-step process is not all that difficult either. Parents just have to realize that the process is learned first by pointing things out after the fact; then, as time goes on, it becomes a natural part of kids' internal language.

Let's review those three steps again, just so they're fresh in your mind. The first step is to teach ways of identifying the urge or impulse to do something. Take the case of eight-year-old Tanya. Tanya is dying to go outside and play with her friends, but she has some homework to do. If she rushes through it and maybe even skips over some of it, she can still get to her friends outside. Tanya is faced with quite a challenge, especially for an eight-year-old child who is desperate to go out with her friends. The challenge is to do the homework right and earn praise for a job well done, or rush through it, play with her friends, and risk whatever problems will result with her parents and teacher about her homework. It is a tough decision, but ultimately the temptation to play with her friends wins out. She does her homework sloppily, and later in the evening when her father checks it, he is very disappointed. How will he handle it? Well, as I said, it is important to identify the urge or impulse. Dad says, "I know you really wanted to play with your friends this afternoon, and I'm sure that is the reason why you didn't take enough time to do your homework correctly. It must have been really hard to think about doing your homework." Second, after identifying the impulse, talk about the action. Tanya's dad continues by saying, "I guess you chose to play with your friends over doing your homework." Third, he points out the sequence of events that leads to the consequence by saying, "You know that means that I won't be able to let you play with your friends after school unless you show me your finished homework and I give you permission."

## FOCUSING ON SELF-TALK

The best way of helping kids learn the three basic steps is to begin by focusing children on what they are saying to themselves. Parents can encourage their children to discuss their decision-making strategy and then help them determine whether it was a good strategy or a bad strategy. Parents are sometimes reluctant to do this because they don't believe children will ever learn anything by simply discussing their behavior. They usually say, "Talking about things is not enough." But when you talk about behavior from the point of view of "What were you thinking about when you made that decision?" you are giving kids a chance to focus in on the relationship between action and consequence.

## A SPRAY-PAINTING INCIDENT

Twelve-year-old Ryan just spray-painted his name on the street in front of his house. The conversation between him and his mother begins with the same question and answer parents have asked and heard a million times. "Why did you do that?" "I don't know." When parents ask children too many questions it puts the parents at a disadvantage. Asking kids questions about their behavior usually does two things. First, it gives kids the opportunity to avoid the topic by shrugging their shoulders or saying, "I don't know." Second, as a result of that, the parent's frustration increases and she presses harder, which in turn causes the child to run from or avoid the topic that much more.

Now look at the situation a different way. Instead of *asking* why, Ryan's mother might have tried *predicting* why Ryan did what he did. "I guess you thought it might look cool to see your name painted on the street." After all, how many other reasons could there be? It certainly wasn't "Gee, Ryan, I guess you really wanted to get into a lot of trouble today." By saying, "I guess you thought it might look cool to see your name painted on the street," Ryan's mom is reminding him of the impulse that put the behavior into action. From this point she can continue by saying, "I guess the fun of doing it stopped you from thinking that it might not be a good idea." By saying this, Ryan's mom begins to establish the link between the action and the consequence. She can finish by saying, "Well, you're going to have to scrub your name off." Other consequences might be that Ryan will have to pay for the cleaning supplies out of his allowance money.

Later on, that evening, Ryan's mother reviews his behavior with him. Instead of relying on punishment, shame, or the tendency to want to keep him on the hook, she tries to be supportive. "Look, Ryan, we've all done things that are stupid. When I saw that you painted your name in the street I got angry. I was just standing there wishing you had used better judgment. I'm not angry anymore. What's important is that you learn what to tell yourself in situations like this to stop you from getting into trouble. For instance, you could have said, 'It might look cool to see my name painted in the street, but what will happen if it doesn't wash off' or 'what will happen if other people don't like the way it looks and they complain to the town or the police?'"

▲

Using these words, Ryan's mom accomplishes quite a bit. She sets up the situation by being supportive. Everyone does things they regret later on.

Ryan's mom loves him, so she does her best to be sincere and communicate forgiveness. When someone behaves in a way that hurts you, it is the hardest thing in the world to put your feelings aside and be forgiving. This is especially true in relationships that are built around love. It is sometimes easier to forgive a stranger than someone who is very close to you. The reason for this is that we expect that if we love

> *Being supportive and forgiving allows your child the opportunity to learn from her mistakes.*

someone they will try extra hard not to do things that cause us embarrassment, hurt, or pain. Parents, in particular, feel this way. They say to themselves, "Gee, you know I've given this kid the sun, the moon, and the stars, but she still does this incredibly stupid thing that hurts my feelings and really ticks me off." These are natural thoughts to have, but they rarely explain what's going on. When the people we love use poor judgment, they usually don't do it to cause anger or hurt. They do it because they are too focused on themselves. They temporarily lose track of the effect it will have on other people. Understanding this somewhat fragile aspect of human nature can help solve many problems in relationships of all kinds, not just between parents and children. Ryan's mom resisted the urge to lower the boom on Ryan or to hold the experience over his head. Punishing Ryan for his behavior will make him feel shame and guilt, but believe it or not, those feelings usually cause the same exact behavior to be played out over and over. Shame and guilt lower self-esteem. The worse we feel about ourselves, the more we tend to act out behavior that is more and more self-defeating. That's why forgiveness is such a powerful tool in relationships. When Ryan's mother decides to be supportive rather than punitive, she tells Ryan that she got angry over what he did, but wants to help him avoid putting himself in that situation again. By forgiving Ryan, she gives him the opportunity to learn from his mistakes.

Now, you might be saying, "If you are too forgiving your children will learn they can get away with anything, and they will walk all over you." That's not true at all. You're not excusing the behavior, and you aren't condoning it either. You can identify the behavior as selfish, irritating, or whatever you like. The part that you are leaving out is the part that says, "You did something wrong, and you hurt my feelings. Now you must suffer." Ryan's mother separates her feelings of anger from the situation and simply points out the consequences. In the end, she encourages Ryan to ask himself in a similar situation whether his actions will lead to consequences he wants to avoid.

## RESIST THE URGE TO INTERROGATE

Whenever you have a hard time deciding how to approach a situation, try to resist the urge to interrogate. Instead, describe what happened and acknowledge the impulse that must have been there. Admit that it must have been fun to do this or that, agree that other kids would probably think that what happened was cool, but then follow up with how the action led to a negative consequence and talk about those consequences. Finally, key the child into the things she should say to herself to avoid a similar situation. Focus on who might get hurt or upset, or whatever the consequences may be.

## USING THE GOOD THINKING DIARY SHEETS

The "Good Thinking Diary Sheets" at the end of this chapter break situations down into two types. One diary page is titled "What I Learned." Parents and kids can fill it out when there is a situation that involves poor judgment. The "What I Learned" page has three sections. The first section on this page is called "What Happened?" It asks for a simple description of the situation. The second section is called "What Were the Consequences?" and asks for a description of everything that happened after the behavior or event. The

> *Acknowledging your child's good behavior is much more effective than pointing out inappropriate behavior.*

third section, "What Should I Say to Myself Next Time?" asks for some self-talk that would help prevent the same thing from happening again. These three sections ask for the event, the consequences, and some self-talk to prevent it from happening again.

Let's look at an example: Seven-year-old Teri pops open the freezer and notices there is only one ice-cream bar left. Dinner is in one hour. She can't bear the thought of either her brother or sister eating it, so she gobbles it up and hopes nobody notices. As she sits down at the dinner table, Dad notices the attractive chocolate ring that outlines Teri's entire mouth and asks whether she had her dessert before dinner. Teri turns bright red, and her two siblings immediately scream, "You ate the last ice-cream bar," and threaten to kill her. Teri's diary entry might read, under the "What Happened?" section, "I saw there was only one ice-cream bar left and wanted to eat it so my brother and sister couldn't get it." Under the section that says, "What Were the Consequences?" she might put, "Everyone got mad at me, and Dad decided that when he went to the store and got some more, I had to give my share to Cindy and Peter." Finally, under "What Should I Say to Myself Next Time?" she might put, "The next time I will say to myself, 'I'd really like to eat that ice-cream bar, but if I do it will cause more trouble than it's worth.'"

The other kind of diary sheet is called "When Your Child Shows Good Judgment." This sheet is important because acknowledging good behavior will take you farther than correcting inappropriate behavior. On this page the first section is "What I Stopped Myself from Doing." In this section you can describe the situation. The second section is "What Could Have Happened?" Here you describe what could have happened if the child didn't exercise good judgment. The third section is "What Were the Consequences?" Here's an example: Eight-year-old Mary faced a very difficult situation. It was her turn to sit in the front seat of the car, but her six-year-old sister Alice jumped in ahead of her and wouldn't budge. Mom was in a tremendous hurry to get home. If Mary started fighting with Alice, Mom would get angry. When everyone got home Mary's mom sat down with her and reviewed the situation. "Mary, I know it was your turn to sit in the front seat, and Alice probably really annoyed you." By doing this Mary's mom describes the situation. Next, she says, "I know that you could have started arguing with Alice about sitting there, but instead you chose to be nice." Mary's mom says this to describe what could have happened but didn't. Finally, Mary's mom describes a more positive set of consequences—the kind that comes when you exercise good judgment. She says, "I want you to know that because you were so helpful we're going to spend some extra time together later reading a story." Mary's mom chose reading a story because that is Mary's favorite thing to do.

Of course, you don't need to fill out diary pages to accomplish what needs to be done in these situations, but you might find them to be useful guides to remind yourself what points you should focus on.

Teaching children to have good thinking skills and judgment means teaching them to avoid patterns of behavior that will get them into trouble. Here are a few more simple ways to focus on the relationship between actions and consequences.

1. *Be a Good Role Model.* If you have a tough decision to make, let your kids know how you solved the problem. Tell them what you said to yourself that helped you make the right choice. When it is something that is appropriate to discuss with a child, explain how you made a bad choice and what you would do differently next time.

2. *When You Observe a Child Make a Good Decision, Ask Him What He Was Saying to Himself When He Did This.* Tell him why his decision was a good one. Always praise good thinking skills.

3. *Tune Your Child in to Choices or Alternatives When They Exist.* Using good judgment involves being able to consider a number of choices, bad ones and good ones, too.

4. *Make Your Child Aware of Situations That Have Been Problems in the Past.* Rehearse strategies for good decision making. If your child wants to play at a friend's house where there's been a history of fighting or arguing, ask your child to tell you what she will say to herself if she gets into a tough situation. Help her come up with some strategies that allow her to use words instead of fighting to resolve the conflict.

5. *Reward Both Effort and Success.* Sometimes you will see your child get right to the point of making a good decision, and then blow it. Use these situations to acknowledge that your child is trying and making progress.

Parenting is a demanding, difficult job. Fortunately for your child, you are dedicated to learning the skills that will help her grow up happy and healthy. Teaching your child good thinking skills and how to make positive choices is hard. Human beings, especially kids, tend to make choices that look like they will bring the most gain, even if it means breaking a rule, telling a white lie, or being selfish. This is often complicated by the fact that whenever breaking a rule, telling a white lie, or being selfish pays off, it provides a kind of reinforcement that allows it to happen again. The older and more independent children get, the more difficult it becomes to sit them down and focus them in on their behavior. That's why it is so important to start when they're young.

## QUICK REVIEW

1. Children have to be taught to think about the connections between their actions and the consequences of those actions. This is all part of how people develop good judgment. This can be a difficult thing for kids to learn because they are used to having people satisfy their needs. Developing good thinking skills often requires us to put our needs on hold and do what is best for others.

2. Learning to use good judgment and thinking skills takes many repetitions to learn, because good judgment is learned largely through experience. Kids have to make mistakes before they can begin to generalize the rules of good judgment in other situations.

3. Punishing a child for using poor judgment never works as well as requiring the child to learn the reasons why his choices were bad and what actions would be more appropriate next time. Punishment rarely deters people from doing the same wrong thing again. It only makes them sneakier and more skilled at not getting caught.

4. It is important for parents to understand and acknowledge why a child used poor judgment. Typical reasons are: "You thought it would be cool or impress your friends if you . . . ," "You thought it might feel good to . . . ," or "You thought it would be fun if you . . ."

5. Always try to get your child to talk about what he would do differently the next time around. Use the situation to develop a way of rehearsing for other similar situations that might happen in the future.

6. Encouraging a child to feel shame and guilt over using poor judgment will only lower self-esteem, and that will usually create more self-defeating behavior. Allowing your child to talk openly about bad choices without punishment will make your child less likely to lie about situations. She will become motivated to correct her own behavior.

7. Be a good role model by admitting your own mistakes and verbalizing what you do to correct your behavior.

# GOOD THINKING DIARY SHEETS

Use these diary sheets to record and review situations that involve using good judgment and thinking skills. Photocopy the sheets so that you can keep track of this behavior over the course of one or two weeks.

## WHAT I LEARNED

What Happened?

Briefly describe the situation or event. (For example: At school I hit a kid who called me a name.)

_____

_____

_____

What Were the Consequences?

Briefly describe what followed the event. (For example: The teacher found out, I got sent to the principal's office, and Mom and Dad got angry and upset.)

_____

_____

_____

What Should I Say to Myself Next Time?

Tell what you should say to yourself when you are in a similar situation. (For example: It is not worth getting into all the trouble I'll be in if I hit this kid.)

_____

_____

_____

## EXERCISES FOR PARENTS

# WHEN YOUR CHILD SHOWS GOOD JUDGMENT

Use this page to reinforce good judgment and thinking skills. You might want to offer reinforcement in the form of a special privilege or treat for filling this sheet out.

What I Stopped Myself from Doing

Briefly describe the situation or event. (For example: At school I felt like hitting a kid who called me a name, but I didn't.)

_____

_____

_____

What Could Have Happened?

Briefly describe what could have happened. (For example: He could have gotten hurt, and I could have gotten into big trouble.)

_____

_____

_____

What Were the Consequences?

Tell what the consequences were. (For example: I didn't get into trouble just because that kid was acting like a jerk.)

_____

_____

_____

# 9

# MAXIMIZING YOUR CHILD'S SCHOOL POTENTIAL  ◄

Why is it that so many bright children have trouble reaching their potential in school, that year after year the comments section on the report card reads "not trying as hard as he could"? Success in school doesn't depend only on native intelligence; it depends on a few skills, some good habits, and some very specific attitudes.

## TEN IMPORTANT SCHOOL SKILLS  ◄

You don't have to be a physics teacher as well as a parent to make your kids more successful in school. The trick is in practicing the following ten important skills, habits, and attitudes and making them a part of your family's value system.

1. Make reading more important than television.
2. Keep in touch with your child's teacher.
3. Teach the secrets of good memory.
4. Help your child develop good homework habits.
5. Give your child enrichment experiences.
6. Be a good role model for learning.

7. Reinforce your child's natural curiosity.
8. Encourage a good vocabulary.
9. Teach your child not to be ashamed of failure.
10. Have high expectations for success.

**1. Make reading more important than television.** This one hurts. I didn't say these things would be easy to *do*; I just said they were easy to *understand*. We tend to think that television is an uncontrollable force that invades our homes without permission. There are positive and negative aspects of having television in our home, and parents need to feel in control of what television does to kids. One way to do this is by taking a practical, balanced look at the role of television in your home while at the same time emphasizing the value of reading.

Television has always provided a very seductive service. It keeps kids occupied and out of your hair. It will even keep siblings from fighting for a few minutes. When we rely on this baby-sitting service for five or six hours a day, of course it will influence our children. How can you not be influenced by something you sit in front of for thirty or forty hours a week? The trick is to start feeding children other forms of media—like plenty of things to read—when they are young. Reading builds vocabulary. It is a skill that requires practice. The more reading practice kids get, the better their comprehension.

> *Television has as much influence on children as parents allow it to have.*

One way to reduce the amount of time kids watch television is to make sure books are out all the time. Encourage your children to read to you. If you start early, ten or twelve hours a day of the television blasting won't become the norm. If it already is the norm, start cutting back. Make sure the television is not a constant source of background noise. When nobody's watching, turn it off. Make a game out of reading the newspaper. See who can come up with the silliest headline by substituting another family member's name in it. Encourage trips to the library, to book fairs and bookstores. Television can be a part of your family activities; it just doesn't have to be the only part.

**2. Keep in touch with your child's teacher.** This secret is much easier to use than the first, because it requires nothing more than your time in the form of a phone call, a brief visit, or a note to your child's teacher. Parents usually have contact with a teacher only after something has gone wrong—a few tests have been failed, a few homework assignments are missing, a bad report card comes home. At this point it is too late to prevent something bad from happening. It is your job to stay on top of your child's school performance, especially if you know she is having trouble. Contacting the teacher before a problem develops can make the difference between passing and failing a test or between a high and a low grade on a report card. Teachers are busy people, but talking to parents who are concerned about their children's academic performance is part of their job. And by the way, there are reasons for talking to your child's teacher besides being worried. Believe it or not, sometimes children actually want to learn *more* than what is being taught in class.

Be sure to contact your child's teacher at the beginning and end of every school year. Actively seek information from the teacher about the class or teacher the child will be going to next year. If you want your child to have a certain teacher or be in a certain class, make your preference known. Teachers will often tell you that they cannot honor requests for a specific teacher, but they will listen to what you have to say and take your comments into consideration when they are making recommendations.

### 3. Teach the secrets of good memory. Some of us are born with a great memory for everything. Most of us, however, are good at remember-

ing some things, not so good at remembering others. Memory is a very important ingredient in learning. If you can't remember what you study, the process becomes very frustrating.

One way to improve your memory and study more effectively is through the use of *mnemonics*, memory tricks to help you remember lists or sequences. You may remember several famous mnemonics from school, such

> *You can help your child improve his memory by teaching him a few simple word association tricks.*

as this easy way to remember the names of the Great Lakes: the first letter of each lake spells the word *homes*—*H*uron, *O*ntario, *M*ichigan, *E*rie, *S*uperior. Another mnemonic helps us remember the colors of the visible spectrum—Roy G. Biv, whose name stands for *r*ed, *o*range, *y*ellow, *g*reen, *b*lue, *i*ndigo, and *v*iolet. Still another mnemonic helps us

remember the names of the notes on the lines of the musical staff—
*every good boy does fine* (e,g,b,d,f). The most effective mnemonic
devices are the ones we make up ourselves. They cue or trigger memory
of other information. The trick to making up a mnemonic is to organize
the  information you want to study, then look for a pattern or an
association. Do the first letters spell anything? Can you rearrange the
information slightly so that it makes a pattern? People can remember a
lot of information using mnemonic cues.

A second way to remember is by creating a list of associations. Let's
say you want to remember these items in a list: fish, ball, light, green,
dark. The first item is fish, so you can imagine a fish swimming in the water. The second item is a ball. Think of a way to connect the two words. Perhaps the fish swallows the ball. Now you have the image of a fish swallowing a ball. Would you like to see what's inside the fish's belly? You'll need a light. Now you have fish, ball, and light. What color is the light? It's green.

> **The trick to mnemonics is to organize the information you want to remember, then look for a pattern.**

What happens when you turn off the light? It gets dark. You can
remember lists of names, places, or terms using this method, called the
*link method.*

Another memory trick you can use is called the *place method.* Let's
say you have to memorize a list of names or facts. Pick a place that is
familiar to you, like your bedroom or the kitchen. For every place in
your bedroom, store a fact or a name. One name goes under your
pillow. One goes in your shoe by the bed, another goes in your light,
and so on. You can aid the process by drawing a picture and writing the
words or facts next to the places in the picture. You can get creative by
using your own body, hiding names of facts goodness-knows-where! In
any case it is a simple method, and it works.

## 4. Help your child develop good homework habits. The two
main facets of good homework habits are developing a regular routine
and sticking with it. Homework should be done in the same place, at the
same time every day. Although some kids like to do homework with the
television or radio on or while eating, these things are distractions and
reduce performance. Tune in early to any tendencies your child has to
avoid homework by "forgetting" assignments or books. Be careful to

observe whether frustration or attention and concentration problems are interfering with your child's work. These may be signs of learning difficulties and should be checked by a psychologist or learning specialist.

## HELP YOUR KIDS GET ORGANIZED

Help your child organize difficult assignments by breaking them into smaller tasks. For instance, with a large report, create a checklist that breaks the task into research and gathering materials. After that, help your child figure out the main subheadings for each of the sections in the report. Space the work out so that a little is done every day. Above all, never sit down and do the work for your child. Give her all the help she needs with organizing and structuring the task. If you let your child depend on you to do her work, she will never become an independent worker. Don't be afraid to enlist the help of your child's teacher. Most teachers prefer to know as soon as possible whether their students are having difficulties with homework. Solving homework problems early is critical. We'll discuss other aspects of homework in the next chapter.

**5. Give your child enrichment experiences.** Parents need to realize that as much (if not more) learning takes place outside of school as inside the classroom. Look for events at your local library, go to a historical reenactment, visit a museum, attend a play, or go on a nature walk or hike. Before vacations or other family travel, take out a map and show your child where you are going. Try to point out whether you will be traveling east, west, north, or south. Talk about the differences in climate, food, nature, or culture.

Enrichment experiences can also be created at home. Take out a book of simple science experiments from the library. There are many books on "kitchen science," experiments you can do with ordinary household materials. Make a compass or volcano or demonstrate simple laws of physics by making a Cartesian diver. Five easy kitchen science experiments are included at the end of this chapter.

Grow a plant in your home or backyard. Even if you don't have a green thumb, kids are fascinated by the way things grow. You may not remember, but you were too as a child. What may seem silly or uninteresting to you might spark a lifelong interest in your child. Take a look at what might be crawling or growing in your backyard. Teach your child respect and appreciation for nature and living things by catching something, treating it gently, observing it, and releasing it again.

If science and nature aren't your thing, try cooking something with your child. Young children benefit from learning to measure and helping you combine materials. Older children might actually learn to cook something that would give you a night off from the chore!

Stimulate kids' curiosity by saving things that you might otherwise throw out. Kids like to invent things out of old paper towel rolls, tape, paper, old plastic containers, empty soda bottles, and anything else they can get their hands on. You might want to keep a small box of your child's favorite "junk" to use as an inventor's workshop. Encourage your child to seek information about the world.

## 6. Be a good role model for learning. If you are the type who never liked school yourself, you might find yourself naturally shying away from anything that seems like school. Sometimes parents who didn't care for or do well in school are also embarrassed to help their children with schoolwork because they don't feel competent. Most parents are surprised by what they remember from school and even more surprised by what they learn the second time around. If you can't help your child directly with something, help him understand the value of things like dictionaries and encyclopedias. If you don't know anything about the subject your child needs help with, go to the library. If you don't know how to use the library, don't be afraid to ask. Learning is a lifelong process. Consider taking a continuing education course at your local school or library.

## READ THE NEWSPAPER

Do you read the newspaper every day? People who read the newspaper are more familiar with what is happening in the world. They have more intelligent conversations and a better vocabulary. They are better at forming opinions and in general are more well rounded. For a good learning experience, make reading the newspaper a family activity. You don't have to make it resemble school; it can be quite a lot of fun. Again, kid around by inserting a family member's name into a news headline. Let one of your children make up a newscast and reel off the top stories of the day. Let your child become the family meteorologist and read the five-day forecast aloud. If one of your children is interested in sports, let her provide a recap of the latest highlights. This is how children become interested in what is happening in the world. It also enhances their reading skills and stimulates an interest in different careers.

It is sometimes so difficult to explain to parents that children don't develop an interest in learning automatically—that, in fact, they won't necessarily get the exposure they need even in school. If you leave it to chance, they almost certainly will not live up to their potential. But if you take just a little bit of time to point them in some direction by exposing them to interesting things and encouraging them to participate in experiences that bring them into contact with learning, then learning will become a part of their everyday experience, a way of life. Things like reading the paper and visiting interesting places help your children become active learners. An active learner is someone who seeks out information as opposed to just passively absorbing it because it is a requirement to pass a test or write a report. Better to have a child who has a sincere and passionate interest in learning and gets only average grades in school than to have a child who studies for the sake of getting good grades but is not really interested in anything.

**7. Reinforce your child's natural curiosity.** Curiosity is an important aid to learning, and most children are born with an abundance of it. You can help your child sustain that curiosity by communicating that there is no such thing as a stupid question and by not talking down to children when they show an interest in something. Many children want to master a large body of information. I've seen four- and five-year-old children become experts at naming dinosaurs and describing their habits and habitats. A seven-year-old child I know is an expert on every type of shark you can think of. He even knows the scientific names for most of them. He knows what they eat, how they swim, and which ones are dangerous. These children are bright, but they are not unusually bright. What they have in common is that they were allowed to explore their interests. When you see a child light up to something, help the child by sharing that interest. Does that mean you have to live your life around sharks and dinosaurs? No, but it does mean you can be a patient listener and participate by bringing home a special book or going to an exhibit or show with your child. Take your child's interest seriously, but don't showcase it by making him recite everything he knows about something to friends, neighbors, and relatives. This can be embarrassing and squash the interest.

If your child is not the curious type, how can you get her to take an interest in things? Once again, the key is to expose your child to as much as you can. Keep your eyes and ears open, and you will see what your child gravitates toward. Be aware that your child will not always share your passion for things.

## A SO-SO FISHERMAN BUT A FABULOUS COOK

The father of a ten-year-old child I know desperately wanted his son to take an interest in fishing. The dad was an excellent fisherman and took an almost scientific interest in the sport. He couldn't wait to get his son out on the water, teach him about navigation and seamanship, and show him what it takes to bring in the big ones. As it turned out, his son only tolerated being on the water and didn't really enjoy fishing. As a matter of fact, he was really disgusted by the idea of having to handle all that smelly bait. What his son was really interested in was cooking. After pushing fishing too hard on his son, Dad accepted the fact that there wouldn't be much joy in father-son fishing trips—until his son got a little older and started to learn how to cook fish! His son then became an invaluable and appreciated member of many of his father's fishing and camping trips, not as a fisherman but as a cook, and a darn good one.

**8. Encourage a good vocabulary.** This, of course, is related to reading, but it also depends on you and your vocabulary. Children will model the vocabulary and speaking style of their parents. If you speak in an intelligent, articulate way, so will your children. A good vocabulary helps children become better at reading, writing, and speaking. A strong vocabulary always communicates intelligence. In school a good vocabulary and strong self-expressive skills will always influence a teacher favorably. Later in life an articulate communication style and good vocabulary will be impressive at job interviews and on the job.

Building a good vocabulary is actually quite easy. Many audiotapes are available to help people develop strong vocabularies. Word-a-day calendars can also help. The simplest ways to build a strong vocabulary, however, are to read and use a dictionary. So many people are reluctant to consult a dictionary when they encounter a word they don't know. I had a fourth-grade teacher who was a pain in the butt (or so I thought at the time) because she refused to define words for us. Everyone had to have a dictionary, and when we couldn't understand a word she would make us look it up. Although it seemed pointless then, I'm much better off for it now. Don't be afraid to post a new word a week on your refrigerator door or to hold family contests to see who can come up with the most creative sentence using that word. Your kids will make fun of you, but sometimes kids have to do that before they allow themselves to have fun with something that doesn't seem "cool." Besides, if they didn't make fun of you for that, they would make fun of you for something else!

Somewhat related to good vocabulary are good grammar and punctuation skills. Schools no longer emphasize writing skills. Many college seniors hand in papers that are poorly written and barely make sense. If your own writing skills are poor, consider taking a writing workshop. It will make you a better communicator and speaker as well as writer.

**9. Teach your child not to be ashamed of failure.** Every successful person—every great president, scientist, inventor, and businessperson—has encountered failures. People who succeed don't enjoy failure, but they don't feel ashamed or guilty either. Our current education system has a very unreasonable attitude toward failure. When students fail, they are identified as "disappointments," "underachievers," or "slow." We have come a long way in identifying children who have learning problems, but a large number of children who do not achieve as much as they should fall between the cracks of the system and never reach their potential.

## FAMOUS FAILURES

One of Thomas Edison's elementary school teachers described him as "dull" and recommended that his mother not hold high expectations for her son. Albert Einstein had a terrible time with what some would consider very basic mathematics principles. History is replete with "dumb" geniuses, gifted individuals who were off on a different track, failing in the mainstream but blazing new trails on their own. Certainly they all must have had to endure failure, but all of them learned to put it in perspective and thrive in spite of it.

Education today still places a very negative value on failure. One reason for this is that teachers have limited options and resources for teaching things creatively. Most school budgets simply do not support much more than a textbook-workbook approach to learning, which is far from stimulating. There are and always will be individual teachers who motivate children beyond their failures and teach them how to turn those experiences into success. Unfortunately they are the exception rather than the rule. It is therefore up to parents to help children understand the value of failure and not to associate it with guilt or shame. One of the fastest ways of ensuring a child will turn off to school is punishing that child for failing or doing poorly.

If your child is having a bad year, sit down with her and examine the learning environment. Get the teacher involved. Come up with a plan that is aimed directly at the weakness. Is she having trouble understanding the work? If so, arrange for extra help with the teacher or consider hiring a tutor. Is the problem with the amount of time spent studying or general motivation? If so, sit down and set goals for studying and reviewing for tests. You may have to be assertive in demanding that your child reorganize her time to allow for more studying, but that is much different from banishing her to her room until she can pass her next algebra test.

Failure, even if it occurs out of laziness or selfishness, is not a criminal offense; it is human nature. It doesn't have to be tolerated, but no one needs to be punished to understand that failing is undesirable. Even the laziest students do not like to fail school subjects. Punishment not only takes the focus away from what they can do to improve their work but also sends the message that as long as they accept the punishment they are relieved of the responsibility for changing.

Instead of punishing a child for failing, try these alternatives:

1. Ask your child to help you come up with three suggestions for improving his work.

2. Keep the focus on the improvement, which is in the future, rather than on the failure, which is in the past and can't be changed.

3. Resist the urge to blame yourself when your child makes mistakes or fails. Parents tend to judge themselves by what their children do, and many feel they have failed if their children fail. That's nonsense. One thing that distinguishes truly great parenting is separating yourself from your child's failures so that you can help her be more successful. If both parent and child carry around the guilt and shame of failure, the situation will never improve. During these times parents need to deliver the message that failure should not be taken lightly but should be examined as a learning experience and left in the past.

**10. Have high expectations for success.** High achievers come from families who place high expectations on them. That doesn't mean that you have to be a tyrant. It also doesn't mean that you should place academic success over everything else. One of the worst things a parent can do is ask "How come you couldn't get a hundred?" when a child receives a test grade of ninety-five. The most successful achievers come from family backgrounds that combine high expectations with warmth, love, and acceptance. Parents need to be aware of their children's potential so they can help set the goals necessary for doing well. Parents who have high expectations are not afraid to sit down and say "Listen, I know you tried your best on your last science test, but if you spend just another hour or two studying next time, I think your grade will be much better."

## TEACHING SUCCESS WILL CARRY THROUGH TO ADULTHOOD

As you can see, there is nothing magical about success in school, and the secrets just discussed are the same qualities that contribute to success in life—developing good work habits, setting goals for achievement, tolerating and learning from failure, remaining curious and interested in the world, and developing a love of learning. Parents can teach and model these skills and attitudes a little every day. The key is to avoid settling into a rut where life is just a series of routines that prevent you and your kids from learning anything new and exciting.

## QUICK REVIEW

1. Television may not be the monster some people make it out to be, but it is a passive, inactive pastime. Don't leave the television on as a source of background noise. Encourage reading, storytelling, and other activities that develop skills.

2. Stay in touch with your child's teacher. Do not wait until your child falls seriously behind in a subject before getting on top of things.

3. Teach your child memory tricks to help him remember information on tests. Make a game out of inventing songs, pictures, and funny sayings to help remember school facts.

4. Develop a solid homework routine. Make studying and homework habits.

5. Provide enrichment experiences for your child. Encourage your child to be curious and explore the world around her.

6. Be a good role model. Take a course yourself or develop hobbies and interests.

7. Encourage your child to be an active learner. If he develops an interest in something, support that interest, even if it's a topic you're not crazy about.

8. Encourage a strong vocabulary. Try to teach one or two new vocabulary words a week. People with good vocabularies make smarter impressions on others, in school and eventually at work.

9. Teach your child to manage failure by looking at it as a step toward mastering something challenging. Failure should never be internalized ("I failed because I am faulty and bad.").

10. Always maintain high expectations for your child's school performance.

## EXERCISES FOR PARENTS

You don't have to be a scientist to enjoy or teach some simple facts about the world we live in. Here are five basic activities that stimulate an interest in how things work.

### 1. SINK THE ORANGE

**Materials:** One or two oranges, a large bowl or small bucket of water.

**Activity:** Does an orange sink or float when you drop it in water? Are you sure of your answer? First drop an orange into a large bowl or small bucket of water. Observe what happens. Now peel the orange and do the same thing. What happens? Why does it float in one circumstance and sink in the other? The answer has to do with the fact that the orange peel is full of trapped air bubbles that makes it light for its size and buoyant.

### 2. TOOTHPICK TUG-OF-WAR

**Materials:** Three toothpicks, liquid dish soap, glass bowl.

**Activity:** This experiment demonstrates how water molecules can pull things apart. Fill the bowl half to three-quarters full of water. Lay two toothpicks next to each other in the water in the center of the bowl. Dip the third toothpick into the liquid detergent. (Don't use too much, just dip the end in.) Touch the tip with the detergent on it in between the other toothpicks. What you will see is the first two toothpicks "run away" from each other and scoot to the edge of the bowl. The surface tension of the water acts as if there is a thin skin stretched across it. The detergent breaks the attraction of the molecules at the surface and takes the floating sticks with them.

### 3. CHEMICAL REACTION VOLCANO

**Materials:** Empty soda bottle, baking pan, one cup vinegar, baking soda, red food coloring, soil.

**Activity:** This is a great example of how chemicals react. In particular, this experiment shows how baking soda and vinegar react to produce carbon dioxide gas. Put the bottle in the pan and heap moist soil around it so that the soil reaches the top of the bottle without getting in. Pour one tablespoon of baking soda into the bottle. Add red food coloring to one cup of vinegar and then carefully pour the red vinegar into the bottle. Red foam will start shooting out of the top of the bottle and down the sides of the "mountain" you created. The baking soda and vinegar combine to produce carbon dioxide gas. The gas builds pressure inside the bottle and forces liquid out of the top. The mixture of the gas and liquid produces the foam that you see.

## 4. TAKE SOMEONE'S FINGERPRINTS

**Materials:** A piece of burned toast, a bowl, a spoon, a white plastic bag, some cellophane tape.

**Activity:** Toast a piece of bread until it turns black around the edges. The black parts are bread that have changed to carbon. Scrape the carbon into a large bowl, then crush the black chunks into a fine powder using the back of a spoon. Have a family member run his fingers through his hair and press his fingertips on the white plastic bag. Sprinkle the carbon powder onto the fingerprints. Shake the excess powder off the bag, and you will see the fingerprints. Cover the prints with tape to preserve them. Whenever you touch something, you leave a slightly oily fingerprint behind. The shiny surface of the plastic bag picks up the prints, and they show up when you cover them with carbon. See if you can make a family album out of the fingerprints of everyone in your family.

## 5. MAKE YOUR OWN THERMOMETER

**Materials:** Glass bottle, food coloring, clear plastic drinking straw, plastic clay, bowl, cardboard, pen, cellophane tape.

**Activity:** This experiment shows that heat makes water expand and that cold makes water contract. You can use this idea to make your own thermometer. Fill the glass bottle almost to the top with cool water. Add some red food coloring, then fill it more until it overflows. Cut the straw so that it is about five inches long. Put some plastic clay around the straw so that one inch of the straw sticks out from the bottom and the rest sticks out the top. Don't crush the straw while you are doing this. Plug the bottle with the plastic clay so that the top of the straw sticks out. Make sure no air can get into the bottle. You should see some water rise in the straw. Put the bottle into a bowl of warm water for a test. You should see the water rise in the straw. Make a scale out of a piece of cardboard by marking off the numbers one through ten about every half inch. Tape the cardboard to the straw. You have now made some temperature markings. Record the temperature at different times of day. Compare it to other thermometers to see how your scale matches other scales.

# 10

# SOLVING HOMEWORK HASSLES ◀

"How was your day?"

"OK."

"What did you do in school?"

"Nothing."

"Do you have any homework?"

"No."

For some parents this conversation is a daily ritual. Homework problems are one of the most common sources of conflict between parents and children. Parents often assume that children don't do homework because they are lazy. That might be true in some cases, but many times it isn't. Children avoid homework for many different reasons, such as procrastination, frustration, poor organization, and poor time management. Sometimes only one of these is at the root of your child's homework problems, but usually a couple are at work.

You can do a lot to resolve homework problems and get kids back on the right track, but you need practical, effective strategies. First, a review of some of the most typical situations.

# THE PROCRASTINATOR

The procrastinator can't do his homework after school because he wants to see his friends. After dinner he wants to play video games. Then he wants to watch his favorite television show. By the time he's finished with everything he wants to do, he's much too tired to do his homework. So the next morning he scribbles out his assignments on the bus on his way to school. With his busy day, who the heck has time for homework, anyway?

Procrastination is a trait that many of us can relate to. Why do something annoying today when we can put it off until tomorrow, the next day, or, if we are really lucky, forever? Procrastination has its good side. For the moment we experience the relief of avoiding something we really don't want to do. Unfortunately, that benefit usually gives way to a gigantic downside—the time crisis. Whenever we try to do a task during a time crisis, we do the work poorly.

Now, why do children procrastinate over homework? Well, one reason is that kids can fill up their time with a lot more interesting things to do. Another, perhaps more compelling reason is that their parents let them. One advantage that children have over parents is stamina. A child who can stay out of sight or artfully dodge a parent's questions about homework for long enough will get away with it at least some of the time. Parents understandably become frustrated by constantly policing their children. Eventually they stop asking "Did you do your homework?" fifteen or twenty times a day.

# HOW TO BREAK THE PROCRASTINATION HABIT

There are several ways to break the procrastination habit. One is to create a house rule that a certain time is homework time. Coming home from school, doing homework, and getting it out of the way suits some children best. Most children, however, need a little time to unwind after school. This can put you in a real bind. Parents are usually sympathetic to the fact that children want to play after school, but you must be honest with yourself about what happens after this winding-down period. Does it become impossible to structure your child's time once she has begun to play after school? If the answer is yes, it is better to have the child bite the bullet and do homework right after school.

The key to staying out of the procrastination cycle is developing good habits. Homework should be done at the same time, in the same place, and under the same conditions every day with few exceptions.

## LOUIS THE PROCRASTINATOR

Nine-year-old Louis comes home from school, takes out his books, lays everything out on the table, and then stares into space, sharpens his pencils for twenty minutes, gets up and down for several glasses of water or juice, or makes several trips to the bathroom. Finally he sits down and does maybe five minutes of homework. Then the staring starts again, the pencils need resharpening, and his thirst returns. Louis is an expert at making a twenty-minute homework project take two to three hours. Louis's mom is completely baffled by all this. The question she asks most is "If he hates homework so much, why doesn't he just take the twenty minutes and get it over with?"

Louis is stuck in one of the worst kinds of procrastination cycles. His nose is right up against the task, yet he still won't do it. Louis is a passive protester. He will freely tell you that he hates homework, whether it is a minute's worth or an hour's worth. Then he will tell you how boring it is. It is, of course, impossible to convince him that the homework is boring because anyone would be bored by sharpening pencils for three hours five times a week.

The advice I gave to Louis's mom about his procrastination was relatively simple: to ask Louis's teacher how long it should take Louis to do his homework and then have a chat with Louis, making a rule that he stop doing his homework after that amount of time. Louis's mom and teacher agreed that Louis's teacher would handle it when Louis showed up short of work. Louis did not like the new arrangement at all. He knew that his mom and his teacher were cooperating with each other and that he would be accountable to his teacher for his missing work.

Remarkable things began to happen. Louis's mom felt tremendous relief over not having to police his homework activities. All she had to do was look at the clock and then tell him when his hour and a half was up. Louis began to get used to the new system, and his work time got shorter and shorter while its quality actually improved because he didn't start and stop a hundred times during one homework session.

Was the new system foolproof? Not at all. Louis would test the system from time to time, and because his teacher had twenty other children to teach, she would from time to time forget to call Louis to task on work that was incomplete or poorly done. Overall, however, the intervention was a success.

Please remember that almost no problem resolves itself 100 percent overnight. For Louis's homework problems to end completely Louis's attitude about homework, success, and achievement had to change completely. Limiting his time motivated him from the outside, but to show real success Louis has to push himself. The solution worked in part because his mom and teacher cooperated. Talk to the classroom teacher at the first sign of homework problems. Children often get away with avoiding work because of poor communication between parent and teacher. Many teachers will note when a child does not do homework, but many are just too busy to do anything about it unless parents bring it to their attention. Change requires action, and parents who want to help their children change their homework habits have to be willing to take it.

## THE HOMEWORK HUCKSTER

The homework huckster has discovered an interesting way to do her homework—she gets Mom or Dad to do it. How can an intelligent adult be fooled into doing a child's homework for her? It can happen a number of ways, starting when parents see their child agonizing over homework. They ask if she needs help. Since most parents aren't teachers, they become frustrated trying to help their child find the correct answers to homework problems. They think that if they do one or two examples or problems for the child she might get the hang of it. Well, maybe three or four answers will do the trick. After that Mom or Dad says, "See, wasn't that easy? We're all done!" Parents also can offer too much help on school reports and projects. Some parents type their children's reports on a word processor and clean up grammar and spelling mistakes while they're at it. Others construct elaborate science projects for their children. In turn children begin to rely heavily on their parents, and they never learn the basic organizational and planning aspects of managing a project.

If you do this, your youngster could end up in the embarrassing situation one third-grader found himself in after winning first place in a science fair. When the award was presented, he was asked how his project worked. He wasn't able to answer because his dad had done it for him. It's easy for parents to get their own issues confused with doing their kids' homework. They worry that teachers will criticize *them* if their children don't perform in school. Good grades tell parents that they are doing a good job. It is during these times that you need to remind yourself that you have already gone through your schooling. It's time to let your child do it on her own. That doesn't mean that you can't help your child with homework. It means that you just have to define some boundaries first. Here are some to get you started:

1.  Never give your child more than a few answers on any homework assignment. If she still can't understand the work, sit down and write a note to the teacher. Say that your child is having a lot of trouble managing today's assignment. Then let the teacher take it from there.

2.  If your child is having trouble managing a report or a project, do not do it for him. Instead help him develop an outline or a checklist of steps that he needs to finish the project. The smaller the steps, the more manageable they become. This helps build confidence. You can help gather materials and make suggestions, but when it comes to doing, back off.

3.  Above all, resist the urge to prove your worth as a parent through your children's grades. Nobody wants his children to fail, but it's unfair to provide a superficial crutch for your

children to lean on. As school becomes more and more difficult and demanding, your child's foundation of skills simply does not develop; then the real problems start in high school and college. You wouldn't believe how often I discovered, even as a college professor, that some of my students still relied on their parents to do term papers and written reports.

## THE PERFECTIONIST

Where some children don't seem to care at all about their homework, the perfectionist is overconcerned.

### ALINA'S NEVER SATISFIED WITH HER WORK

Ten-year-old Alina used to come home from school each day and put herself through a very strenuous ritual. She would sit down, lay out her schoolbooks and homework, and begin her assignments. If she made a single mistake or didn't like the way something looked, she would tear up her work and start again. Alina's handwriting was overly neat, actually compulsive. Her letters all had to be the same size. Many days she would bring herself to tears out of frustration and disappointment. Alina liked school, and she idolized her teacher. She didn't want to disappoint her teacher or her parents.

Some children acquire unrealistic expectations from their parents, but many acquire those expectations on their own or even from their teachers. The best way to handle behavior like this is to schedule a conference and ask your child's teacher to tell your child she is putting too much pressure on herself and her work can be of excellent quality even if she makes one or two mistakes. Next look for reasons for your child's perfectionism. Stress from high parental expectations or other sources close to home like divorce or fighting between the parents can also play a role. Children who are perfectionistic feel inadequate and usually have very low self-esteem. Special care must be taken to discourage those negative perceptions and encourage more positive and reasonable ideas about themselves and their performance. If the perfectionism continues, it is always a good idea to seek counseling from someone who is qualified and has experience in working with children.

## THE FRUSTRATED CHILD   ◀

Frustration, the mental equivalent of having to walk ten miles over a hot desert with a large pebble in your shoe, is a factor in every type of homework problem or battle. An irritating force that wears all children down, it is the main factor in the trouble that children with learning disabilities, hyperactivity, and attention problems have with homework. Frustration usually occurs when schoolwork or homework is either confusing or understimulating. The natural response to frustration is avoidance.

Imagine for a second that our government decided what each of us would do for a living. Then imagine that your job is to fix carburetors, but you're neither very good at it nor very interested in it. So you work all day long fixing these irritating carburetors with all these stupid little parts and levers—and you come home exhausted and just glad to get away from it all. About a half hour after you return home from work every day, your doorbell rings. It's always one neighbor or another, telling you that his car is having trouble. It's always the carburetor. Would it be possible for you to spend an hour or two working on the car? After all, it will be good practice for what you have to do at work tomorrow. In a world like that, how long do you think it would take you to learn to avoid answering the door? You might even bury yourself in a room somewhere and try to get lost in a television show. On really bad days you might even answer the door and

> *Frustration, especially when it's experienced every single day, can result in anger and depression in your child.*

have a temper tantrum in front of your neighbors while you scream, "I'm not fixing your stupid carburetor! I have enough of this garbage all day at work, and I'm just not doing it anymore!"

The point is that frustration is not only a bad mental state to be in but also a difficult one to get out of when you experience it every day. Over the course of months—even years in the case of children in school—frustration can totally and completely turn a child off. In a very powerful way frustration can actually train children to avoid homework and school-related activities: Your child becomes frustrated trying to do some work in school. It's either difficult, confusing, or boring. Since frustration is an irritating state to be in, the child is likely to look for a way to get out of that state. The best way to put an end to frustrating schoolwork is simply to stay away from it. Not doing homework can have an unpleasant consequence, but you experience that consequence only if you get caught.

This is exactly the point at which homework problems begin. A child comes home and lies about not having any homework. The parent believes the child, and the child goes to school and lies about forgetting to bring in his homework. The teacher believes him. There is little if any consequence. The child has learned that lying about homework reduces the frustration of having to deal with it. The next day, a new set of lies. More relief from frustration. This isn't so bad. The next day, the child does a little of his homework, copies the rest from a friend on the school bus. The teacher isn't exactly thrilled with the quality of the work but doesn't say anything. Over the next few days or weeks, more lies about homework, more dodges from the teacher at school.

> *Getting children to do their homework is easier if you establish and follow a daily homework routine.*

The next report card that goes home to the parent includes a note about a lot of missing homework. At this point the parent says, "I didn't know you weren't doing your homework. Why have you been telling me that you don't have any homework?" This is the first time in weeks that there has been any real negative consequence concerning the avoided homework. The usual response of the child is to make believe the teacher is crazy. "I don't know what she's talking about, Mom. Maybe I missed one homework the entire marking period." At this point the parent either checks with the teacher or doesn't, but in most cases not enough is done about it. The net result of the whole situation is that all the relief this child has gotten from avoiding doing his homework is well worth getting into a little trouble once every marking period. The next marking period, a new set of lies and dodges. The process can go on for an entire year—even several years if nothing is done about it.

## ENCOURAGE CLEAR COMMUNICATION ◀

There are many ways that you can break the frustration-avoidance cycle. The single most important way is to allow and encourage your child to tell you when homework is too frustrating. This is where you have to be a bit careful. *Too frustrating* doesn't mean that the child can't stand to be inside while her friends are outside; it means she has a problem learning the work. To help determine whether your child is chronically frustrated by schoolwork done at home, ask yourself these questions:

1. Does your child have a history of learning problems?
2. Does he rip up or destroy his papers during a homework session?
3. Does your child refer to herself as dumb or stupid when she doesn't understand the work?
4. Does your child speed through or scribble work in poor quality just to get it done?

If the answer to any of these questions is yes, don't wait to see what happens. Make special arrangements to get your child back on track, or things will only get much worse.

## TIPS TO HELP YOUR CHILD OVERCOME FRUSTRATION ◀

When your child is frustrated, you must take action to prevent the situation from becoming worse. Here are some things you can do immediately after you determine that frustration is contributing to your child's homework problems.

1. Schedule a conference with your child's teacher. Explain some of the behavior you see at home that indicates frustration. Ask your child's teacher for suggestions. Discuss with the

teacher or your child's pediatrician the possibility of having the child evaluated for learning difficulties.

2. Discuss with the teacher the possibility of having your child hand in less work but of very high quality as opposed to all of the work of poor quality. For instance, let's say twenty-five math problems are assigned. A child who has trouble concentrating might be overwhelmed by the sheer number of problems. She might try five or six with good attention, then give up and write or scribble any answer on the sheet just to get the work done. An alternative is to tell the child that if she does twelve of the examples and can show that she understands the work and can do it neatly, that's all she will have to do. Your child will feel less frustrated with a lower volume of work to tackle. Your child's teacher will advise you on how much work needs to be done to reinforce the lessons learned in school that day. After all, there is no hard-and-fast rule for how much homework is needed to reinforce a concept. If the child does half the work but can demonstrate good comprehension of the material, the main goal of homework is accomplished. If your child does higher-quality work, even if it is less work, at least there will be a solid basis for praising the child and building up her self-esteem. More praise of homework will in turn reduce frustration and might actually change perceptions about homework.

3. Examine what part of the homework process actually causes the frustration. Many children have fine motor difficulties that make it very hard for them to write neatly, so the physical act of writing itself is what causes the difficulty. Kids who are very creative may avoid expressing themselves in writing because of this problem, coming up with "I like fish" when asked to write a sentence with the word *fish* in it instead of "The fish that live around coral reefs are brightly colored and beautiful."

There are ways to reduce the frustration associated with writing tasks. For instance, dictating into a tape recorder and then copying the sentences from the tape separates the tasks of writing and thinking, so the child has to manage only one part of the task at a time. Learning to use a word processor can also be helpful, but learning how to use a word processor will make children (and most other people) *less* efficient at first because of the time it takes to learn keyboarding skills and to operate the word processor. I believe, however, that the time spent learning to type and use a word processor is more than worth the effort and the temporary decrease in productivity.

Please remember that the most important step to solving almost any homework problem is to make contact with the classroom teacher or, in the case of an older child who has more than one teacher, the guidance counselor. A good way to keep your child honest about homework assignments is to set up a weekly progress report to be filled out and sent back to you every week. Most teachers do not mind filling out a very short checklist, but a lengthy report every week might be looked at as an imposition.

## HOW YOU CAN HELP YOURSELF, TOO ◀

You don't have to solve this problem yourself. Here are three ways that you can get help to improve the situation.

1. Whenever possible, work as a team with your spouse so that one person doesn't become the sole member of the homework police.

2. Communicate with your child's teachers when things get rough. If you are afraid that they will think you are a pain in the butt, don't sweat it. If you are polite, they will not mind, and if they do that's too bad. Listening to parents is part of their job.

3. Bow out when you don't feel capable of being patient. Don't let your own frustration contribute to making your child feel "dumb" for not understanding. When you don't feel as though you have the patience to help your child with her homework, consider a homework tutor, someone from outside your family to help your child with her homework. If your

child has no special needs, a responsible high school student might be more than adequate to help with homework. If your child has learning difficulties, there are many qualified tutors who can help. When choosing a homework tutor, it is always a good idea to check references. Also be advised that quality tutoring doesn't really have to cost a lot of money. Tutoring sessions should never last for more than ninety minutes and are more effective for shorter periods a few times a week.

## A CHECKLIST TO HELP YOU CONQUER HOMEWORK PROBLEMS

It's possible to set up a checklist geared to helping you solve your child's homework problems.

The first step involves identifying what the causes of homework problems are. See if you can identify whether the problems are related to

- poor after-school time management,
- difficulty understanding what's been happening in the classroom,
- difficulties with attention and concentration, or
- frustration.

If poor after-school time management is a problem, structure a period of time after the school day when homework can be done. Contact the teacher and ask for cooperation with a system that limits the amount of time a child spends doing work at home. Set up a schedule with the teacher and stay in communication to check on progress. If homework problems are due to difficulty understanding the classroom material, consult the teacher for advice immediately. Consider hiring a homework tutor to help. Make sure the tutor is in contact with the teacher. If there are attention and concentration problems, it is a good idea to have your child evaluated by a psychologist who is trained in the assessment of attentional disorders. (Attention difficulties may influence as many as one in ten children, and they are found more frequently in boys than in girls.) Finally, if your child seems to be caught in the frustration-avoidance cycle, increase her accountability for homework by setting up a weekly progress report that goes to the teacher or guidance counselor. Try to find the reason why your child is avoiding homework. Give your child the opportunity to express openly her confusion or even lack of interest in the material. Schedule a conference with the teacher or guidance counselor.

Above all, remember that homework problems can become serious only when they are left alone. The longer you wait to start solving them, the further behind your child will fall in school and the more ground there will be to make up. Some subjects like math build on material learned in the beginning of the year and are practiced in homework. If a child falls behind in this situation, it is much more difficult to make up.

Also remember what I said about your having gone to school already. If you really want to do homework again, enroll yourself in a stimulating college course. Then at least you'll get the credit for it. When it comes to your kid's work, the most important thing you can help teach is independence.

## QUICK REVIEW

1. Children neglect their homework for a number of different reasons. Eventually, avoiding homework becomes a bad habit or a pattern. Some common patterns include procrastination, manipulation, perfectionism, and frustration.

2. Never let homework problems go on for too long without consulting a teacher or guidance counselor. Working with you and your child to get things back on track is part of his job.

3. Establish a routine that sets a regular time and place for doing homework, then stick to it—no exceptions.

4. When your child is having trouble with homework, suggest to the teacher that she do less work but of better quality. In other words, instead of doing forty math problems and getting only ten right, have her do thirty and get twenty right.

5. If your child seems frustrated, fatigued, and unable to concentrate, have him evaluated by a learning specialist. The earlier learning difficulties are detected, the more effectively they can be corrected.

6. If you don't think you have the patience to help your child with her homework, look into the possibility of ¡a homework tutor (if the child has trouble learning basic skills and concepts, try to find someone with teaching experience) or a homework helper, a high school or college student who can look over the situation and see that homework gets done.

**EXERCISES FOR PARENTS**

## COMMUNICATING WITH TEACHERS AND GUIDANCE COUNSELORS

Parents sometimes get flustered when communicating to teachers and guidance counselors about school matters. Use these sample notes as guidelines to help you act early.

> Dear Mr. or Mrs. So-and-So:
>
> My son, Mark, seems to be having difficulty understanding his math homework. I would like to schedule a brief conference with you at your earliest convenience to discuss how we can get him some help before he falls too far behind.
>
> Thank you for your consideration,
> Mrs. Greene

Here is another example.

> Dear Mr. or Mrs. So-and-So:
>
> My daughter Hillary has returned from school only twice in the last two weeks with homework assignments. She informs me that she does most of her homework in school. Can we have a brief talk so that I can find out whether she is getting all of her work done with good effort and performance?
>
> Thank you,
> Mr. Browne

**EXERCISES FOR PARENTS**

Finally, here is a note to request help in monitoring that homework is done and handed in.

> Dear Mr. or Ms. So-and-So:
>
> We are trying to help our son, Justin, become more conscientious about doing his homework. Would you mind filling out this checklist and sending it home to us, once a week, so that we know he is doing his work? Please call us at 555-6734 if you would like to discuss this.
>
> Sincerely,
> Ms. Blocke

Use the Weekly Homework Progress Report on the next page to keep on top of your child's homework and school performance. Always reward good reports and do not hesitate to contact the teacher for a conference if things are not going as well as they should.

**EXERCISES FOR PARENTS**

# WEEKLY HOMEWORK PROGRESS REPORT

Week of: __ / __ / __

Dear _____,

Would you please be kind enough to fill out this weekly homework progress report for our child, _____?
Thank you for your cooperation.

| Subject | Homework handed in? | | Quality of work | | |
|---|---|---|---|---|---|
| English | ☐ YES | ☐ NO | ☐ excellent | ☐ OK | ☐ needs work |
| Reading | ☐ YES | ☐ NO | ☐ excellent | ☐ OK | ☐ needs work |
| Spelling | ☐ YES | ☐ NO | ☐ excellent | ☐ OK | ☐ needs work |
| Soc. Studies | ☐ YES | ☐ NO | ☐ excellent | ☐ OK | ☐ needs work |
| Science | ☐ YES | ☐ NO | ☐ excellent | ☐ OK | ☐ needs work |
| Math | ☐ YES | ☐ NO | ☐ excellent | ☐ OK | ☐ needs work |
| Language | ☐ YES | ☐ NO | ☐ excellent | ☐ OK | ☐ needs work |
| _____ | ☐ YES | ☐ NO | ☐ excellent | ☐ OK | ☐ needs work |
| _____ | ☐ YES | ☐ NO | ☐ excellent | ☐ OK | ☐ needs work |
| _____ | ☐ YES | ☐ NO | ☐ excellent | ☐ OK | ☐ needs work |

Comments, missing work, assignments due:

_____

_____

_____

_____

## ORGANIZING PROJECTS AND PAPERS

Create an outline and a schedule for completing tasks for major projects and assignments:

Name and nature of assignment: _____

_____

Date due: ___/___/___

| | |
|---|---|
| **Step One:** Determine best places to get information. Gather research—go to library, bookstore, encyclopedia, etc. Take out books, copy articles, or talk to whomever you need to contact so that you have all necessary materials for completing assignment. | **Step One:** Complete no later than: ___/___/___. ☐ DONE! |
| **Step Two:** Assemble materials, read, and take notes so that you can begin creating an outline of project. | **Step Two:** Complete no later than: ___/___/___. ☐ DONE! |
| **Step Three:** Create outline or prototype. Jot down sentences that are critical to the project so that you don't forget to include them. Decide on major headings and subheadings for reports. | **Step Three:** Complete no later than: ___/___/___. ☐ DONE! |
| **Step Four:** Fill in main ideas and secondary ideas. Be sure everything is in an order that makes sense. Finish with a strong conclusion. | **Step Four:** Complete no later than: ___/___/___. ☐ DONE! |
| **Step Five:** Go over paper/project. Check for spelling errors or important ideas you might have left out. Do your title and/or cover page. Don't forget to pack it up to take to school. | **Step Five:** Complete no later than: ___/___/___. ☐ DONE! |

# 11

# SOLVING SLEEP PROBLEMS ◀

Whenever a parent corners me at a party with the opening line "Dr. Favaro, I know you're not working now, but I just need to ask you one little question about my child," I can bet the question has to do with getting a child to sleep at night. The "right" versus "wrong" way to get kids to sleep has become one of the most hotly debated topics in all of behavioral pediatrics.

Perhaps it has to do with the increase in two-career families and the changing roles of mothers and fathers. Today's parents value their rest and the preservation of their energy and make a good night's sleep a very high priority, especially when facing a full workload the next day. Staying up all night with a crying toddler or a child who is asking to sleep in your bed is not on most parents' agenda.

Before we begin, understand that you shouldn't consider the information in this book a substitute for a doctor's visit. If your child's sleep problems persist or if your child seems uncomfortable or in pain during the night, please contact your pediatrician.

# AN ANTHROPOLOGICAL PERSPECTIVE

Imagine yourself a prehistoric man or woman living in a cave. Inside, you and your mate huddle around a fire. Outside the cave the night is still, yet to ensure your safety you listen for the rustling footsteps of a fierce saber-toothed tiger. Hopefully there will be no encounters with this man-eater tonight. Your infant child is in the cave with you, and it is time for bed. How likely is it that you will move your child to another cave before you retire for a peaceful night's sleep? Not likely at all. In prehistoric times parents probably slept very close to their children because of the relative lack of security in their living environments. What that should suggest about "natural" sleeping arrangements is that long ago we had a strong behavioral mechanism for sleeping with our children. A human infant is far too helpless and defenseless to sleep alone in a hostile environment. It is easy to forget these prehistoric roots today when we have the luxury of sleeping apart from our children in our own comfortable beds, but this perspective shows us that sleeping apart from our children is not natural at all. It is something we do for convenience.

# A CULTURAL POINT OF VIEW

On the whole Americans have much different views about sleeping with children from people in other parts of the world. Living in a prosperous culture affords us the luxury of having more than one sleeping room in the house to begin with. In cultures where economic or space limitations prevail, there is never an issue about children putting themselves to sleep, because everyone sleeps together out of practical necessity.

Also, our cultural norms and values have sometimes made us equate sleeping in the same bed as children with causing them to have premature sexual feelings, thoughts, and fantasies. These ideas probably originated in Puritan and Victorian times, yet they still influence our thinking today, even though there is nothing to suggest that sleeping with your children causes them to develop abnormally in any way. Of course acting in a sexual manner toward a child would always be harmful to the child.

## IS A "FAMILY BED" THE SOLUTION?

I am not going to suggest that the way to solve your children's sleeping problems is for everyone to pile into the same bed. What I *am* saying is that you need to understand some of the evolutionary and cultural reasons for our sleeping patterns. You can *choose* to sleep with your kids if you want to, without fear that it will damage them psychologically. You can also choose to *teach* your children to sleep in their own beds, but after all I've explained, it should be clear that the emphasis is on the word *teach* because children sleeping apart from their parents is just not natural human behavior.

## SLEEP PATTERNS

Every single one of us wakes up about two or three times a night. We might not remember doing so because we're used to it and we just fall back to sleep. It's quite different for a child, who might wake up and get frightened or upset. When kids get frightened, they want Mom and Dad, of course.

Infants spend more than half of their time sleeping, but they don't really put in that many hours in a row. Three-month-old children can sleep about four hours in a row. By four months, pediatricians tell us, children can go a full eight hours without food, and feeding at night might actually lead to a series of psychological and physical events that can make for an uncomfortable night's sleep for parent and child. If you are feeding your baby through the night, be sure to hear what your pediatrician has to say about it. On a simply practical level, if you get into the habit of feeding your child through the night, you will actually train her to feel hungry at night and then wake up and cry to be fed. By six months most kids can sleep about six hours in a row.

As children get older, they pass through some very critical ages and stages that affect their sleep patterns. The first of these periods occurs between nine and twelve months, the next at fifteen months. During these periods of life children, even during their waking hours, have a difficult time being separated from their parents. These periods of separation anxiety often coincide with sleep disturbances, which is only logical since things are so much scarier at night.

Three years is also an interesting age for sleep problems, but for entirely different reasons. At about age three children begin to develop the mental abilities needed for fantasy play. A good friend of mine had a three-year-old who made up a big hairy gorilla to accompany him on his fantastic imaginary journeys. It is at this age when kids begin to conjure up imaginary friends and make up dramatic fantasy stories, and this aspect of development does tend to interact with sleep patterns.

## THREE YEARS OLD: A CRITICAL AGE

Three-year-old children are just beginning to get in touch with their imagination. One side effect of all this imaginary play is that they tend to blur the line between fantasy and reality; they are not fully aware of what is real and what is "just pretend." Parents must do a lot of explaining about what's real and what's not at this age, and even though children don't understand the distinction at first, they soon learn through example and association. If you want to get a good night's sleep, try not to let your three-year-old watch too many scary television shows before bed. *The Wizard of Oz* is famous for putting terrible frights into kids. Also, as wonderful as they are, many Disney animations have images that can be very frightening to young children. Surprisingly, even shows that don't seem so scary can give kids a hard time. One parent told me that the scene from the movie *Raising Arizona* where two men pop up from under a manhole cover terrified her three-year-old son because he thought it was possible to be walking along and just see men popping out of the ground at any time.

Another interesting mental event that occurs at around three years old is that children begin reporting their dreams. Dreams at this age can be disturbing for a number of reasons. Many three-year-old children lack the verbal ability to explain what happened to them during the night when they were dreaming. The anxiety the new experience causes, along with the frustration of not being able to explain it, can make for many rough nights. Children usually begin reporting their dreams by talking about animals. Research seems to suggest that animals inhabit children's dream worlds before people do. When people do start playing roles in children's dreams, it can be frightening. Children wake up and report that a man or sometimes a monster is following them. You might have heard that children this age tend to be egocentric, which just means children tend to believe that they are at the center of everything. Because of this egocentrism, your children don't know that you didn't have the same dream that they did. Instead they believe you saw everything they did and can't quite figure out why you are having a difficult time understanding what has happened to them.

## STAY OR GO?

What should parents do when their three-year-old child walks into their room and cries in fright about a man or a monster or some other creepy nighttime creature? The answer to this question is "It depends." Your first decision must be whether you want to allow the child to use your bed as a source of comfort during these times. If you do, then be prepared to be called into service regularly and often. It can be quite nice snuggling right in between Mom and Dad, and a smart three-year-old will figure out that the ticket for this ride is free as long as the story is good enough. At this point parents usually ask me if letting their child sleep with them fosters "dependence" on it. *Dependence* always sounds like a description of a disorder to me, so I tend to stay away from this term. What is actually happening is that the child may develop the *habit* of sleeping with parents and then not feel comfortable in her own bed anymore. If you let yourself give in to your child's request to sleep with you even once every so often, it won't stop her from asking every night since it's always possible that this might be one of those special nights. So if you want to get a peaceful night's sleep, you have to decide on the rules, then stick to them. If you decide to let your child come into bed with you, that's what you will have to adopt as the norm.

## COMPROMISES AND CHOICES

If you let your child know that sleeping with you is not an option, you can try to arrange a compromise that keeps everyone happy.

One compromise is to allow your child to come into your room and sleep on a blanket or towel next to your bed. The advantage of doing this is that your child will never get too comfortable sleeping on the floor and will eventually move back into his own bed. Another compromise is to agree to meet your child in his own room and sit with him until he falls back to sleep. More often than not you will fall asleep first, and that works out fairly well, because without you awake to talk to the child gets bored and falls asleep as well.

## SHOULD I LET MY CHILD CRY AT NIGHT?

Regardless of what you might have heard, letting your child cry without tending to her at all is not, in my opinion, a good way of handling this situation. Some people recommend that you let your child cry for thirty minutes or more so that she can "get used to" her own bed. Think about it a different way. Sleep is a habit. There are good habits and bad habits. Do you want your child's early sleep experiences and memories to be associated with that much unpleasantness? It just doesn't make any sense. Your child will follow just about any routine that you set. If the routine calls for you to get upset and irritated with each other before settling in to sleep, that pattern will be followed. If the routine is that your child is allowed to touch base with you and feel comforted or you will come in and touch base with her, the experience will be a lot more pleasant for both of you. Once again, the key to getting your two- to five-year-old to sleep is in developing a routine or habit. Whatever happens most of the time becomes a habit, and you are the one who should determine what happens most of the time. Many parents have tried Dr. Richard Ferber's method for putting kids to sleep. In his book *Solving Your Child's Sleep Problems*, Dr. Ferber suggests that you put children, even infants as young as five months old, to bed, comfort them briefly, then walk out of the room. If the baby cries, wait five minutes, then go back in. Dr. Ferber recommends that you soothe the child briefly but that you do not stay in very long. He also recommends that you leave the room while the child is still awake. Repeat the process as many times as necessary during the night, waiting for longer intervals each time. Many parents have had success with Dr. Ferber's method, but in my own clinical experience this method does not work for every child. What is good about Dr. Ferber's method is that it encourages children to regulate their own sleep patterns and establish their own sleep habits. This method will prevent children from relying on Mom or Dad to get them to sleep at night. The downside is that children who have difficulty adjusting to the process might feel distressed and upset. No single method is foolproof, so use your common sense and good judgment to determine whether a method like this is too stressful.

## SOME COMMONSENSE STRATEGIES ◀

Here is my own quick list of commonsense tips to help you develop bedtime habits and routines.

**1. Don't wait until the last possible second to get young children ready for bed.** Having to rush to get pajamas on, teeth brushed, and so on will immediately raise the level of tension. As tensions rise, children get more stubborn and parents have to behave more forcefully. Also, bedtime fights tend to charge up both parents and children. Getting all wound up from fighting for fifteen minutes before bed doesn't help ease a child into a peaceful night's sleep. That sets the stage for stalling, drink requests, bathroom requests, and so on. That's when bedtime battles usually begin.

**2. Cue your children to get ready for bed by rehearsing what the after-dinner schedule will be.** Simply set aside some quiet time after dinner, when you are reading a story or playing a game, and say something like "OK, now we are going to read a story, then we'll get into our pajamas, watch a little television, and then it will be time for bed." Present bedtime as being an upper limit rather than a lower limit. In other words, instead of saying "I want you to be in bed by eight-thirty," say "You can stay up as late as eight-thirty."

**3. Try to make the right-before-bedtime activities fun but not too stimulating.** This information is especially important for dads to hear. I can't tell you how many times moms have told me that just as soon as they've gotten their kids settled in and relaxed, Dad comes along and starts a wrestling match or some other stimulating activity that has everyone wired for the next few hours. Storytelling, snuggling, and reviewing the day's activities are preferable to sports matches or invigorating video-game challenges.

**4. Use the time right before bed to review your child's behavior during the day.** Praise the positive behavior and talk about negative behavior in a neutral, nonpunitive way: "You know, Allison, today you were very helpful to Mommy because you set the table all by yourself. That was just great, and I want you to know that I appreciate it. You know I also saw you pushing your sister around, which I don't think is too good. Do you think that tomorrow you can be a little nicer to her? If you have a problem with her, you can show her you're angry with words, but we don't allow hitting or pushing. OK?"

## KIDS WILL TAKE THEIR CUES FROM YOU

Your behavior will help set the tone for bedtime. If you've had a rough day and can't wait to get the kids out of your hair, they will most certainly sense the stress and fight you about bedtime. Although it is much easier said than done, it is always more effective to move kids through the bedtime ritual by being calm. Again, a key to this is not putting time pressure on yourself. If you feel the stress of getting everyone washed up and ready for bed, the struggle will put you right over the top of the stress scale. In two-career families it is essential that both parents participate so that one parent doesn't always have to shoulder this difficult burden.

## WHEN OLDER KIDS STALL AT BEDTIME

Did you know that most kids over the age of six believe that right after they go to bed, the living room floor transforms itself into a basketball court and Mom and Dad run around all night shooting hoops and having all the fun while the kids suffer in their bedrooms? That's why they have to keep coming out of their rooms. They want to see it happen, and they want to play, too. Most kids hate going to bed, especially if they are not tired. Adults can't relate to this at all because they're always tired. If life happened the way people wanted it to, parents would be asleep by eight o'clock every night and kids would be watching MTV and eating Pop-Tarts until four o'clock in the morning.

## STICK TO YOUR GUNS—DON'T NEGOTIATE ◀

The first and most common mistake is to let yourself lose a negotiation because you are too tired to stick to your guns. On Monday your child asks for an extra hour to watch a television show. You stick to your guns and win—he goes to bed. On Tuesday you are talking on the phone when it is time to get your child to bed. Your phone conversation ends fifteen minutes after the time your child has to go to his room. He is sitting very quietly. He is almost invisible. You have to look extra hard at his chest to make sure he is breathing. So you feel sorry for him and then generous, and you let him stay up for an extra half hour. Mistake. You'll see why the next day.

On Wednesday you try to put him to bed at his regular time. "But you let me stay up last night. Why can't I go to bed at the same time tonight?" Good question. After all, what was the harm? He has a leg up on you. You can't tell him that the real reason is because you want an extra half hour to yourself. Besides, if you told him that, he would argue with you for a half hour just to make your life as miserable as his. You give in again out of sheer exhaustion. On Thursday you are having someone over for coffee. You want him out of the way. He won't go. You put your foot down. Out of desperation you say, "In five minutes this is going to get ugly." He convinces you that for a measly ten minutes he'll go to bed without a fight. You give in. Twenty minutes later you are asking him why he still isn't in bed. So far the score is you, one night; him, three nights. I don't think I need to go on. This has been painful enough. The point of the story is that, once you waver, you're dead in the water. The keys to getting your child to bed are structure, predictability, and routine.

## INCENTIVE PROGRAMS FOR OLDER KIDS

I recommend two systems that work very well to get your older kids to bed on time. The first system involves a coupon and works like this: Make a coupon out of construction paper or plain white paper. Tell the child that she can use it as a pass to get out of bed and watch television or sit outside the room for fifteen minutes, *or* she can trade it in for fifty cents the next morning. The coupon cannot be used more than once a night. This system can be used as a way to give out allowance, which makes it even more powerful, because the amount of allowance received is related to how well the child listens and goes to bed.

The second system allows a child to stay up ten minutes later the next night provided he goes to bed on time the night before. By the time the weekend rolls around, the child has earned an extra hour, which is about right for weekend nights. Here is an example involving a child with an eight o'clock bedtime. If the child goes to bed at 8:00 on Sunday, he can stay up until 8:10 on Monday. If he goes to bed on time Monday, he can stay up until 8:20 on Tuesday. If he continues to go to bed on time he will stay up until 8:30 on Wednesday, 8:40 on Thursday, 8:50 on Friday, and 9:00 on Saturday. If the child doesn't go to bed on time one of those nights, he has to start over again at 8:00 the next night.

Either system works well provided you stick to it. Again, the key is to utilize it in some kind of *routine*.

## SLEEP PROBLEMS

There are also a couple of common problems that children have once they are actually in bed. Nightmares are the most common bad sleeping experience, and people of all ages have them. They can be particularly scary for children, especially if they are recurring nightmares. One six-year-old girl I know had recurring nightmares that the school bus would not drop her off in front of her house, and she would wake up frightened that she would not be able to find her way home. You can teach most children to interrupt their nightmares and wake up simply by telling them that once they see the familiar signs of a bad dream they should shout, "Wake up!"

Another way to help children deal with nightmares is to encourage them to think pleasant thoughts before falling asleep. Eight-year-old Martin puts himself to sleep by imagining he is the last batter up with two outs in the bottom of the ninth inning at the World Series. Naturally he hits the game-winning home run. This story that he tells himself before he goes to sleep dispels some of the negative or anxious thoughts he has and prevents him from having or remembering his bad dreams. Nightmares can and do stem from anxiety or stress, so parents should encourage children to talk about the stressful events in their lives if they are reporting sleeping problems or bad dreams. For some children, encouraging them to draw a picture of the dream and then rip it up is a symbolic way of exerting some control over a situation that seems uncontrollable. If bad dreams cause so much stress that they interfere with your child's sleep for long periods of time, consult your pediatrician or a child development expert for guidance.

Another childhood sleep disturbance is something called a *night terror.* A child who is having a night terror looks wide awake and often screams or may even get out of bed. In reality the child is dreaming. Parents wonder whether they should wake children up in the middle of these night terrors. The answer to this question is no. Your child won't even remember the incident in the morning, and waking her up will probably be *more* disorienting to her than simply letting her "sleep through it."

Sleepwalking is another sleep disturbance that occurs in children from about three to twelve years of age. As with night terrors, parents should do their best to guide children back to their rooms with a minimum of fuss. Night terrors and sleepwalking usually subside on their own but can be related to going to sleep feeling agitated or overtired. As always, consult your pediatrician for advice if these behaviors persist.

# BED-WETTING

Parents also worry a great deal about bed-wetting, which is more common in boys than it is in girls and can persist from early childhood into adolescence. Many theories attempt to explain why children wet the bed. Some professionals believe that bed-wetting is a sign of inner turmoil and that any child who wets the bed is suffering from emotional problems. I do not find that this is always the case. Many children who wet the bed are actually very deep sleepers who do not wake up in

> *Patience and understanding are the keys to managing your child's bed-wetting problem.*

response to bladder pressure at night. The increase in bladder pressure may be enough to stimulate a dream about going to the bathroom, which in turn causes a child to urinate in bed. The experience is embarrassing for children and frustrating for parents. Children who are undergoing the stresses and strains of something like divorce may begin wetting the bed, and it is likely that these instances are related to emotional distress.

Several techniques employ devices that wake a child up if he is urinating at night. Their effectiveness is mixed. Some pediatricians try medications like Tofranil to help a child stop wetting the bed; again, this has limited effectiveness. The onset of puberty usually marks the end of bed-wetting. Parents must take special care to monitor the child's feelings of shame and embarrassment and to reinforce the notion that he is not at fault or "a baby." Aside from being sure that a child does not consume large amounts of liquid before bedtime and trying to wake the child up to go to the bathroom in the middle of the night, patience and understanding are the keys in this situation.

## KEEP AT IT!

Please understand that there will always be times when you'll have trouble getting your kids to do what you want. As children grow up, they want more and more control over their time and their lives in general. One day, like you and me, they will regret it and pine for the days when they could pull the blankets up over their heads at 8:00. Parenting isn't easy, but with a few helpful hints it can be easier.

1. Sleep patterns vary from child to child and situation to situation. You need to develop a consistent style for getting kids to sleep, and you need to make individual decisions about things like whether to let kids sleep in the same bed as you.

2. It is natural for your child to want to sleep with you. From infancy children are more comfortable sleeping close to a parent's body. Also, our biological heritage suggests that sleeping with parents satisfies needs for comfort and safety. This doesn't mean that you have to sleep with your children; it just means that they will need to be taught to sleep alone.

3. Different ages and stages that children pass through will influence their sleep. During the third and fourth year as children's imaginations develop they will be more likely to be frightened at night and wake up looking for Mom or Dad.

4. Establish routines for bedtime. Don't wait until the last second to get everyone ready for bed. Cue your children to get ready for bed while there is still plenty of time.

5. If you begin to negotiate bedtime for special occasions, be prepared to argue all the time about bedtime and extra time.

6. Nightmares, sleepwalking, and night terrors are all part of normal development, but if they persist, see your pediatrician.

7. Bed-wetting can be a psychologically stressful thing for kids. In almost all cases it resolves itself by adolescence. It can be related to emotional stress, but it doesn't have to be. Sometimes children are very deep sleepers who don't respond well to bladder pressure cues during the night.

## EXERCISES FOR PARENTS

## BEDTIME ROUTINE

Fill in this list to help create a bedtime routine for your kids.

### AT BEDTIME

| By this time . . . | You should . . . | Check |
|---|---|---|
| _____ | _____ | ☐ |
| _____ | _____ | ☐ |
| _____ | _____ | ☐ |
| _____ | _____ | ☐ |
| _____ | _____ | ☐ |
| _____ | _____ | ☐ |
| _____ | _____ | ☐ |
| _____ | _____ | ☐ |
| _____ | _____ | ☐ |
| _____ | _____ | ☐ |

## EXERCISES FOR PARENTS

### BEDTIME CONTRACT

You can use this simple contract to make your child's bedtime an hour later while reinforcing the idea that a strict bedtime must be adhered to.

---

# CONTRACT

This contract will allow _____ (name of child) to change his/her bedtime from _____ (current bedtime) to _____ (an hour later) under the following conditions. Bedtime will be twenty minutes later each week for three weeks. If bedtime responsibilities are not met, we will go back to the original bedtime and start over. If bedtime responsibilities are met, at the end of three weeks we will consider the new bedtime permanent.

Signed,

_____ Parent

_____ Parent

_____ Child

# 12

# HANDLING SIBLING RIVALRY ◀

"He hit me."

"She pushed me first."

"He took my toy."

"She wasn't playing with it."

"She's been taking my bras out of my drawer."

"She spit all over the last ice-cream bar so I couldn't have it."

"I never get to do anything, and he always gets to do everything."

"You like him more."

"She never gets into trouble."

"Why do I always get treated like the baby?"

Does any of this sound familiar? If there is more than one child living in your house, it should. Sibling rivalry is probably the single most frustrating and aggravating part of parenting. This chapter will outline some commonsense strategies for managing sibling rivalry so that your job as a parent is less stressful.

## OUR SIBLINGS BRING OUT THE WORST IN US ◀

Given what we all went through growing up with our own brothers and sisters, it is a wonder that parents ever decide to have more than one child. With two or more children, parents are guaranteed to see all of the worst that can come out in people—jealousy, envy, aggression, greed, spitefulness, even hatred—right there in their own children. Parents are often frightened by how calculating and mean their children can be toward one another. Sisters sneak into each other's room and cut each other's hair while brothers routinely send each other to the hospital for stitches after knock-down-drag-out brawls. Then there's the cursing, name-calling, and mental torture that take place every day, day in and day out, which can leave psychological scars for a lifetime. The good news is that, except in the worst cases, your children will actually grow up to seek out each other's company from time to time. But before this happens you will already have gone through a great deal of trouble trying to prevent them from scalping one another.

## "WE'RE BRINGING HOME SOMEONE NEW!"

There is an analogy that is often used to describe how one child feels when another child is about to enter—or shall we say *invade*?—the family. It goes like this: Imagine that your husband or wife wakes you up one day and tells you a new spouse is coming to live with you. He or she will be cute and cuddly, and we will all have to do the best we can to make him or her feel welcomed and loved. The new spouse will take up a lot of time and attention, and in many cases, especially in the beginning, you will have to put your needs aside so that the new spouse can be tended to and taken care of. It's not hard to imagine feeling enraged at the thought of someone "taking your place" in the family and upsetting the balance of things, especially when you have gotten used to your share of love and attention. Kids are no different. It is helpful to try to adopt your child's frame of mind for just a second so that you can see how confusing it is to have both positive and negative feelings for a sibling when you are growing up.

## CHILDREN ARE SELFISH: THEY HAVE TO BE

Let's take it one step at a time. Even when there's only one child in the house, children are selfish. They don't know how to be any other way. They are used to having things done for them. Their selfishness is a function of their dependence. There's nothing wrong with or bad about it, it's just the way things are. When another child enters the picture, kids have to become less selfish. They have to share things like toys, cookies, and television-watching preferences as well as emotional things like love and attention. This kind of sharing creates a lot of discomfort. On one hand all of a child's natural inclinations are to resent a brother or sister for causing that discomfort. On the other hand every day parents give very strong messages to siblings that they have to love one another and get along and play nicely. As shocking as it may seem, kids *are* influenced by that. So they wind up having conflicting feelings: "I hate this pain in the neck for interfering with my world and my stuff" versus "This is my brother [or sister], and I love him [or her]." Now throw into the mix the fact that brothers and sisters actually act in loving ways toward one another some of the time, even when their parents *don't* tell them to. This reinforces for them the idea that they should love their brothers and sisters. Finally, add the fact that brothers and sisters often do mean and terrible things to one another, which reinforces their notion that they should hate and antagonize their brothers and sisters. What a mess!

## REDUCING ANTAGONISM ◀

Parents need to understand the double-sided nature of the relationship between siblings so they can deal with all the ups and downs that go along with it. Parents also need to know how they can capitalize on the loving aspects of the relationship while reducing the antagonistic parts. Let's take a look at how we can reduce antagonism first.

▼

## MICHAEL AND EMILY

Unless your children are identical twins, chances are they are quite different. Take eight-year-old Emily and five-year-old Michael. Emily is active, distractible, and very physical. She is fidgety and has trouble concentrating on anything for a long time. Michael is quiet, reserved, and very gentle. He looks up to his older sister, but she doesn't even give him the time of day. She takes his toys whenever she wants, but she won't share hers. She walks into Michael's room whenever she wants, but heaven forbid if he goes anywhere near her room or her property.

Michael and Emily's parents are at their wit's end with Emily's inconsiderate behavior. In their minds they have labeled Michael as the "good, loving" child and Emily as the "bad, selfish" child. By doing this they have, without realizing it, intensified the antagonism between the two children. Emily's complaint is that her parents do everything for Michael and nothing for her. In a way she's right, because Michael and Emily's parents always feel as though Michael gets the short end of the stick from Emily, so they try to make up for it by giving him extra love and attention. This is not an entirely bad strategy. As you will see later on, I do recommend that you give more attention to the sibling who is being mistreated. In Michael and Emily's case, however, Mom and Dad make a point of yelling at Emily and giving her strong "you are bad" messages while they are comforting Michael. This only serves to give Emily a script or a role to act out. As the years go by, she will come to accept the role of Michael's tormentor.

Chances are that although siblings possess certain family traits and characteristics, some learned and some inborn, they are different. The goal is to teach children how to coexist despite their differences. Of course, this is much easier said than done. In the example of Michael and Emily, Emily doesn't have very good people skills. She is very independent and doesn't like to cuddle or be cuddled. Michael is warm and will say "I love you" to his parents and even his sister. It is only natural that their parents gravitate toward Michael. The point is that Michael and Emily's parents have to find reasons to build Emily up. For instance, Emily excels at sports. Mom and Dad need to fuss over her sports skills and accomplishments so that she feels appreciated for who she is and what she can do. In the end this will help reduce the antagonism between her and Michael.

## TRY NOT TO PLAY FAVORITES ◀

Another way of reducing antagonism between siblings is to be careful about each parent choosing a different favorite child and then identifying with that child. In many families it is mother and daughter against father and son or mother and son against father and daughter. This kind of teaming up can create intense antagonism between siblings.

## FAMILY FEUDS

Penny and Rob have been married for twelve years. They have an eight-year-old son and an eleven-year-old daughter. Penny and Rob have had their share of marital difficulties. Penny openly calls Rob "stupid" and believes he is unmotivated and incompetent. She often tells the children that they don't have enough nice things because their father doesn't make enough money. Rob gets angry at Penny and complains about her being mean. Penny is closer to their son and gives him more attention. Rob is closer to their daughter and gives her more attention. When the children are together, they often bicker just like their parents. Not only do they have role models for hostile behavior; they also feel the need to protect the parent they are closest to. The situation amounts to a disaster.

Children will be loyal to a parent who favors them, and when each parent favors a different child problems between the parents become problems between the children. Another important point that comes out of this example is that when parents bicker, yell, and fight, the children will pick up these behaviors and use them as a way of interacting with one another.

## EVERYDAY SIBLING PROBLEMS ◀

The following are practical ways of handling some of the most common day-to-day problems that pop up with siblings.

# EQUALITY: "SHE GOT MORE THAN ME!"

As soon as kids learn how to count and measure (which can be very young), they learn how to compare. Regardless of the item being dished out, don't be fooled by the complaints. What your children are really comparing and measuring is love. Let's take this conversation between nine-year-old Jordan and his mother.

"Ma, April got more pancakes than me."

"No, she didn't, Jordan. I gave you exactly the same number as I gave April."

"Hers are bigger. I want hers."

"No, they aren't. They are all about the same size."

"Hers have the better syrup."

"I gave you the same syrup."

"Hers are better."

"No, they are exactly the same."

"Why do you always give April the good stuff while I get the junk? You love April more."

"No. I love you exactly the same."

"Well, then why do you always treat her better?"

This conversation could go on forever. So many parents take great pains to make sure their children are always treated equally. When it comes to love and respect, of course it is important to treat your children as equals. But treating two people as equals doesn't mean that they have to have the same possessions or privileges. Remember, children, especially children younger than ten or twelve, can be very concrete thinkers. They are more likely to see love and attention as commodities than as feelings. It is your job as a parent to communicate that all of your children are special in their own way. Don't let yourself get caught in the trap of trying to do everything exactly the same for your children. For one thing, regardless of how you try, someone will always be disappointed. For another, you will add a tremendous amount of stress to the already difficult task of raising two or more children.

Instead of trying to dole out everything in equal amounts, confront the issue more directly. Take aside the child who is complaining and say, "You really seem to think that I treat your brother [or sister] better than I treat you. Let me tell you that each one of you is a special person to me. I love you because you are . . . ," then choose something unique about the child. Finish the conversation by saying "There are times when your brother might get a little more, and there are times when you might get a little more, but what is more important is that I love you both in your own way." By doing this we avoid comparisons, which can cause quite a bit of trouble. Some of the most troublesome comparisons have to do with comparing an older child to a younger child. Not too long ago I heard a parent tell an older brother, "Why don't you have any table manners? Your two-year-old sister has better manners and behavior at the table than you do." Comments like this just place more distance between siblings. The goal is to communicate an appreciation of what is different and unique about each of your children. This way they don't have to compete to live up to the standards of some imaginary ideal that you have set.

## POSSESSIVENESS AND TERRITORIALITY

Human beings are no different from many other types of animals that protect their territory. The way we tend to fight and bicker with our neighbors over property lines and fences shows this very clearly. Siblings constantly fight over territory, rights to property, and privileges.

### TWINKIE WARS

Twelve-year-old Anne had been eyeing the last Twinkie in a box in the cupboard for days, wondering whether her ten-year-old brother would swoop down on it. Although she didn't really feel like eating it, she didn't want her brother to eat it either. After all, from what she had seen over the past week, he had eaten almost the whole box by himself. She would never let him have the last one. Every day when he came home from school she watched him like a hawk. Then finally it was too much for her. She took the Twinkie out of the cupboard and hid it carefully in her room. He'll never get it now, she thought. The next day her brother walked into the house and announced that he was looking for that last Twinkie. Anne dashed into her room, devoured the Twinkie, and emerged victoriously. Anne had staked a claim on that Twinkie.

    I'm sure anthropologists and biologists would be quick to point out that this kind of competitive behavior once ensured that if there was ever a famine only the strongest and most cunning members of the species would survive. But who the heck cares about that when you've got two kids who are ready to kill each other over a Twinkie?

Parents have devised elaborate schemes to try to prevent squabbles over territory or possessions. Unfortunately these almost never work, because once again you are forced to divide everything up equally, and no matter how much you try, your kids will not be happy about the final tally. Then what should you do? The best thing to do is not let yourself become involved in any fight over who is eating the last one of anything. Sit back, observe the situation, and make those snacks more and more scarce until one of the kids says, "Hey, how come we never have Twinkies in the house anymore?" Your reply will simply be "When we had them, all you guys did was fight over them, so I decided we just couldn't handle having them around." Then let a brief time pass and start loosening up on the restriction. Eventually they will get the message that sharing a smaller portion of something good is better than having none at all.

A typical example of fighting over territory involves "prime real estate," like a favorite chair for watching television or the incredibly popular front seat of the car. For some reason children have universally agreed that the front seat of the car is one of the most desirable places on earth. They would gladly risk their own lives and the lives of everyone else in the car to sit there. Parents contribute to the perception that the front seat is a prized spot by offering it as a reward for good behavior. "If you're a good boy, I'll let you sit in the front seat of the car." When children bicker too much over the front seat, you can send them both to the backseat, where they will torment each other for the entire ride, until you have to threaten to pull off the road and do things that we probably shouldn't discuss here.

> *It's natural for a child to resent a brother or sister horning in on her territory or time with Mom and Dad.*

How can you handle front-seat or favorite-chair disputes? If you have two kids, the easiest way is to say that one child has rights to the front seat on Monday, Wednesday, and Friday and the other on Tuesday, Thursday, and Saturday, and the kids would draw straws for rights on Sunday. Is this a foolproof system? Of course not; there will still be plenty of fighting and claims of unfairness. A second way of dealing with it is by trading off privileges. The person who sits in the front seat has to give up the favorite chair for the rest of the day. A third way is to let them decide for themselves. If you have the time, or if you know there is going to be a problem with the front seat before you have to leave to go anywhere, ask the kids to decide for themselves who is going to sit there. You can increase their motivation by telling them that they will both have to sit in the backseat if they can't come up with anything. In many cases you will be amazed at how cooperative and inventive kids can be when they are asked to come up with solutions on their own. You will also see that the solutions they come up with are often completely unfair in terms of equality but are still acceptable. Please try to stop yourself from fine-tuning a bargain or negotiation after it has already been agreed on. If your children have solved a problem on their own, praise them for it and enjoy the few minutes of peace and quiet it affords.

## SPACE INVADERS

What do you do when one of your children invades the space or possessions of another? Let's look at an example. Kendra, age seven, and Richard, age nine, both have their own stack of video games. Richard will think nothing of going into Kendra's things and playing with his sister's video games. Kendra resents this and will often retaliate. The solution that worked in this case started with a strategy meeting among Kendra, Richard, and Mom. Mom explained that it was rude to take someone's things without asking first. Mom asked Richard and Kendra to explain how they felt when the other just took whatever he wanted. Neither one liked it, and of course both claimed that they never did it. With siblings you can often observe strange medical phenomena such as "spontaneous memory loss" and rearrangements of reality. It's truly amazing. In any case Kendra and Richard's mom made them sign an agreement that stated if Richard took one of Kendra's toys without asking, Kendra would have the right to take and temporarily own any one of Richard's possessions for twenty-four hours—and vice versa. The strategy meeting is an excellent way to diffuse tense situations between siblings, work out acceptable compromises, and teach conflict resolution. The keys to having a successful strategy meeting are:

1.  Make sure you do it after everyone has calmed down, not during a screaming fight or a brawl.

2.  Let each child fully express what he feels is happening.

3.  Suggest only a single solution and from that point allow the children to discuss that solution and modify it to a point where they feel comfortable.

4.  Walk away. Don't beat the issue to death. Let the kids do most of the compromising and negotiating on their own.

## WHEN A YOUNGER CHILD TAKES ADVANTAGE OF AN OLDER CHILD

One of the most disruptive things in six-year-old Brian's life is when his toddler brother, Andrew, waddles into his room and starts pulling down his stuff. At first Brian tried to be patient, but after Andrew started drooling all over his prized possessions he just couldn't take it anymore. The only way Brian was able to get Andrew out of the room was to bop him on the head or push him over. Mom tended to side with Andrew on most of these matters because Brian, being the big brother, should know better. But in this situation siding with the toddler isn't always fair. Limit setting is an important part of parenting a toddler, and Brian does have some rights to privacy. Mom should be sensitive to this by doing her best to pluck Andrew out of Brian's things whenever she can. She can also instruct Brian to let her know when Andrew is into his things so she can intervene accordingly.

## TEASING

When siblings tease one another, it can run from gentle good-natured kidding to sadistic, nonstop tormenting that can and does leave serious emotional scars on the receiver. A lot of brothers and sisters have the process so fine-tuned that they can send the object of their teasing into a rage by simply muttering one word.

### PHYLLIS AND DIANE

Eleven-year-old Phyllis and eight-year-old Diane are sisters. Phyllis has always been jealous of Diane because, according to Phyllis, their mother pays more attention to Diane. Diane is a bit overweight, and Phyllis learned that she could torment Diane by teasing her about her weight. After calling her "jumbo," "whale," and "Diane the African Elephant," Phyllis found that the word *lipid*, the scientific word for a molecule of fat, drove her sister absolutely insane. Maybe it was because Diane didn't really understand the meaning of it or because all of the other abusive terms had taken their cumulative toll and worn her down. Now that Phyllis knew how to push this button, she used it at every opportunity. It got to the point where Phyllis's mom forbade her to use that word in the house and threatened to punish Phyllis if she didn't stop. Threats didn't help. Phyllis would walk by Diane and mouth the word without actually saying it. Or she would just make the sound "llllllllll" whenever she passed Diane or would use variations or soundalike versions of the word. Phyllis and Diane's mother finally decided to put a stop to it when Diane became so depressed by all the teasing that she started talking about wanting to kill herself.

One way to handle this kind of name-calling and teasing is to take the teasing child aside and say, "I know that you have been teasing your sister. If you are trying to hurt her, you are doing an excellent job. Every time you tease her you are making her feel worse and worse about herself. When she grows up, she will probably not like herself very much. I don't think it's fair, but I know that if I ask you to stop you won't. Tell me, what would you do if you had two friends, and one friend was always teasing the other and making her feel terrible?" See if you can get the child who teases to identify with your role as a person who cares for two people but doesn't want to see either one hurt by the other.

When two children tease each other, you can also create a fine or a penalty system. One parent told me that she had great success with this system: whenever one of her children teased the other, the one who teased had to forfeit a quarter of allowance to the other. You can also use chores as a penalty. When one child teases, he has to do a chore that is usually assigned to the other child. For techniques like this to work, parents must stay on top of them and dedicate the time and energy needed to carry them off fairly.

Another important way that you can cut down on teasing is to be sure it isn't a family style. In some families teasing is pretty much a constant form of communication. Please be aware that constant teasing and taunting erode self-esteem and create anger and resentment in the long run. Since there is anger behind all teasing, it is important to give the child who teases an opportunity to express that anger in a more appropriate way. Acknowledge the angry feelings by saying "I know you don't like your sister and sometimes you even hate having her around. If you want to tell me how much you don't like her, that's fine, but teasing is mean, and I won't allow you to do that." Allowing the child to express anger and acknowledging angry feelings lessens the child's motivation to tease.

> *Constant teasing and taunting by siblings can erode a child's self-esteem and create anger and resentment.*

## BICKERING ◀

Bickering is another form of behavior that occurs regularly if not constantly among siblings. Bickering often escalates into loud arguments, and loud arguments sometimes progress to fistfights and other forms of aggression. As a parent, you need to know when to step in and when to let things work themselves out. If you intervene every time your children bicker, they will soon learn that bickering is an easy way to get your attention and bring you right into the middle of things. That's why I advise parents to be cautious about stepping into the middle of a disagreement. If you tend to step into the middle even just to add a comment or stick up for the one who is getting the short end of the stick, try sitting back and watching what happens. You will be surprised to see that a lot of squabbles work themselves out just fine without you. The outcome might not be fair in your eyes, but at least you will see that the problem comes and goes. No one knows your kids better than you do; that's why only you know the signals that indicate an argument is going to turn nasty. When you see or hear these signals, it is time to step in. Then the question becomes "What is the best way to intervene?" The best way is to encourage the children to do their own problem solving. The first step is to approach them and briefly describe what you see.

The second step is to remain neutral, describe the situation, let both kids put in their two cents, suggest a strategy, offer as an alternative removing the object in dispute, and then walk away. Will this work every time? No, but it will probably work better than whatever is happening now, and over time it will lead to more and more situations where your kids solve their own problems without your intervention.

## HOW TO HANDLE BICKERING

As an eight-year-old and a six-year-old are playing in another room, you hear bickering followed by a loud thump, the six-year-old crying and saying "Give me that back," and the eight-year-old saying "Shut up, you baby." You walk into the room and see the six-year-old on the floor and the eight-year-old with the toy they were fighting for. Your first response is to call it the way you see it without giving either child the chance to speak. "Greg, you are on the floor complaining, and Susan, you are standing there with his toy in your hand. I guess he doesn't want you to have the toy, and you want to play with it." At that point, step back from the situation and let both children tell their side of the story. After they finish, lay out a series of choices, one of which includes removing the toy from both of them. It might sound like this: "Let's see how we can solve this. Either you can figure out a way for both of you to play with the toy, or I can put it away and you can find something else to do." Then remove yourself from the situation altogether by saying "I'll be back in a few minutes to see what you have decided to do." Believe it or not, if you follow these simple steps, you won't often have to go back a second time.

## BRAINSTORMING

An important part of parenting strategies aimed at helping kids solve their own problems is helping them understand the importance of brainstorming. Let's say two of your children want to watch different television shows at the same time. You can see a rumble brewing as they furiously switch channels back and forth. You can step in front of the television and ask the children to come up with a solution that would make both happy. If the children reach an impasse, you can always turn the television off so that neither of them wins. Encourage both children to make suggestions for how to solve the problem and let them speak freely regardless of how ridiculous the suggestions sound. If there is an older child and a younger child who can't speak for herself, do most of the talking and negotiating for the younger child, but let the older child express himself. After the children agree on a solution, finish up the problem-solving session by going over details that might mess up the solution. If Johnny decides to let Ellen watch her television show in exchange for letting Johnny watch his show later, ask Johnny what he will be doing while Ellen is watching her show.

## WHEN TO STEP IN AND SEPARATE

If things have gotten completely out of hand and children are on the floor punching and hitting one another, it is not a good time to initiate a problem-solving session. When children have gotten to the point of hitting, it is time for a cooling-off period or time-out. Step in by separating the kids and by describing the situation as neutrally as possible: "I see you two are really upset with each other. I think you both need to separate and cool off before we can figure out what's going on here and what we should do about it." When tempers are running hot, time apart is necessary to bring things back into focus. This is true for children as well as adults. Try to bring the children back together to work out the problem after about ten or fifteen minutes. Use the same steps as before. Describe the situation as you saw it. Give both children the chance to tell their side of the story. Offer a solution. Provide the alternative that they can stay away from each other for the rest of the day if they want. Then leave. The funny thing about situations like these is that, even if kids are killing each other, they don't like

> *Believe it or not, kids are influenced by your words, "be nice to your brother or sister."*

to be told to stay away from each other. Feelings among siblings aren't so black and white even if they seem that way on the surface. On a rainy day, when there is no one else around, most siblings are pretty grateful to have a brother or sister in the house to play with.

1. When another sibling arrives on the scene, there is a natural tendency to feel displaced and pushed aside. Children get used to whatever family pecking order exists and resent newcomers impinging on their territory.

2. Appreciate the individuality of each of your children. Try not to compare them or give the message "I wish you would be more like your brother or sister."

3. Try to avoid aligning yourself too closely with one child, especially if she is having a discipline problem with your spouse. "Teaming up" with one child against a spouse or a sibling creates resentment and hard feelings that are difficult to chase away.

4. Do not be so concerned about treating children equally. While you shouldn't play favorites, the other side of the coin is that there will be circumstances when one child gets the better end of a deal and other circumstances where another child will. If you go out of your way to measure everything exactly, your kids will still accuse you of giving the other one more!

5. When one sibling is being hurtful or aggressive to another, give the positive attention to the child who is being taken advantage of and no attention to the child who is being aggressive.

6. To resolve conflicts: First, require that everyone calm down and use a reasonable tone of voice. Second, let both children tell their side of the story without letting the other one interrupt. Third, suggest a reasonable compromise and tell them if they want to work out something different that's fine with you. Fourth, walk away. Allow the children to come to their own resolution. Fifth, if they continue arguing, split them up and send them both to time-out until they cool off.

7. Don't let yourself get into the middle of bickering. Intervene only when things get out of hand. You would be surprised at how many situations tend to resolve themselves. When you step in, kids are more motivated to prove that they are right in front of you.

## EXERCISES FOR PARENTS

### CALLING A TRUCE

Petty fights can go on indefinitely, escalating into daily shouting matches, sabotage, and mental torture. Try having your kids sit down and sign this truce to help end the warfare.

---

# TRUCE

This truce is being called by:

_____

_____

It is hereby declared that _____ will cease and desist (in other words, "stop doing") the following thing(s) that annoy _____ :

(1) _____

(2) _____

It is also hereby declared that _____ will cease and desist (in other words, "stop doing") the following thing(s) that annoy _____ :

(1) _____

(2) _____

It is finally declared that any party who goes back on his or her word and does something promised not to do will have to give up the following privilege or favor or payment to the person he or she broke the promise to.

_____

Signed,

_____ and _____

## EXERCISES FOR PARENTS

How to fill out the truce:

1. Have both siblings put their names on the first two lines.
2. Have each sibling state what he or she will do to stop annoying the other; e.g., It is hereby declared that John will cease and desist ("stop doing") the following thing(s) that annoy Susan.
   (1) Stop barging into Susan's room and making noises when she is on the phone with her friends.
3. Have the kids agree on some kind of penalty if they don't stick to their end of the bargain; e.g., John has to do one of Susan's weekly chores, Susan has to give John fifty cents if she breaks her promise, etc.

## BOARD GAME

This game is most appropriate for kids between the ages of five and ten. It is designed to increase cooperation among siblings. On a large piece of oaktag, have the kids draw a board game with about twenty-five squares and start and finish lines. Make sure some of the squares say things like "free turn," "skip two spaces ahead," etc. Do not add penalty squares like "go back to start," "lose a turn," and so on. Make a game spinner out of a piece of cardboard or use a single die from another board game. If you don't have either one of these, you can decide on how many spaces to move by tossing four pennies onto the table and going as many spaces as there are heads. The object of the game is to go from start to finish. Each time a child reaches the finish line, he or she earns 100 points. The kids will not reach the finish line at the same time, so the child who reaches it first must wait for the others to get there before going back to start to earn more points. Decide on a certain number of points (400 at first, then 600). When they reach that number, reward them each with a prize, treat, or privilege. Here's the catch: Children can take a turn only when they do something nice for or cooperative with their sibling(s). The goal is to get them to rely on one another to win the game.

# 13

# SEX, DEATH, AND OTHER
# UNCOMFORTABLE TOPICS ◀

There are few things more perplexing than having to answer a three-year-old child's innocent query, "Mommy, where do babies come from?" It's no wonder that folk wisdom has created the stork, the pumpkin patch, and the many other colorful stories people invent to avoid telling kids where babies really come from. Children will even make up their own stories. Just ask four-year-old Amy where babies come from, and she will tell you with scientific certainty: "Well, the mommy goes to the store and buys a watermelon. She takes it home and cuts out the pits. She finds the best pits and puts them on a dish [she hesitates, then emphasizes], a *clean* dish, and she waits. In the middle of the night God picks up one of the seeds and pushes it into the mommy's belly button, and then in two years a baby comes." And then, as if to demonstrate her total and complete mastery of the subject, she ends with "And that's all there is to it." When I inquire about what, if anything, Daddy has to do with this process, Amy puts her hands on her hips as if to admonish me for my utter foolishness. "Daddy works and gives us the money for the new baby!"

# HOW MUCH TO TELL AND HOW SOON?

The answer to this question depends on how interested your child is in knowing about sex and babies. Some three- and four-year-old kids are very curious, especially if a little brother or sister is on the way. Other children are very interested in kissing and sex. Some children's interest, however, goes way past curiosity and borders on preoccupation. This sometimes but not always indicates a problem. When there *is* a problem, it can mean that a child has been exposed to an incident of molestation or abuse or sensitized to sex by viewing it on television or through other media. If your child seems preoccupied with sex, it is definitely a time to explore where that knowledge came from and why the interest is so strong.

It is always best to give children under five or six years old only as much information as they ask for and will satisfy them. If you launch into a complicated medical explanation, you run the risk of confusing or even frightening them.

In your general explanation about sex, make certain you cover these points:

- Sex is something that Mommy and Daddy decide to do together to make a baby or as a special way of showing that they love each other. If the child asks whether mommies and children or daddies and children have sex (after all, they love one another, too), explain that mommies and daddies have other special ways of showing their children they love them, and sex is not one of them.

- If the child under the age of five or six asks about the mechanics of sex, you can say that to make a baby mommies and daddies have to share a special part of themselves. The daddy has something called *sperm*, which is in his penis, and the mommy has an ovum, which is in a place near her tummy but not her tummy. It's generally not a good idea to tell children that Mommy has eggs, because children can get these eggs confused with the kind we eat for breakfast, which can be unsettling.

    You may continue by saying that the sperm and the ovum are both needed to make a baby, so the man puts his penis into a special opening called a *vagina*, and that's how the sperm and the ovum get together.

By the time you finish telling children these details, their curiosity will usually be satisfied, or they will be bored.

As children get older, you can fill in some of the details around this basic framework. In today's complicated and dangerous world you must convey the importance of monogamy and proper attention to health issues as well as the importance of love and intimacy.

## BRAD'S EARLY EXPOSURE TO SEX THROUGH VIDEOS

Six-year-old Brad had always been more interested in sexuality, kissing, and where babies come from than most kids. It seemed, however, that Brad was passing through a phase of intense interest in sexuality. He was exposing himself to some of the other children on the school bus, using profanity, and telling stories about women sucking on a man's penis. A counselor at school was alerted when Brad approached a girl at school and asked her if she wanted to touch his penis.

After several counseling sessions Brad reported that he had been watching videos that his father had at home, and this is where he was getting much of his information. The counselor alerted his parents, and his father took precautions to stash his videos in a childproof place.

There is nothing inherently unhealthy or perverted in adults owning or watching videos. Many couples watch erotic movies to stimulate their sex lives. Adults can make this choice because presumably they know the tender, intimate aspects of sex as well as the mechanics depicted nonchalantly in these films. Children, of course, do not, and exposure to erotic materials can be confusing and can prematurely sexualize them. The message here is: keep your private things private and reinforce the values of intimacy, love, tenderness, and monogamy when explaining sex to your child.

# PROTECTING CHILDREN FROM SEXUAL ABUSE ◀

Unfortunately, thousands of children every year are sexually abused. You can help protect your children from sexual abuse by teaching them the following important facts, starting at about age three:

1. There are certain places on your body that are private. These places include the genitals and the buttocks. No adult should touch or put anything inside these parts. The only time it's OK for an adult to be near those places is if you are having trouble going to the bathroom and you ask for help. If any adult ever touches these private places, you should tell Mommy or Daddy immediately.

2. Adults should never ask you to touch or kiss these private places on them, because that is wrong. You should tell Mom or Dad right away if an adult ever asks you to do that.

3. You should tell Mommy or Daddy immediately if an adult or an older child ever shows you his or her private places or asks to see yours.

4. If someone is kissing or hugging you in a way that feels uncomfortable, funny, or frightening, get away from that person and tell Mommy or Daddy.

5. If any adult or older person does any of these things and you are in a place where other adults are around, yell for help as loud as possible and run away.

Please take your children's comments about who touches them or makes them "feel funny" very seriously, even if it involves a friend or family member that you would never dream of thinking anything bad about. The sad fact is that a great many cases of child sexual abuse are perpetrated by friends of the family or family members. These are usually people who have a great love for children but express it in a very unhealthy way—a way that can scar or damage a child for life. Please stay on guard and listen carefully to what your children have to say.

## IF YOU SUSPECT YOUR CHILD
## HAS BEEN SEXUALLY ABUSED

If you suspect that your child has been sexually abused, you must safeguard his physical and emotional health. A physician should give your child a physical examination to see if there is damage to the genitals and later to test for the presence of disease. In the case of girls who are past menses, a pregnancy test should be performed. It sounds like a horrible prospect to face, but you must be sure that your child's physical health is protected and preserved. Begin by contacting your pediatrician, who might suggest you come in to the office, or take your child to the local emergency room.

Since these experiences are almost always emotionally devastating, your child should also be seen by a mental health worker who has specific experience and training in detecting the emotional signs of sexual abuse. Many of these professionals use anatomically correct dolls to help children express how and where they were fondled or touched. Children will often reveal experiences and details to a sympathetic professional outside the family faster than they will to a parent or guardian. I can't tell you how many times parents have called me unsure of whether their child had been sexually abused and then the child has reported in detail the story of abuse or assault only fifteen minutes after arriving at my office.

Parents can quickly go numb at the thought of their precious child being sexually abused. This numbness can lead to denial or lack of action, both of which compromise the child's physical and emotional health. The bottom line is: if you have any suspicions, please act on them.

## CHILDREN AND SEXUAL EXPERIMENTATION

Children are naturally curious about sex. It's common for children between the ages of three and seven to remove their clothing in front of one another and play doctor. If children have observed or heard about sexual acts, it is also not uncommon to experiment with sex. Because sexual stimulation at any age produces pleasurable sensations, this kind of experimentation could go on for quite some time until parents discover it. When you do discover it, try to put the behavior in perspective. Young children do not think of sex in terms of morality or right and wrong; they are simply imitating behavior that they have seen elsewhere or exploring a natural curiosity.

Becoming excited or punishing children for sex play can have a negative impact on their sexual development. A very effective way of approaching children who are experimenting with sex is to talk to them in terms of etiquette, not sexuality. In other words, you don't want to say, "Bobby, you are a bad boy for taking your clothes off in front of Peggy," especially if Bobby is only three or four years old. Instead, present it in these terms: "Bobby, taking off your clothes is a private thing. We don't do that in front of friends because it is bad manners." Then leave it at that.

When children past the age of eight experiment with sex, it is a more serious issue and should not be taken lightly. In some cases sexual experimentation is the result of sexual abuse. Professional counseling is necessary to sort out the reasons for and the history behind this behavior.

## TALKING TO CHILDREN ABOUT AIDS

By the time our children reach sexual maturity AIDS will kill millions, perhaps tens of millions of people every year, given the current rate of the epidemic. AIDS is a deadly disease spread through sexual contact, specifically through the exchange of body fluids, and as I write this book there is little hope for a cure in the near future. As much as the general population would like to believe the AIDS virus is confined to specific subgroups like intravenous drug users or homosexuals, AIDS is epidemic in the heterosexual population and will continue to claim the lives of people from all walks of life. Talking frankly with your children about AIDS can literally save their lives, but how do you do that without communicating the message that sex is simply something that can kill you? This is truly a new parenting problem and concern. It has never been easy to teach children to grow up to be sexually healthy creatures; in today's society the job is especially challenging.

Although there is tremendous controversy surrounding the best way to educate your child about AIDS, I advocate the following:

1. Begin teaching your children about AIDS as soon as they are capable of understanding what it is. For most children this is as early as six or seven years old.

2. Communicate that AIDS is a virus transmitted when people have sex.

3. Explain that AIDS can make people very sick and many people die from it.

4. Explain that not all people who have sex get AIDS, but people do need to be careful. People can avoid getting AIDS by not having sex, and they can prevent AIDS by learning about safe sex from a doctor.

5. Reinforce the values of love, intimacy, and monogamy—that sex is a very special grown-up thing that people do when they love each other very much, but only after they make sure they are healthy and don't have AIDS.

Awareness from a very early age is most definitely a key to prevention.

## CHILDREN AND HOMOSEXUALITY ◀

Homosexuality was once considered a perversion and a disease. Since the American Psychiatric Association revised the standards and criteria for diagnosing mental illness in the 1970s, homosexuality has been reclassified not as a disease but as a type of sexuality. Twenty years later, most estimates place homosexuals between two and three percent of the general population, yet our culture still opposes homosexuality. In fact most parents are frightened and upset by the prospect that their children might "grow up" to be homosexuals.

Is homosexuality determined by genes or environment? As I write this, no one knows for sure. There is some scientific evidence to support the theory that homosexuality is a genetically determined trait, but members within the scientific community are at war over the validity of these findings. We do know that many homosexuals report that they became aware of their sexual orientation at a very early age.

Parents first begin to worry about their children's sexuality when they find their three-year-old male children expressing a preference for girl's clothing or girl's toys. Before the age of five children's gender identity, their sense of being a boy or a girl, is not firmly established, so it is very common to see this behavior in little boys. We rarely worry about girls' tomboy behavior because, quite frankly, women of all ages are likely to be perceived positively when they show male traits at least some of the time. Boys, on the other hand, are considered "wimps" and "sissies" when they exhibit feminine traits. We live in a society that values male characteristics and devalues and demeans feminine characteristics, so we tend to worry if our boys act too much like girls. Playing with dolls or even wanting to wear a dress is not a sign of homosexuality. The majority of adult homosexuals are not cross-dressers and did not cross-dress as children.

> *When discussing sex with your child, emphasize the importance of love, monogamy, and responsibility.*

As children approach adolescence, thoughts about homosexuality are normal. For children who are confused about their sexuality and believe they might be gay, preadolescence and adolescence can be an extremely painful phase of life. That is why it is critical to establish an open line of communication with children that gives the message "You can talk to us about anything; we will always love you."

## FIFTH GRADE AND ALREADY DATING!

Talking to hundreds of kids every year tells me that dating begins at around fifth grade. A typical fifth-grade date involves going to the movies or for pizza with a group of other kids with a rough one-to-one ratio of boys to girls. A boyfriend or girlfriend is someone you write notes to in school or give a present or token of affection to. Yes, there is some kissing, especially at parties, where kids play the same kissing games, such as post office and spin the bottle, that have been around for about a hundred years. This rite of passage is occurring about two to three years earlier than twenty years ago, and some consider it a sign that kids are growing up too fast. If this is the case, it is time for children to learn about what it takes to be a good partner in a relationship—kindness ("I'll help you with your books") empathy ("I know you must be feeling terrible that you didn't make the soccer team"), support ("I can lend you a really good book for your next book report"), and loyalty ("I won't talk about you behind your back").

These very adult concepts can be taught only when parents model them to their spouses and children. There is no way to reverse social trends. If kids are going to date at eleven and twelve, then that is what they will do. Sure, you can keep your children locked up in their rooms until they are thirteen or fourteen, but wouldn't it be better to teach them how to be not just a "good date," but a good friend?

## DEATH AND DYING: ANOTHER UNCOMFORTABLE TOPIC

Parents hate to see their children in pain. When a grandparent, a parent, another relative, or a friend passes away, parents want to know how to explain death to the children who were emotionally attached to the person. When I am confronted by this, I wish that my training in psychology had come with "the magic book" of all the right things to say to people when they feel sad. The truth is that most people never really adjust to the thought of someone close to them dying. It *always* hurts. It makes us cry and grieve. People never have to be taught the "proper" way to grieve. The difficulty usually comes when they are prevented from grieving as others admonish them to "be strong," "be a fighter," or "get over it." Most fifty- and sixty-year-olds can't make sense out of the world when the people they love dearly get sick and die. How can we expect a six-year-old to handle it?

The best we can hope for is to teach children about the natural process of grieving while giving them the emotional room to experience and express it. Some of the best guidelines I can give parents involve what *not* to do with children:

- Don't force children to attend funerals or wakes. Do not criticize them for being afraid or upset. Unfortunately, they will have an entire lifetime to get used to the idea of paying their respects, because the older they get, the more they will experience death.

- Do not equate death with "sleeping for a long time." This can be very confusing to young children, who might become frightened about going to sleep.

- Even if you are very religious, and perhaps especially if you are very religious, be very careful about how you explain God's role in someone's death. Children do not possess the cognitive skills to understand the abstract nature of religious concepts. You run the risk of turning children away from religion if you make them angry at God for "calling upon" someone they love.

- Do not criticize a child for expressing negative emotions, anger, or sadness after someone dies. Do not encourage children who are crying to "be brave" or "be grown up." At the same time, do not be surprised to see children letting out anxious laughter or playing at a wake or funeral. Everyone else around them is probably denying the death or loss, but because they are adults, they are simply doing a better job of hiding it.

Instead of falling into these common traps, encourage your children to grieve appropriately and allow them to see you grieve appropriately as well. Encourage them to talk about their feelings, draw pictures, write letters, or otherwise express themselves.

Remember that children under five years old do not possess a sense of the finality of death. It is sometimes hard for them to grasp the fact that the person will never come back. When they finally comprehend this, you may see a strong grief reaction well after the fact.

While it will never spare a child from the strong emotions associated with the loss of a loved one, I always encourage parents to keep pets like fish, newts, hermit crabs, and small lizards. When these pets die, children experience on some small scale the irreversibility of death and some of the sadness and loss associated with it.

## PREPARING CHILDREN WHEN RELATIVES ARE VERY SICK

You can and should help children prepare for the possibility of death if a loved one is terminally or critically ill. You can say to your child,

"I think you know that Grandpa has been very sick lately, and that we are all worried about him. It's sad to talk about this, but we think he might die." This will lessen but not eliminate some of the painful feelings associated with death.

I do not think it is a good idea to tell children that the deceased person is simply away or has moved. Children will feel upset if the person who has supposedly moved doesn't try to contact or visit them. One family I know told a five-year-old child that his favorite person in the world, his great-grandfather, "was out at the store," when in reality he had died. Every time the child visited his great-grand-father's home, he was told the same thing. After a few visits the child began to believe that the great-grandfather simply did not

> *The best way to help your child cope with the loss of a loved one is to share your own feelings of grief.*

want to see him anymore and was very hurt. When the child finally found out what happened, he felt guilty about being angry at his great-grandfather, sad about the loss, and furious at his parents and other family members for lying.

This anecdote should emphasize the importance of preparing children for the death of someone close and respecting their right to know and grieve over the loss.

1. A good rule of thumb for children under six years old is: always give children the answers to the questions they have about sex and nothing extra. Young children are often curious about sex but disinterested in the biology or mechanics of sexual activity. Giving them too much detail at a young age can be confusing.

2. When explaining sex to your child, always communicate the importance of love, intimacy, and being with just one special person, as well as the responsibility that comes along with deciding to have a baby.

3. Children's early exposure to erotic materials can prematurely sexualize them and cause them to act out in inappropriate ways. These materials tend to depict sex as mechanical and superficial. Keep your erotic videos and other materials in a private place.

4. Protect your children from sexual abuse by talking to them early (by three years of age) and often about "private" body areas, about "good touch" and "bad touch," and about the importance of telling Mommy or Daddy if an adult or older child touches them or tells them to do something that they shouldn't.

5. If you suspect that your child has been sexually abused, act on it immediately. It is natural for parents to want to deny that something terrible has happened to their child, but please do get help from qualified medical and mental health professionals.

6. Children are naturally curious about sex and will tend to explore their sexuality with other children. Refrain from presenting this behavior to them as an issue of right or wrong. Instead, present it as a matter of etiquette and good manners to keep your clothes on when with friends.

7. Begin teaching your children about AIDS and other sexually transmitted diseases as soon as they are old enough

## QUICK REVIEW

(between five and seven years of age) to comprehend what sex is and that people can get sick from having sex if they are not careful.

8.  Homosexuality is not a disease; it is a genetically influenced trait. Children who feel they might be homosexual must have an open line of communication to parents, as well as their love, support, and understanding.

9.  Accepting death at any age is difficult from an emotional point of view. Allow children to experience the normal process of grieving without suggesting that they be "strong" or "grown-up."

10.  Allow your children to see you grieve. The death of a loved one will not make sense to them if they perceive it as something tragic and upsetting but see you behaving as if unaffected.

## EXERCISES FOR PARENTS

### DISCUSSION

Have a discussion with your spouse or a few good friends about how sex was explained to you as a child. Listen carefully for how the stories you tell and your friends tell correspond or conflict with what you are telling your child.

### "GUESS WHY" GAME FOR INCREASING AWARENESS OF GOOD TOUCH AND BAD TOUCH IN CHILDREN UNDER AGE FIVE

Use these vignettes to help children verbalize the difference between appropriate and inappropriate sexual behavior from adults.

*A man came over to a little boy and tried to show the little boy his penis. This was not good. Can you guess why?*

(Because adults are not supposed to show their private places to children.)

*A teenager asked a little girl if she would lift up her dress and show him her vagina. Guess why this was not a good thing to do.*

(Because older kids are not supposed to ask to see little boys' or girls' private places.)

*A man once asked a little girl to touch his penis, and the little girl said, "No!" in a very loud voice and ran away. Can you guess why?*

(Because adults are not supposed to ask children to touch their private places, and when they do children should run away.)

*A man once touched a little boy in one of his private places, and the little boy became very upset. He went right home and told his mommy and daddy what happened. Can you guess why he told his mommy and daddy what happened?*

(Because whenever an older kid or an adult does something like this, the little boy or girl should go home right away and tell Mommy or Daddy.)

# 14

# ALCOHOL AND OTHER DRUGS ◀

There are plenty of statistics that report on children and alcohol and drug abuse. The real problems, however, are never tallied. Statistics don't tell us how many kids in grade school and high school burn out or fall short of their potential because of drug-related problems. These are kids from every ethnic and socioeconomic background.

Alcohol is considered a drug, just like cocaine, heroin, and prescription pills. This chapter focuses mainly on alcohol because that is the drug that children usually come into contact with first.

## WARNING SIGNS ARE CLEAR, BUT PARENTS TEND TO IGNORE THEM ◀

The best advice I can give to parents about preventing drug and alcohol abuse in their children is: don't ignore the warning signs. There isn't one type of kid who gets wrapped up in drugs or alcohol. Some kids from some backgrounds are more likely to, but the captain of the football team and the scholarship winner, the straight-A student and the quiet little girl who sits in the corner are all candidates as well.

Most parents have some idea that their children are drinking, and their first clues are usually pretty strong ones—the smell of alcohol on a child's breath, empty liquor bottles in the house, an overheard telephone conversation. Yet most parents decide to do little or nothing about it. It is an uncomfortable subject to bring up with a child. What do you say? Do you come right out and say, "I know you are drinking?" Do you say, "I smell alcohol on your breath?"

You're certainly not stupid; you were a kid once yourself. You know what you did, and you know how strongly you denied what you did when your parents accused you of it. That's the incredible thing about being a teenager. I'll bet you remember doing something wrong, then getting caught, denying it, and sticking to your story so closely that in your own mind it became the truth. So you started getting annoyed at your parents for accusing you of something you actually did but convinced yourself you didn't do. You started accusing your parents of not trusting you, of treating you like an infant, of being unreasonably worried all the time.

The whole process can become quite intimidating to you as a parent. It causes you to doubt your own original observation. Your motivation to believe your child is increased because you don't want to have to deal with the reality of being right. You would rather be *wrong*. In this chapter I'm going to present two stories, both true. They are two simple illustrations of what can happen when you don't act on what you see.

## JENNY: TOUGH, OUTGOING, AND FREE-SPIRITED

Jenny had always been a rebellious kid. She didn't like being directed, taught, asked to do anything. "Not a bad kid," her mom would say, "just a tough kid to raise." Her independence and outspokenness made Jenny a popular kid in school. Other kids were attracted to her free spirit. She won class elections, always had other kids fighting over being her friend and jockeying for her attention. She was a leader. She had mixed success with teachers. Some teachers hated her for her energy and saw it as a challenge to their authority. They would go head to head with Jenny and invariably lose. Jenny would always do well enough academically to steer clear of any real trouble, but she was known as being somewhat of a behavior problem (bratty and a little disrespectful but never bad enough to be suspended or thrown out of school). Her report cards typically contained the awful phrase "not working up to her potential." (I say the phrase is awful because so many times it should actually read, "Teacher not teaching to his or her potential.") Every once in a while Jenny would be lucky enough to get a special teacher, the kind that wasn't intimidated by Jenny's strong style and actually enjoyed her energy and assertiveness and realized that there is often a very fragile kid under the strong, street-fighting exterior, the kind that Jenny presented.

Another group of kids attracted to Jenny were older kids—boys, girls, it didn't matter. Jenny was favored by everyone. Since older kids were considered cooler to hang out with, Jenny loved being "adopted" by big brothers and sisters in the higher grades. In eighth grade she began to get invited to high school parties. Naturally, she thought her parents were ridiculous when they questioned the wisdom of going to parties with older kids. Jenny was quick to point out that most of the people were only a year or two older than she was. She was also quick to point out, using her impeccable teenage logic, that her parents had friends who were five or even ten years older than they were. As usual, her parents were being hypocrites. A solid week of whining, arguing, and ornery, nasty behavior finally wore down Jenny's mom, who gave her permission to go to such a party, with an early curfew of eleven-thirty.

Jenny left the house looking much too old for thirteen. She would get a lift home from Joshua's mom. There was absolutely no possibility that Jenny would allow her mom to pick her up. Jenny's mom knew Joshua's mom and agreed because she seemed like a concerned mother.

At eleven forty-five the phone rang, and Jenny's mother, already on pins and needles, listened to Jenny tell her that Josh's mom was running late. Could she stay at the party another hour? "I would rather pick you up, Jenny," her mother said. "Don't do this to me, Mom. Just don't do this to me. She'll be here soon. Everything is all right. Don't blow a hissy on me. If you pick me up, it will create a scene." Jenny's mom clenched her teeth and muttered, "Be in this house one minute after twelve-thirty and you are grounded for a month." Jenny's anger withdrew; she had gotten what she wanted. "Thanks, Mom. I'll see you in a bit. I love you." Click.

Jenny arrived home at twelve-forty. Two other kids had to be dropped off first. The fact that she was ten minutes late was not her fault. As Jenny walked by, her mom smelled cigarette smoke on her clothes. A tense dialogue began.

"Were kids smoking at the party?"

"Smoking what?"

"Smoking *anything*."

"I guess some kids were smoking cigarettes."

"Were they smoking anything else?"

"Not that I know of, Mother. Are there any more questions, or is the interrogation over?"

"No, as a matter of fact I'm *not* finished asking questions. Was anyone there drinking?"

"Drinking what?"

"Alcohol?"

"Yes, some of the older kids were drinking a few beers."

"And Joe's parents didn't care that there were kids drinking in their house?"

"Yeah, they cared. They had a rule. Anyone who smelled like beer had to have a ride home."

"Yeah, but they *let* underage kids drink in their house."

"You see, Mom, this is why I think you are totally out of it, and this is why we fight. You asked me a question. I told you the truth. I am not Joe's parents. Don't get pissed at me over their house rules. Besides, do you think it would be better if Joe's parents said 'no drinking' at the party and had kids drinking their beers out in the car unsupervised?"

"Did you drink?"

"No."

At this point Jenny's mom felt old, and she was tired from worrying and arguing. In a way Jenny was right. Joe's parents made the house rules. Was it actually possible to stop kids from drinking? Wasn't it better, after all, to supervise? As she was trying to fall asleep, she tried to imagine Jenny being around kids who were drinking and tried to imagine her not joining in. Jenny was tough and stubborn. She could say no if she wanted to, but did she want to?

The fact is that Jenny had lied. She had drunk a beer. It was a single beer; she hadn't even finished it. She just kind of held it, blended in. It made her feel cool. It was kind of like an accessory, she thought.

When her mom asked her if she had had anything to drink, she didn't feel as though she were lying. She didn't drink to get drunk. She held a beer to keep from calling attention to herself. She didn't want anyone pressuring her. With a beer in her hand she was in control. These were things her mother would never understand.

The next time Jenny drank was two months later. The weather had turned warm. School let out early. She was hanging out with some of her older friends in a car. Her mother would have killed her if she had known that Jenny was riding around in a car with seventeen-year-old boys. They bought a case of beer. The afternoon went by so fast. Just hanging out, swigging the beer. She got tipsy, and at first it scared her, but it also made her curious. She kept drinking and got drunk, really drunk; and she liked it. She stayed out late, made an excuse that she was over at a girlfriend's house doing research for a paper. When she walked into the house, she walked quickly past her parents, went straight to her room, and closed the door. It seemed odd to Jenny's mom, who figured she must have been tired from doing all that work. For a brief second Jenny's mom considered the other meaning of a kid's rushing by her parents to get to her room. She flashed back to when she was a teenager, coming home drunk on a Friday night and blowing past her parents to get to her room. Jenny couldn't be doing that, she thought. You're just being paranoid, she told herself.

*Children have opportunities to drink and experiment with drugs every day and almost everywhere.*

Jenny soon became a regular with the older crowd. She drank a little every weekend, mostly beer. She didn't really enjoy the taste, but she liked the buzz. What she did enjoy was Jell-O shots—Jell-O made with vodka and poured into cute little cups. It made a shape in the cup so that you could peel back the cup and suck down the Jell-O in one gulp. It didn't even taste like alcohol, but after four or five you were totally gone. Cherry was her favorite.

The end of the school year was bad news. Jenny had her worst report card since she began school. Jenny's dad lectured her about not letting her social life get in the way of her schoolwork. Jenny admitted she had screwed up, but she had gotten really terrible grades only in her last quarter. In September she would buckle down and start high school off right.

High school was great. The other kids in her grade felt uncomfortable and out of place, but Jenny had her older friends. She sneaked out for lunch with the seniors, drank beer at the football games, and continued to get drunk on weekends. One night she came home and threw up in the bathroom. Her mom heard her, but the door was locked behind Jenny, so she could not really tell what was happening. When Jenny came out, she was pale and said she had the flu. Jenny's mom tried to remember if Jenny had looked like she was coming down with something. She quickly convinced herself that she did think that Jenny had looked pale for a couple of days.

> **Today, every child in the country is at risk of developing drug and alcohol problems.**

The next night Jenny went out, over her mother's objections that just yesterday she had been complaining about having the flu. Her curfew was twelve-thirty. She had been drinking beer all night and looked at her watch. She was within walking distance from home, but it was a long walk, and if she walked she would be late. A guy she hung out with but didn't know that well offered her a ride with a friend of his, whom she didn't know at all. She took the offer because she didn't want to be late. The guy she knew decided to hang out a while longer. His friend still offered to drive her home. It was less than a ten-minute drive. She never made it home. He was drunk. She nodded out in the car. He swerved, hit the divider, and flipped the car into oncoming traffic. She was killed in her sleep.

Unfortunately, stories like these are quite common and often have the same catastrophic ending.

# BRIAN: THE YOUNGEST OF THREE COOL BROTHERS

Brian was the youngest of three brothers, growing up in a family that did everything "right." Dad had a great job as an investment analyst but spent plenty of time with the boys. Mom was a dedicated homemaker who made sure everything always got done—the house was spotless, and everyone got to where he or she needed to be on time, all the time, whether it was soccer, baseball, choir practice, or the movies. People envied the way the three boys cooperated and the "team spirit" everyone showed. Brian's house was always populated by friends of the boys, who were always welcome to hang out. After all, with the boys in plain sight they couldn't possibly get into trouble.

Brian knew that his two older brothers, now sixteen and eighteen, drank beer. He heard them talking about going to "keg parties." Brian's dad had even given permission to his eldest son to drink a beer or two at a party but to make sure he used "good judgment" about drinking. Dad's philosophy was that if you made alcohol a "forbidden fruit" kids would be more attracted to it and therefore sneakier about how they used it. In the summer, from time to time, Dad even let Brian's oldest brother have a beer with him if it was a really hot day.

Then, one day when Brian was fourteen, his oldest brother asked him if he wanted a beer. Brian was scared to try it, but he looked up to his older brother and desperately wanted to be cool. At first he didn't like the taste, but he did like the way it made him feel. Brian was a very shy kid, but drinking a beer with his brother made him feel tough and powerful, something he had rarely felt in his life.

Brian joined the basketball team in ninth grade. He was tall, like his brothers, and athletically superior to most kids his age. Brian had always belonged to a family of "jocks." Excelling at sports was something the family was known for. Brian wasn't crazy about sports, but he played them because he figured that's what he was supposed to do. He was good, but he didn't like being watched, and he felt uncomfortable at being envied by some of the players who weren't as good. He knew that there were some kids who wanted to get more play time because they loved playing and really wanted to be there. He felt guilty about playing more than they did. In his mind Brian often considered quitting basketball, but he knew his father would be disappointed. It was a funny thing about Brian's dad. He never yelled or reprimanded the children, but if he was upset or disappointed about something it was so much worse. Brian used to wish his father would lose his temper instead of sitting him down for one of those talks where he would tell Brian that he was "hurt" about this or "disappointed" about that. That was awful.

In December of his freshman year in high school, Brian went on a school ski trip with some of his friends from school and roomed with a few kids from his basketball team. Late at night, after lights out, one of the kids took out a bottle of Jack Daniel's whiskey and started passing it around. Brian remembers that he felt as if he shouldn't do it, not even take a sip. The first few times the bottle came around, he just put his lips on it and made believe he was drinking. Then, on one pass, he took a hard swig from the bottle and felt the effects almost immediately. He became silly, started telling jokes. The kids in the room laughed and joked back. For the first time in his life Brian felt comfortable in a social situation.  He was always so worried about what people thought, so self-conscious about his behavior. Later that night one of the other kids threw up. Brian and another kid helped him get cleaned up and into bed. The next morning the kid was embarrassed but thanked Brian and the other boy, and they all laughed about it.

> *Children of alcoholics are seven to ten times more at risk for alcoholism than kids of nonalcoholics.*

Brian became closer with these two kids, and they made it a point to sneak a drink whenever they could. By the end of his ninth year in school Brian was drinking one or two times a week. Around this time Brian also discovered wine coolers. Two wine coolers made him just buzzed enough to be the funny, wisecracking, relaxed person he began to like more and more. It was his "drinking personality." Brian found that he could get wine coolers really easily. The guy in the deli near school would sell a six-pack of wine coolers to almost anyone.

That summer Brian met Jill, his first real girlfriend. Jill was the friend of one of his basketball buddies. She was free-spirited and French-kissed him on their first date. She made Brian feel cool, and she liked to drink with him and his friends. Unfortunately, the relationship never made it beyond six weeks. Jill explained that she needed to be free, and she was beginning to get tied down. Brian was crushed. He didn't even feel he could face his friends. The wine coolers that he drank every day made him feel better, though, at least for a little while.

All the time that Brian was drinking, his parents remained completely unaware of what was going on. They knew that he was upset over losing his girlfriend and gave him tons of sympathy. They saw Brian as going through the normal storm and strife of adolescence and believed he would get over it. They made sure they told Brian that they loved him and that before he knew it another girl would come along.

His brothers teased him about it at first, but even they were supportive. That's the way Brian's family was.

Brian was a sneaky drinker. He was careful about where and how he drank. He kept his wine coolers hidden very well and could control himself when he had to. He was using the money from his paper route to buy his wine coolers, almost all of it, but it was worth it. Drinking those wine coolers was his only ticket to being the cool and relaxed version of Brian that he wanted to be.

The rest of the summer Brian kept mostly to himself and didn't bother much with girls. He was very interested in them but didn't want to get hurt again. Sophomore year was coming up. He wasn't a lowly freshman anymore. Things would be looking up.

Things did look up. Sophomore year wasn't the adjustment that freshman year was. Brian had grown another three inches over the summer, so he was now about six feet, two inches tall. He was asked to play on both the junior varsity and varsity teams, something that allowed him to gain a lot of prestige in school. The varsity team was a traveling team, and the players loved to get together after the games and drink. The coach was known to hit the bottle quite hard from time to time and always warned the players that they would be suspended if they were caught drinking, but he knew the team drank beer, and even though the warnings were stern he never did anything.

> *By the time your child reaches adolescence, his friends will have more influence over his behavior with drugs than you will.*

The first time Brian actually got caught drinking was after the varsity play-offs. The team won, and there was tequila. Everyone was drinking shots. Another kid mixed up some kamikazes—vodka, triple sec, and lime juice—and he had a few of those too. Brian came home "wasted" that night and couldn't hide it from his parents. He threw up in the bathroom, and the next morning he found his dad sitting at the foot of the bed and giving him a lecture about not disappointing him or Mom. Brian was amazed at how calmly his dad was taking it and how he said he had done the exact same thing at Brian's age. Aside from hating to hear his father say how disappointed he was, everything was OK. His mom asked if he was feeling all right but said nothing more and was her usual sweet self, acting as if nothing had happened. Everything was OK—except, of course, for his head. He had a pounding headache. That night Brian drank two wine coolers just because the day had stressed him out.

The middle of sophomore year was the roughest time of his life. Now, more than ever, he wanted to be accepted by a certain group of kids at school. There was a girl he was madly in love with in this group who wouldn't give him the time of day. Then, one day, she started paying attention to him. She went out with him a couple of times, then promptly attached herself to a college guy, and that was the last she ever wanted to hear from him. Brian's drinking got worse. He drank whenever he could, with whoever was around. His brothers heard about his reputation and went to their parents. The family went for counseling. The counselor was totally taken with the love and concern of Brian's parents and implied that Brian was just going through a tough phase and that a lot of kids drank, almost all of the high school kids. The counselor recommended that they set up a contract about drinking with Brian and watch him very closely.

> *Begin talking to your child about drug and alcohol issues when she is about three years old.*

Brian's parents discussed the issue between themselves. They asked for their other two sons' input. Based on the counselor's conclusion and what they all wanted to believe, Brian would be OK.

Brian quit drinking hard liquor for the rest of the year and cut his wine cooler drinking down to weekend nights when he was going to hang out with his friends. Brian's mother even found a wine cooler bottle while she was cleaning under the bed and confronted Brian about it. Brian said it must have been there from when he was having "his trouble."

The summer before Brian's junior year in high school was a good one. Some of his friends had cars. Everyone around him drank, and he started drinking heavily again. One night things got so bad that he came home, began throwing up, and got so dehydrated he had to be taken to the hospital. A social worker at the hospital suggested that Brian go into an inpatient detoxification program. "You want my son to be put in an alcoholism program?" his father asked. For the first time in his life Brian heard anger in his father's voice. "Not even a remote possibility." Brian's father was adamant. Instead his father found a psychiatrist who agreed to treat Brian four times a week on an outpatient basis.

Brian couldn't keep a four-times-a-week therapy program because of school and sports. His parents always called the doctor to cancel and always made sure he went at least once a week. Brian liked the psychiatrist but never really told him the truth. He was afraid that his parents would find out how long, how often, and how badly he had been drinking for what was now three years.

The psychiatrist had family meetings every month for the first six months, then every other month. After a year the psychiatrist said there was nothing further that could be done. Privately the psychiatrist took Brian's father aside and said, "Look, I have to be straight up with you. Although Brian participated in the therapy, I don't really feel I ever got a good grasp on him. A lot of kids can sit here week after week and pass the time because that is what their parents are making them do. If you ever find out that Brian is drinking again, even if it's just casual or mild drinking, take him to a detox program. That's where he should have been this time around."

*Don't ignore warning signs that your child is using drugs or alcohol. Take action immediately.*

Brian's dad thanked the psychiatrist and agreed with him, but in his head he kept repeating, "There isn't going to be a next time." Brian's dad made sure to spend more time with him and suggested he do less sports and maybe look for an after-school job. He figured that having some job responsibilities might keep him away from the element that caused him to drink. Brian got a job at a gas station, pumping gas and running their convenience store. He was a good worker, but he continued to drink.

In the early summer before his senior year, the police caught Brian drinking in a park with some of his friends. They took Brian home and didn't arrest him. Brian's mom and dad finally took him to a detox program. They took him out of state and made it look as if he was going away for the summer. It was a place in Colorado where there were a lot of people with serious drinking problems. The doctors were all very helpful and concerned. Brian's mom and dad were finally beginning to see that there were serious problems, although Brian's dad kept calling Brian's problems "potentially" serious.

Senior year was uneventful. Brian got into a decent college, considering all of his difficulties. His other two brothers were already out of the house. Brian's mom pleaded with Brian to stay close to home, but Brian wanted to go to an out-of-state college that a few of his friends liked.

Brian's roommate at college was a big partier. Brian wisely told his roommate about the problems he had, but one night, out of sheer boredom, Brian smoked some pot with his roommate and then drank some vodka.

Brian dropped out of school in his third semester. He went to detox again, but his future doesn't really look too good. Just shy of his twentieth birthday Brian is a chronic alcoholic. He misses alcohol when he is sober, and is easily pulled back to an alcoholic lifestyle. Every time he comes out of detox he says he's quit for good. Soon after that he convinces himself that he can drink a beer or two just to hang around with his friends. From there he drinks every day. Brian's mom and dad refuse to discuss the issue, even between themselves. They blame Brian's problems on poor supervision at school. How could they allow children to drink alcohol at school functions? Why aren't there programs to stop this before it becomes a big problem? They can't see where they went wrong. They gave Brian all the love and support any child could ever wish for; they still do. But Brian still drinks.

It is never a good idea to condone a child's drinking, as Brian's parents initially did with his oldest brother. Regardless of how mature your child may seem, youth and peer pressure make it virtually impossible for him to know how to "use good judgment" when it comes to drugs. And although it may seem drastic, alcohol and drug problems need to be treated *immediately* by people who are trained to deal with such problems. If a relapse occurs after treatment, professional help must again be obtained immediately. Waiting for the problem to go away on its own is never a wise strategy.

If you've read the stories about Jenny and Brian, you might be tempted to say, "How could these parents let so much slide by?" But when it is happening with *your* child, in *your* house, it is so much more difficult to see. You can tell from these two stories that kids from "normal" homes can develop serious problems. You can probably also ell that peers seem to have a lot more influence over kids' drinking and drug taking than parents do. Unfortunately, the research seems to suggest that's true.

## DEVELOPING STRATEGIES TO PREVENT ABUSE: FIRST REALIZE THAT THERE ARE LOTS OF OPPORTUNITIES TO DRINK ◄

By the time kids finish eighth grade, over half of them have had drinks with their friends. It happens at parties, where, believe it or not, parents allow the kids to have the run of the house with little or no supervision. There are parties that are supervised where parents of fourteen- and fifteen-year-olds will actually allow beer. It also happens on the school bus, in the school yard, before school, after school, and at sports functions. Kids drink in their friends' cars, parked or on the road. Kids drink on school trips. Kids drink in the basement of your house when you are not around. They also drink in their rooms. Considering the fact that there are lots of two-career families and many single-parent households, the opportunities for your preteen or teen to drink with friends are tremendous.

So, we have established that there is opportunity. There is also motivation—even more motivation than opportunity. Let's look at some of the factors that encourage your child to use alcohol from a very young age.

### We live in a culture that heavily endorses alcohol use and abuse. Alcoholism in adults is one of the nation's most severe health problems. As a culture we rely on alcohol for a number of reasons: to enjoy watching sports, to celebrate, to make us feel better when we are depressed, to entertain our friends, to stimulate our appetite or enjoy a meal, to unwind after work, to name a few. Our children are very careful observers of adult behavior. Much of what they do is modeled on what we do. Although it sometimes happens for the right reasons, children really do want to grow up to be just like us.

Obviously if you drink alcohol frequently, or if you are a heavy consumer of alcoholic beverages, your children will be influenced by your behavior. If you have a serious drinking problem, your child is seven to ten times more likely to abuse alcohol too. Boys are at somewhat greater risk than girls, but both cases represent serious risks.

Even when you put your liquor under lock and key, if it's there regularly and kids want to get at your booze, they will.

## Getting drunk is a childhood rite of passage. Most fifth-, sixth-, and seventh-graders (kids ages ten through twelve) look forward to becoming teenagers, because it is synonymous with being cool and having freedom. There's dating, driving, and hanging out to look forward to. There's also drinking with your friends. By the time children reach age thirteen most are intimately familiar with the names of different alcoholic beverages and mixed drinks. Ask your kid what a kamikaze, a Jell-O shot, or an Alabama slammer is, and you will probably be quite surprised by his response.

Getting drunk on beer is a typical introduction. Beer is usually around the house and easy to get hold of. A missing beer or two usually won't catch the attention of parents, especially if beer is always in the refrigerator. Also, most kids don't perceive beer as a "bad" type of alcoholic beverage because it is so popular and because most parents will let their kids have a sip of beer from time to time.

The picture of two best buddies in their preteen years sipping a can of beer, giggling, may at first glance seem almost charming. The truth is that it is usually the start of drinking rituals that will lead to the consumption of more and more alcohol so that by the time these best buddies reach college that one can of beer can be a case or a keg or more, and the beer drinking might not stop until both are passed out and dangerously close to death.

By the end of high school kids who are into drinking will have parties that are completely focused around drinks, drinking games, "doing shots," and whatever it takes to get totally and completely drunk. All of this is woven into the day-to-day fabric of their lives, because for days after a party or after a weekend of drinking there are stories that bring the group together—stories about who got the sickest, stories about who wound up drunk and in bed with someone, stories about parents almost finding out, or finding out. The stories help solidify the group and sometimes give great social power to the kids who can drink the most (especially in the case of girls who can drink as much as boys).

> **Advertisements and other forms of media have a definite influence on children's attitudes about alcohol.**

A particularly scary aspect of what motivates children to drink is the fact that peer groups seem to have much more influence over drinking and drug taking than the values or behavior of parents. As we will see, becoming involved with your children's friends and allowing your home to be a place where your kids' friends can feel comfortable lets you observe important aspects of their behavior and demeanor that can tell you a lot about the likelihood that they are drinking.

**The manufacturers of alcoholic beverages create advertisements that appeal to kids.** I don't believe that it is important to determine whether beer and liquor companies are purposely trying to influence children to drink. What's more important is that their advertisements *do* have an impact on children. The Anheuser-Busch company recently began a campaign that delivers the message that parents should teach children not to drink and that alcohol is dangerous to them. To my knowledge this is the only company that dedicates full-page ads to communicating this message. This is in stark contrast to other ads printed by the same company and the rest of the industry that show drinking beer coupled with beautifully choreographed slow-motion shots of windsurfing, volleyball, and other exciting activities, all featuring perfectly tanned and physically perfect young adults enjoying themselves tremendously.

One of the most seductive advertising campaigns to children today is that of a certain vodka manufacturer. It has now become fashionable for high school students to collect the company's ads, hang them as posters, and wear T-shirts sporting the company's logo and sayings.

Is implying that this kind of advertising influences children fanatical or unfair? I must admit to feeling a little guilty about casting aspersions on an entire industry. After all, everyone has the right to earn a living, and I also believe that adults have the right to consume alcohol in responsible ways. Advertising is a competitive industry and therefore relies on pairing positive, pleasant, and exciting images with products to create positive perceptions. But the fact is that any casual review of print and television ads for beer, vodka, wine coolers, and many liquors will suggest that there is a heavy emphasis on "youthfulness" in the models used, the language of the ads and voice-overs, and the activities shown.

Culture, parents' attitudes and behavior, the media, and peers—all highly powerful influences on their own—work simultaneously to influence children's perceptions about drinking. Taking these factors into consideration, do you as a parent have reason to worry that your child will become one of the many statistics that are related to drinking? Worse, regardless of all the millions of recorded statistics, how about the hundreds of millions of people who are touched negatively by drinking who never become statistics, like all the high school children who never realized their academic potential because they drank too much in high school or the kids who wasted their parents' money in college because they drank their way through every semester?

Parents can do a lot to prevent alcohol abuse, but they have to start very young, when children's ideas are more influenced by their parents than their peers.

# EIGHT IMPORTANT STRATEGIES FOR PARENTS

The following strategies will help you deal with the problem of drinking as your kids grow up.

**1. Check the role models that influence your children.** Do you come from a drinking family? Children do not have to grow up in an alcohol-free environment to avoid problems with drinking. Besides, even raising them in an alcohol-free environment wouldn't guarantee that they wouldn't have problems with alcohol later on. Children should, however, grow up in an environment where alcohol is consumed intelligently and not for the sake of getting drunk. One of the worst things a child can grow up with is a parent who gets drunk frequently. It frightens children, creates a tremendous feeling of shame and embarrassment, and causes children to assume responsibility for taking care of the parent. Older brothers and sisters can have a similar negative impact on a younger sibling's behavior.

**2. Start making children aware of the dangers of drug and alcohol abuse as early as possible.** Even a three- or four-year-old child can begin learning simple refusal skills when parents role-play situations like "What should you do if someone asks you to have a sip of beer or alcohol?" This should continue throughout your child's childhood and preadolescence. Providing the message to "just say no" is not enough to steer a child away from drug or alcohol abuse. You must also teach effective ways of saying no. You also need to teach children that it will seem as if their friends don't want to be their friends if they don't have a drink. It's critical to communicate to children how important maintaining a sense of individuality is. Trying to accomplish this when your child is already eleven or twelve is difficult if not impossible, so please stress the importance of independent decision making by allowing your child to make choices and participate in family decisions early.

**3. Understand that poor self-esteem and drinking and drug abuse go hand in hand.** Children who feel bad about themselves are more apt to look for a peer group for acceptance. If the group is into drinking or drugs, the price for membership in that group is simply doing what everybody else does, and sitting around drinking will not seem like a high price to pay for children who feel they haven't been accepted or valued by their families.

**4. Don't be afraid to talk openly to your ten- to fourteen-year-old children about how frightening it is to know that children their age are drinking.** Using a neutral rather than a threatening tone, make it clear to them that you know that kids are experimenting with drugs and alcohol early.

**5. As kids get older, don't ignore the warning signs that your child may be drinking.** If your child comes home late, then rushes past everyone and up to her room and closes the door, that's a warning sign. If you know your child is spending time hanging out in parking lots, in back of stores, or in other dark secluded places, that's a warning sign. The signals are usually quite clear. Many parents who have gone through the experience will say that it was right in front of their noses all the time, but they were too frightened to confront the problem.

**6. Don't assume that just because your child is an "all-American" type who plays on sports teams and gets good grades in school he or she is immune to getting involved with alcohol or drugs.** Kids who lead "perfect" lives on the outside often put tremendous pressure on themselves and fall into drinking to deal with that pressure.

**7. Try to tolerate your child's friends hanging out at your home from time to time.** You will get a chance to see who is influencing your child, and that can be very important. The more you see of your kid's friends, the more information about them will be passed back to you, even without snooping or prying.

**8. If anyone in your close family has drug or alcohol problems, seek professional help.** Drug and alcohol problems are passed down from generation to generation. As you might already know, denial of the problem is what feeds it and makes it stronger. Alcoholics Anonymous, Al-Anon, and Alateen have chapters and branches in every state. You will be surprised by how nearby the closest meeting place is.

Drug and alcohol abuse has claimed the lives of hundreds of thousands of children and teens. Don't let your child become a statistic.

## CIGARETTE SMOKING

I can't think of one single parent who looks forward to seeing a son or daughter smoking a cigarette. By now it is clear to everyone (except for the people who run the cigarette industry) that cigarette smoking is an extremely harmful habit—unhealthy and addictive.

Just as with alcohol, by the time your child reaches adolescence her friends will have more influence over whether she smokes cigarettes than you will. That's why it is so important to start early. Over half the people who smoke start before their thirteenth birthday.

You can do a number of things to prevent your child from developing this unhealthy habit:

**Don't smoke.** It is absolutely ridiculous for you to demand that your child not smoke while you puff away. Children are very tuned in to hypocritical behavior in their parents, and your words will mean nothing if you don't back them up with actions.

**Promote a healthy lifestyle.** Smoking is a choice made by people who do not value a healthy lifestyle. If parents emphasize things like eating right, exercising, and participating in sports, children will see cigarette smoking as counterproductive.

**Never allow your child to smoke in or around the house.**
Many parents get so tired of catching their children smoking with their
friends that they throw up their hands and allow the child to smoke
at home. If you can't get your child to refrain from smoking cigarettes,
don't make it easy for him to fall further into this addictive habit by
allowing him to smoke at home.

## WHAT IF YOU CATCH YOUR CHILD SMOKING? ◀

If you catch your child smoking, don't be afraid to confront her, and
don't let her sell you on a story that she was "just holding" the
cigarettes for someone else.

    If you punish a child for smoking, it will probably do no good
whatsoever. Remember, in most cases friends have more influence over
your child's smoking than you do. Among the things you can do is having
your child sign a "no smoking" contract. Parents sometimes think that
signing a contract has no power to influence a child's behavior, but
I have found that it has. Before you make up a contract or an agreement, accompany your child to the library and pull out some articles
on cigarette smoking. The exercise is not meant as a punishment but to
increase your child's awareness of the dangers of smoking. It is something
you should do together.

    Next, construct a contract specifying the following.

1. Smoking is a dangerous activity that is harmful to your
   health. Because of that, and because we are responsible
   for your health, until you are old enough to leave the
   house and be on your own, you do not have permission
   to smoke.

2. You may not bring cigarettes into the house at any time for
   any reason.

3. Ultimately, even though we forbid it, smoking is a matter of
   choice. If you choose to smoke, be mature enough to inform
   us that you are doing it. It's bad enough to choose to smoke.
   Don't be sneaky and a liar on top of it.

4. As an incentive for not smoking, we will provide you with an incentive or privilege (e.g., an extra hour on curfew) that you will not enjoy if you choose to smoke or if we catch you smoking.

The fourth point is extremely important. It involves giving your child a privilege or reward for not smoking. In effect what you are doing is creating an incentive based on trust and mutual agreement. The idea is to create a situation that is more desirable than smoking. It is also a privilege that can be revoked (not as a punishment but as a consequence of breaking the deal) if the bargain is not adhered to.

# MARIJUANA

Marijuana is often the next "buzz" after drinking. Children who start drinking and like it usually have no problem experimenting with marijuana. Marijuana produces a range of effects, from mild psychedelic effects (distortion of time and reality) to relaxation and peacefulness. Marijuana can be smoked in a rolled cigarette called a *joint* or smoked in a water pipe called a *bong* or baked in brownies.

Marijuana is dangerous because marijuana smoke can cause serious damage to your lungs. In addition, research suggests that marijuana can alter DNA and damage chromosomes. Perhaps the most dangerous aspect of marijuana smoking is that there is no control over the quality or mixture of the material being smoked or consumed. Marijuana is frequently adulterated with many dangerous substances, including PCP or phencyclidine ("angel dust"), a powerful and dangerous mind-altering substance that can cause convulsions, flashbacks, and even death.

In the past few years I have seen two very disturbing trends. One is that children who smoke marijuana steal it from their parents, and that is their introduction to it. Many of today's parents got high as kids and never matured out of the habit. That is unfortunate. Aside from the health and legal risks associated with frequent marijuana use, it also reduces motivation, and one thing that is absolutely required for raising kids is motivation. If you have kids, and you still get high, you might be a decent parent when you are straight, but getting high when you have kids is just plain stupid—period.

The second disturbing trend I have observed is that some parents actually smoke pot with their children. This is worse than stupid; it's child abuse. I'm sure there are other philosophies and points of view on this. The one I prefer to stick with is a simple two-point philosophy:

1. The world is a complicated and difficult place to succeed in.

2. Screwing around with drugs and alcohol can make the difficult parts easier to tolerate but will always increase your problems in the long run.

## LSD, COCAINE, CRACK, BARBITURATES, AND HEROIN ◀

LSD is a hallucinogenic drug that severely distorts reality, causes the user to have "psychedelic" experiences, and significantly alters brain chemistry. LSD was very popular in the 1960s and is making a strong comeback among adolescents and young adults in the 1990s. LSD is cheap, easy to manufacture, and easy to purchase. It comes in many forms, including tablets and stamps where the LSD can be licked off to administer the dose. LSD is an extremely dangerous substance. While some people tout it as a "mind-expanding" drug, overdosing on LSD can produce disturbing flashbacks, permanent changes in brain chemistry, and suicidality.

Cocaine is in the stimulant family. The effect of this drug is to make you feel powerful, invincible, "up," and confident. Cocaine is expensive, very habit forming, and fairly easy to acquire. The expense usually makes it difficult but not impossible for children to acquire. Cocaine is usually snorted in powder form but can also be injected with a combination of other drugs like heroin (this is how the famous comedian John Belushi died). Kids who get hooked on cocaine are often enlisted to sell the drug as a way of supporting their habit. Since the law cannot penalize minors for dealing drugs the way it can penalize adults, kids are often used to make drops during drug deals. Overdosing on cocaine can cause death.

Crack cocaine is a crystalline form of cocaine that is smoked. It is easy to manufacture and far less expensive than cocaine in powdered form. A "hit" of crack costs about ten dollars. One characteristic of a crack high is a quick "up" phase followed by a period of intense depression and irritability. The quick high is the hook, and the depression and irritability make it necessary for the crack user to get back up as quickly as possible.

Heroin is another drug that was popular in the 1960s that is making a comeback today. A member of the opiate family of drugs, it is a narcotic, or painkiller, in the same class as codeine, Darvon, and Percodan.

Drugs like heroin are sometimes called *euphorics* because they increase your feeling of well-being and make you feel as if nothing in the world can bother you. Heroin is easily manufactured and distributed, relatively inexpensive, and extremely addictive. Withdrawal can cause convulsions and death. Heroin is usually shot into the arm or leg with a needle, but it can also be smoked or snorted.

Barbiturates work by relaxing your muscles, decreasing inhibitions, and increasing feelings of well-being. Valium, Librium, and Xanax are frequently prescribed to adults because these drugs have anxiety-relieving properties.

## THE BIGGEST MISTAKES PARENTS MAKE WHEN THEY DISCOVER CHILDREN USING DRUGS OR ALCOHOL ◀

The single biggest mistake parents can make when they discover their children using drugs or alcohol is to try to deal with the problem alone. Most parents don't want to consider the fact that their children may already have a problem, so they sit down, have a family meeting, deliver a stern lecture, and hope it never happens again. *But it almost always does.*

If you discover that your child is using drugs or alcohol, you *must* get help from a qualified professional. Sometimes a well-meaning uncle, cousin, or other family member that the child respects will step in and try to talk to the child. That's fine—the more support you can get, the better—but you still need outside assistance. If you don't know where to look, speak to your child's pediatrician or guidance counselor or your pastor, minister, or rabbi. Call the local chapter of Alcoholics Anonymous for the best possible advice on alcohol-related problems. Just be sure to speak to someone. Drug and alcohol problems go from bad to worse very quickly, and sitting back, even if it is from fear, always means running the risk of an addiction or overdose.

## QUICK REVIEW

1. Drug and alcohol abuse is a problem that spans every ethnic and social boundary. Kids start drinking when they are in grade school, and you should get to know the early warning signs as soon as possible.

2. Kids are more influenced by their peers, who tell them that it's "cool" to drink, than by their parents, who tell them not to.

3. Advertising for beer and liquor pulls younger kids into thinking that drinking is cool because it always pairs drinking with fun, exciting activities, and very attractive people.

4. We live in a culture that promotes drinking to celebrate, to relax, and to reduce tension.

5. If you suspect that your child is drinking, don't ignore it. Take the time to find out who your child's friends are. Require that she check in whenever she is going to be out at night. Do not allow her to attend unchaperoned parties. Encourage her to sign a contract about drinking and drug use.

6. Begin discussing the harmful effects of drugs and alcohol early, when your child is five or six years old.

7. Tune in to "normal" pressures of preadolescence and adolescence. Be open to talking about friends, dating, school, and things that are important to your child. Resist the urge to criticize. If your child doesn't feel comfortable seeking support from you, he will turn to a peer group that might value partying more than talking things through.

8. Try to make your home available for your kids to hang out in from time to time. This will help you get to know the kids your child is hanging around with.

## EXERCISES FOR PARENTS

### PARENT-CHILD CONTRACT

The following contract can form the basis for an agreement between parent and child regarding drug and alcohol abuse, rides home from parties, and driving drunk. Please take the time to do this simple exercise with your preadolescent to teenage child. It might not always prevent the worst case from happening, but often it will force a child to think twice before doing something she will regret.

# CONTRACT

This contract is between _____ (name of child)

and _____ (name of parent)

and _____ (name of parent).

**Section One: Responsibilities of Child**

I promise to avoid people and places where alcohol is served or drugs are used. I realize that it might be impossible always to know when drugs and alcohol are present, but whenever I have knowledge that drugs or alcohol will be present ahead of time, I will not let myself be part of that activity or event.

I promise never to get into a car that is being driven by someone who has had any amount of alcohol or drugs (even if supposedly only one beer) or who smells like alcohol.

I promise never to drive a car after I have had even one drink.

I promise to call home to ask for a ride in the event that my friends who are driving have been drinking or taking drugs.

If I am caught drinking or taking drugs, even once, I promise to attend an AA meeting and a session with a counselor who I may choose. I understand that there will be no punishment handed to me, but I must seek help.

**Section Two: Responsibilities of Parent**

I promise to trust that my child will use good judgment. I understand that I may ask where my child is going for the evening, and expect a "check in" call, but I may not hound or interrogate my child in an untrusting way.

I promise to drive my child home from any event that he or she calls me from to tell me that people are drunk or out of control, or when the ride he or she has gone with has taken alcohol or drugs.

I promise not to punish my child if I catch him or her using drugs or alcohol. We agree that we will attend an AA or similar meeting and meet with a counselor to see if there is a problem.


Signed, on this day (__/__/__)

by _____ (child)

_____ (parent)

_____ (parent).

# 15

# KEEPING PEACE IN
# THE TWO-CAREER FAMILY

◀

If you live in an "average" two-career family, your life is a hectic stream
of nonstop appointments—play dates, baseball games, Girl Scouts,
doctor appointments, and parent-teacher conferences, and that's only
Monday's schedule. Financial needs make the two-career family an
absolute necessity. How do you balance the stresses and strains of
this chaotic lifestyle, while retaining control of your senses and even
squeaking out five or ten minutes of peace and quiet for yourself? The
main goals of this chapter are to help you learn to organize your time
a little better, reduce stress in general, reduce strain on your marriage
in particular, and, most of all, prevent parent burnout.

## IT'S IMPORTANT TO CLARIFY ROLES

◀

The toughest obstacle to conquer is defining the roles of each parent in
a two-career family. Managing a household with children directly brings
to light the partnership aspect of a marriage. To make any partnership
work, you need three very basic and very important ingredients: a basic
trust and respect for your partner, a clear-cut understanding of responsibilities, and a willingness to give a little extra in a pinch. This can be

more difficult than it sounds, especially if both partners are employed in positions of authority or control over other employees. It then becomes very important for parents to switch roles from manager to partner.

## MARK AND JUDY: MANAGERS AT WORK, PARTNERS AT HOME

Mark and Judy both hold management positions in their respective companies. Each is responsible for more than twenty employees. Both individuals are good at delegating work, because that's what good managers do. The problem arises when they are at home and start delegating tasks to each other. Neither Mark nor Judy really likes being told what to do, and that's what probably made them managers to begin with! One of the ways they have gotten around this is to try to look at the other partner's request as a favor rather than an order.

Another thing that helps both partners is reserving the right to say no if something else important is engaging them at the moment. Does this system work 100 percent of the time? No, but it works a heck of a lot better than fighting over who is bossing around whom. Many people who are good problem solvers on the job forget that they possess this skill when they are at home. Organizing, scheduling, setting deadlines, and assigning tasks are all part of what it takes to make a household run smoothly. Families aren't supposed to be run like businesses, some would say. That's true—you don't have to cook your boss meat loaf, and you don't have to tuck the shipping department into bed at night—but the principles of good management that apply on the job often apply at home too.

## DIVIDING UP CHORES

Dividing up child-related chores is a necessity from infancy on up. When both parents have to get up early for work the next morning, both must be willing to put in the long hours at night feeding, comforting, or checking up on a baby who is sick and needs attention. Here is where flexibility plays an important role. Sharing this chore, for instance, doesn't always mean on Mondays I stay up all night, on Tuesdays you stay up all night, and so on. It means sticking to the schedule as often as you can, but on some nights one partner might have a more pressing need than the other, and as a result someone might have to put in a couple of nights in a row. A schedule that alternates a baby task should not be used as a way to create conflict or engage in scorekeeping. "I changed seven diapers in a row, and you changed only four. You owe me three." The much better way to do it would be for the partner enjoying the lighter share of work to say, "I know you have been helping me out with diaper changing lately. Thanks." Then give back when you can. In other words, don't wait for your partner to feel unappreciated and overworked. Pay attention to what's going on and provide appreciation and support. If both partners follow this simple rule, it will set up the kind of environment that feeds on and grows from kindness as opposed to just wearing down with stress.

*Set reasonable, attainable expectations for creating a family atmosphere around the dinner hour.*

As kids get older, household chores like cooking and chauffeuring should be divided up as well. When it comes to dividing up tasks, no one should be exempt from a turn at bat.

## HOW IMPORTANT ARE FAMILY DINNERS?

Dinnertime can become a very large issue in the two-career family. Many of us grew up with the idea that dinnertime is a sacred time, with no interruptions and nothing else going on. In an ideal world the dinner table is a place where stimulating conversation prevails and everyone shares the events of the day. Have you noticed, however, that we don't live in an ideal world? Usually the boys are antagonizing each other with various sharp objects, and the baby is creating abstract landscapes using the full palette supplied by the strained vegetables that are oozing around on the tray table of her high chair. Glasses are shattering in response to the high-pitched squeals and noises that slice through the dinner ambience. Grandma and Grandpa would be appalled at the sight, but what can you really expect? If you have reasonable expectations for creating a family atmosphere around the dinner table, you will not endure the stress of trying to achieve the impossible.

Parents always ask me whether family members should be allowed to eat at separate times. There is more than one way to look at it. The traditional view holds that having a specified dinner hour lends structure and routine to the day. From the point of view of establishing dinnertime as a family responsibility, eating together seems like a worthwhile goal. The contemporary point of view holds that people should eat when hungry. Some of the latest diet and nutrition ideas tell us that we should pay more attention to when our bodies tell us they are hungry and eat until we are satisfied, then stop. As kids get older, after-school activities may crisscross around dinnertime, and grabbing a bite here and there is all that will fit into a busy activity schedule.

Another situation that arises is the case of young children who can't wait until eight or nine o'clock at night when the second parent comes home to eat. Should one parent and the children eat early and let the other parent fend for himself? Should the children eat by themselves and then the two parents eat together? Should the parent who is home early eat twice and suffer the dietary consequences? You have to decide for yourselves, but there is nothing wrong with creating whatever schedule produces the least amount of stress. Maybe two nights a week one parent and the children can eat together, and the other three nights both parents can eat together.

By the time kids are teenagers, they don't even live on the same planet or keep time using conventional methods. If you are getting your teenager to eat with you more than two or three nights a week, you have made a noteworthy accomplishment.

How do you reconcile two points of view so far apart? It depends on your own personal comfort level and family schedule. If you are comfortable with informal eating arrangements but feel guilty because your parents made a big deal out of dinnertime, try it your way for a while and see how it turns out. As a comfortable compromise, work out one or two nights a week when attendance at dinner is absolutely mandatory, no excuses accepted. Finally, if your choice is to be a traditionalist and that is what is important to you, then communicate the importance of a family dinner hour as a loud-and-clear house rule, but remember there will always be times when you'll need to make exceptions.

## KEEPING A COMMON SET OF RULES ◀

Dinnertime routines are just the tip of the iceberg when it comes to decisions. Nothing could be more important than the fact that both parents should always be working from the same set of rules. When parents are divided, children will conquer.

## SNEAKER MADNESS

Let's take a look at how a seemingly innocent gesture by one parent can undermine the efforts of the other. Eleven-year-old Billy wanted a pair of leather sneakers and had been hounding his mother about them for months. The sneakers cost a hundred and twenty dollars. Billy's mom couldn't justify the expense because she knew that Billy was growing fast and that in a month they wouldn't fit.

When Saturday rolled around, Billy's dad decided to do Mom a favor and take Billy sneaker shopping. While they were out, Billy began his campaign for the pair of sneakers he wanted. Dad knew that Billy and Mom had been going head to head over the sneakers for weeks. Then he looked down at Billy and thought, God, what a great time we're having today. This kid is terrific, and look, he's the spitting image of me. Billy's dad then went through a predictable thought process: you're only young once, and things had been going pretty well with the business, so they could really afford the sneakers. Before you knew it, Billy was trying on those hundred-twenty-dollar sneakers, and Dad was thinking that maybe he should get a new pair of sneakers and a helmet too—for when Mom found out and started chasing him around the house swinging something large and heavy. At the cash register Dad recommended that Billy and he tell his mother that the sneakers were actually on sale. Now the two of them were sharing this evil little secret and together would put one over on Mom.

The downside is obvious. Over time Billy will learn to ignore his mother when what she says doesn't suit him, and Dad will get his just desserts too because when Billy doesn't get his way with Dad, he will just work on Mom in the same way. Mom and Dad will begin to resent each other and sabotage each other's authority, and ultimately each will lose a share of parental authority. All over a pair of sneakers? You bet. It's sneakers and karate lessons and video games and just about every other petty thing that creates the stage for power struggles and sabotage tactics in the family.

# TELEVISION TURMOIL

Television-watching privileges can create a lot of conflict in the family. Mom is attending a school conference in the evening while Dad is home watching the kids. The kids are well aware of Mom's rules forbidding various television shows. She has in fact been known to block the entire screen with her body when even the commercials for certain shows come on, and on top of that she once pulled the plug clean out of the wall when a show she considered too violent was polluting the family atmosphere.

When the television set goes on, Dad is largely unaware of exactly which shows are blacklisted but becomes suspicious when he hears the various sounds of explosions, beheadings, and machine-gun rattlings. "Uh, guys, are you supposed to be watching that stuff? That's the show that Mom objects to, isn't it?" The reply is "Mom didn't say we couldn't watch this show," which is not a lie because Mom hasn't seen this exact show, only forty or so just like it, all of which she has banned. Dad figures the kids aren't killing each other at the moment, so what's the harm?

The problem in this story is a lack of clear communication about television-watching rules and the tendency for Dad not to want to look like a bad guy. In this case he wants to be the ever-popular, popcorn-popping, let's-stay-up-and-have-some-laughs Dad, which is great as long as Mom is let in on the fun too. When she isn't, Dad is contributing to the good-cop, bad-cop family dynamic that creates problems.

## DON'T LET KIDS PLAY ONE PARENT AGAINST THE OTHER

Whenever you are not sure of what the other parent has said about something, postpone decisions until you get the correct feedback. But remember, kids can be very crafty. They will sometimes pressure you by asking your permission to do something right before it is supposed to happen.

## DID YOU DISCUSS THIS WITH MOM?

Mom is out of the house, and twelve-year-old Veronica comes running up to Dad, singing, "Anna and the girls are coming over, and they are going to the mall. Can I go?" Dad hasn't a clue as to whether Mom has sanctioned the trip to the mall. He vaguely remembers several small arguments where Veronica was complaining that she is treated like a baby because Mom won't let her go to the mall. Did they straighten that one out? Dad himself doesn't feel too comfortable with the idea. What's he going to do? Should he be mean and say no since he hasn't spoken to Mom about it, or should he be the Best Dad in the Entire Universe and tell her to go but be back early, preferably before Mom returns? The answer is that he should say no. He remembered arguments that Veronica and Mom had, and he shouldn't take the chance that he is going against something Mom feels uncomfortable about. It is best to make a house rule that says that anything you ask for on short notice is subject to a no if both parents aren't around to talk about it.

## SHOULD MOM LET HER KIDS CHEAT ON THE FAMILY DIET?

In Dave and Marge's house, Dave is a health food lover. A chiropractor, he wants the family to eat tofu and sprouts and all kinds of natural healthy things. Marge tolerates Dave's eating habits and supports them because she knows they are healthy, but whenever Dave isn't around the kids beg, I mean beg, with outstretched arms and salivating mouths, to eat at fast-food restaurants. It is during these times when Marge starts to pine for a carton of greasy french fries herself. Should she take them out for fast food when Dave isn't around and swear the kids to secrecy? Or should she have a discussion with Dave about how the kids are reacting to the whole notion of the "forbidden fruit," or burger in this case? If the truth be told, kids who grow up banned from all types of fast food tend to gravitate toward it when they become more independent. Food is a tender issue in many families, but there is always some wisdom in compromise.

## THE FAMILY BULLETIN BOARD

When things are hectic the way they are in two-career families, it is easy to lose track of house rules, promises, and privileges unless you communicate. It may sound corny, but it does help to write things down and keep a family bulletin board. The family bulletin board is such a beautifully simple and effective concept that it should almost be a state law. It can be the family information clearinghouse for schedules, important phone numbers, upcoming school activities, special events, sports activities, telephone messages, and the ever-popular list of chores, which we will talk about in a minute.

## BRINGING THE KIDS INTO THINGS

Now that we have talked about the relationship between the two heads of the house, let's figure out how to get the kids to pitch in and help out. In a two-career family, engineering the environment and teaching chores and responsibilities go hand in hand. In a busy household kids have to learn to pitch in because it is a good and important part of their character development and because it is necessary to keep things running smoothly. Responsible habits should be developed starting very early. Even three-year-old children are capable of doing simple chores like washing the vegetables before dinner and picking up after themselves. Sometimes having a parent nearby can help jump-start the behavior. From about age five and up kids can help with the dishes, set the table, and keep their own things straight. I am a big fan of keeping boxes and bins in kids' rooms because it makes straightening up a lot easier.

When a number of chores have to be done, and more than one person is available to do them, try making a spinner, like those used in board games. Put a chore in each section of the spinner and have the kids spin for their weekly chores. Be sure to write down who is doing what chore so there are no mix-ups. This adds a little bit of fun to the routine and distributes the more difficult or annoying chores by chance. So when someone spins and gets "clean the hamster cage," Mom and Dad can't be blamed for favoring one child over another by giving the hard chore to the child they love less.

> *Even three-year-olds are capable of doing simple chores like washing vegetables or picking up toys.*

Although time is precious, *always* take the time to praise a job well done, especially when someone takes the time to do a little extra. It's very easy to become frustrated and lose your temper when things aren't going well, and that is when people tend to communicate most strongly. A little extra peace and quiet around the house usually means things are running well. Now is the time to enjoy that peace and quiet, but be sure to acknowledge it, because acknowledgment is actually what maintains it.

## HELPING CHILDREN DEVELOP ROUTINES ◄

Routines are chores that develop out of habit or repetition. Morning routines, homework routines, and evening routines are the most important. For the morning, it is best to prepare as much as possible the night before. School clothes should be out and in a folded pile on top of the dresser or near the bed. In large families bathroom times might have to be assigned so everyone can get out of the house on schedule. With older children and teenagers bathroom times are even more crucial.

Homework routines should be established from kindergarten on up. Homework should always be done in the same place and approximately at the same time every day (see Chapter 10 for details). Some parents favor homework to be done right after a child comes home from school. Some will allow a child to do or at least finish homework after dinner. What works best varies from child to child. If your child has the stamina to do homework before dinner, that system will probably smooth out some of the other nighttime routines.

Some parents are very tired and frazzled after work and make poor homework helpers. If you feel you are fighting with your child over homework instead of helping, consider a homework tutor or high school homework helper to help with projects and test or quiz reviews. Always leave time to look over your child's homework and stay in contact with teachers.

## NIGHTTIME RITUALS

Good nighttime routines can make the difference between giving you that ten minutes of breathing room you desperately need at the end of the day and pushing you right over the edge. When kids give you a hard time about going to bed, actions speak louder than words. Don't hesitate to shut the television off and hustle them off to bed. Although it's tempting to give in to kids who want to stay up longer, doing so only sets a precedent for problems in the forthcoming nights. This is one situation where it helps to have both parents around, especially when you have more than one child. One parent can get the first child off to bed with a story while the other begins the nighttime routine with the next child.

## LET YOURSELF LEAN ON HELP WHEN IT'S AVAILABLE

Successful working people tend to think they should be able to do it all and are reluctant to rely on the help of family or friends. When help is available, provided it is good help, use it. If Grandma and Grandpa want to take the kids for a weekend, take them up on their offer. You don't even have to go anywhere; just lock yourself up in the house and relax.

Many parents feel guilty about "skipping out" on their kids on the weekend after being at work all week, and kids sometimes reinforce this by acting as if you are torturing them There is absolutely no need to feel guilty. You are taking some time so that you can give your children more of the good, relaxed parts of yourself. The stress your children endure being without you for a weekend will harm them much less than doing without your patience and stamina on a regular basis.

> *Sitters, nannies, and housekeepers influence your child's self-esteem as well as her health and safety.*

Combining resources with friends is also a good idea. Carpooling can be a tremendous help, but it has to be done right. Get to know the people in your carpool and don't be afraid to decline if you sense that any of the parents may be unreliable. Joining an undependable group can cause more work than it alleviates, especially if you feel you have to pick up the slack for a parent who cancels out at the last minute. Be sure to work out what happens in certain situations. For instance, if it is your turn to drive, and your child gets sick, are you still responsible for driving?

## SITTERS AND HOUSEHOLD HELP

Also in the area of building a support team are people like sitters and household help. A good baby-sitter is worth her weight in gold. Always get references from baby-sitters and then call them. Be sure to review safety procedures, household routines, and emergency phone numbers with sitters. Don't be shy about laying down some house rules, such as not having friends over and limiting the use of the telephone. If at all possible, use a new sitter for only a few hours the first time. Take some extra time leaving the house so you can observe the interaction between the sitter and your children for the first few minutes.

A lot of the rules for sitters also apply to nannies and other household help. A special consideration with nannies is how long they will stay; the biggest problem that parents have with good nannies is that they move on. Your child, especially a young child, will feel as attached to a good nanny as to any other member of the family.

Another problem that people have with nannies is that they become too dependent on them. After having gone through so much trouble locating one in the first place, some parents find it hard to confront a nanny who is not getting along well with the children or is treating them too harshly. Do not be afraid to sit down and have a heart-to-heart talk with a nanny in this situation. Often the problem can be resolved. The bottom line is that this person does have an influence on your child's developing sense of self-esteem, as well as his health and safety.

Please be aware that language barriers can also have an impact on young children whose language skills are developing. Some nannies spend eight or more hours a day with the children, who need to be cared for in an environment that stimulates language development. Cultural differences also may have an impact, such as on discipline.

An open line of communication must be maintained between the nanny and Mom and Dad. If things don't seem to be working out, don't hesitate to find another, more suitable person to help take care of your children.

## TAKE CARE OF YOURSELF

My final piece of advice to parents in two-career families is to make sure that you set some time aside for yourself. Plan your own quiet time and give it up only in the most pressing of circumstances. You are working for more than one reason, and all of them are important: financial betterment, job satisfaction, giving your kids a good life, and achieving personal growth. The bottom line is that you will be of no good use to anyone if you let yourself get so caught up in the day-to-day grind that you have no time for yourself. Make the time and enjoy it.

## QUICK REVIEW

1. A good working partnership between the two heads of household is essential for managing the hectic life of the two-career family. The essential ingredients are a basic trust and respect for your partner, a clear-cut understanding of responsibilities, and a willingness to give a little extra in a pinch.

2. Try to focus on appreciating what your partner does for you. Engage in supportive, positive communication, not scorekeeping and complaining.

3. It is sometimes necessary to modify expectations so that things run smoothly, rather than to try to achieve unrealistic ideals such as cooking a family dinner seven nights a week.

4. Parents must operate under the same set of rules. Both parents must have equal authority—no good-cop, bad-cop routines, and no undermining the other parent just to score popularity points with the kids.

5. Whenever you are unsure about a rule, curfew, or other privilege, try your best to touch base with the other parent to make sure you are not crossing a boundary the other person has drawn.

6. Try to develop routines, especially around morning, nighttime, and homework. Try to accomplish as much as you can the night before for morning routines.

7. Use support whenever it is available and reliable. When your relatives offer to take the kids for a day or weekend once in a while, take them up on it.

8. Program some time for yourself. Don't forget to enjoy some of the fruits of your labor!

## EXERCISES FOR PARENTS

### OUTLINING DISCIPLINE RULES AND REGULATIONS

Don't let the kids divide and conquer because you and your spouse haven't communicated clearly about bedtimes, curfews, or privileges. Take a few minutes to jot down limits that you both agree on. Start off with the major categories:

**Bedtimes (Schooldays and Weekends):**

______________________________

______________________________

______________________________

**Curfews:**

______________________________

______________________________

______________________________

**Homework:**

______________________________

______________________________

______________________________

**Food, Candy, and Snacking:**

______________________________

______________________________

______________________________

## EXERCISES FOR PARENTS

Other Important Issues (e.g., clothes, friends, acceptable places
to hang out):

_____

_____

_____

## CREATING A FAMILY BULLETIN BOARD
The following items should be included on the family bulletin board:

| Weekly Chores | Special Events | Messages |
| --- | --- | --- |

Emergency numbers
School telephone numbers and teachers' names and when they
can be reached
Names and numbers of children who can be relied on for
information such as:
- missing homework
- dates and times of special events that you are missing
  information on
- names and numbers for at least two reliable baby-sitters
- name, number, and parents' names for current "best friends"
  (including addresses and directions to their house)

## EXERCISES FOR PARENTS

### TAKING CARE OF YOURSELF AND YOUR PARTNER

Have you taken the time to do something for yourself this week? Write down three things you will absolutely do for yourself and three things you will do for your partner.

**For myself**

1. _____

2. _____

3. _____

**For my partner**

1. _____

2. _____

3. _____

# 16

# SINGLE PARENTING ▶

Part of the work I do with children involves making recommendations
to the courts about proper custody, residence, and visitation arrangements
when parents are divorcing and can't agree on these things. It is, by far,
the most stressful part of my clinical work; it is very unsettling to be a
stranger evaluating someone else's family and making recommendations
on a decision that will influence children for the rest of their lives. During
the most difficult moments in the process I wonder why parents can't
put their differences aside and jointly plan a strategy that will protect
the most valuable thing in their lives.

## A CORDIAL AND
## BUSINESSLIKE RELATIONSHIP ▶

There are divorced parents who do manage to rise above their differences
and come to terms with the fact that they can no longer be partners in
marriage but will still participate fully and completely in their children's
lives as equal parents. These people have the rare ability to remain
focused on the best interests of their children. It doesn't take a degree

in child psychology to be able to understand that the children from these situations fare much better in life and in their subsequent relationships.

Many of the people I work with just cannot make it to that point, and the children become the vessels for all of the problems, communication difficulties, and incompatibilities that ruined the marriage. Sometimes the children become a symbol for proving the goodness or righteousness of the parent who eventually wins custody. It's almost as if the parent who gets custody is the better person, so by logical extension the problems in the marriage couldn't possibly have been that party's fault. Of course, nothing could be further from the truth.

When parents cannot make it past the hurt of a failed marriage, it is still necessary to communicate about the children. When the parents engage in sarcasm, put-downs, constant complaints, coldness, indifference, or outright abuse, the children are the ones who suffer in the end, and they suffer badly. For their sake you must develop a cordial relationship with your ex-spouse. The kind of relationship I describe has an analogy in the business world. Let's say that you are either a supplier of goods or one of a group of customers who purchase these goods. The supplier needs customers, and the customers need the product. If you are the customer, imagine that you can obtain your goods only from one supplier. If you are the supplier, imagine that your universe of customers is very small and you can't do without any of them. Now, from time to time, the customer is going to dislike the supplier and vice versa, but smart businesspeople will retain a cordial, polite, and businesslike demeanor to keep things running smoothly. In business there is always financial security at stake, so motivation to be cordial is high—that is, if you are a smart businessperson. With children there is something more valuable than money on the line—their emotional health and well-being—so the motivation to be pleasant, cordial, and smart should be even higher.

## GUIDELINES FOR MANAGING CHILDREN AFTER A DIVORCE

These guidelines are designed to help you put your differences aside and cooperate in the best interests of your children. After a divorce certain commonsense rules can help resolve conflicts and minimize the damage to the children:

1. Sit down and fill out a calendar that lists an entire year's visitation schedule. Include weekends, vacations, and holidays. Sign each month and forward a copy to your attorneys. One of the most common things that parents argue about is which has the children for which weekend or holiday. This is easy to avoid when things are worked out in advance.

2. Always prepare your children for a visit by getting them excited about seeing their Mom or Dad, by speaking about the experience in a positive way.

3. Do not argue with your ex-spouse during the visitation switchovers. If it's your turn, spend the time greeting the children, getting them ready to go, and communicating that you are happy to begin a visit with them. If it's your ex-spouse's turn, do not use the switchover time to argue about money, whom your ex-spouse is dating, how much you hate your ex-spouse's family, and so on.

4. Be considerate and have the children ready to go on their visit at the appointed time. Do not return the children late or arrive early or late for a pickup. By the same token, when your ex-spouse has a legitimate reason for being late (traffic or other unavoidable circumstances), don't give him or her a hard time.

5. Be reasonable when the child is feeling ill. If the child seems too sick to travel, don't make a big deal out of it. Arrange for makeup time and let the child rest. If the child is just a little sniffly, don't use this as an excuse to withhold visitation. If you can't decide what to do, call and let your pediatrician's word be final.

6. Don't interrogate your child during a visitation or when the child returns to the custodial residence. This is one of the worst things you can do to a child. It always makes her feel uncomfortable and as if she is betraying the other parent.

7.  Don't complain about your ex-spouse to your child, and *never* discuss money matters with him. He can't do anything about it and may feel responsible for it if you complain.

8.  Agree to participate jointly in important decisions regarding school, doctors, social activities, and religion. If you can't agree, try talking to a family counselor who has experience in resolving postdivorce conflicts or find a mediator who can assist you.

9.  When you will be taking your children away from home, provide your ex-spouse with a telephone number where the children can be reached at specified times. It is wrong to forbid your children to talk to your ex-spouse on the phone during a visit. It is also wrong to call your children constantly while they are visiting with your ex-spouse, interrupting their private time together.

10. If you cannot make a visitation switch without fighting, please try to enlist the help of a neutral friend or family member whose home you can use as a drop-off. Subjecting your child to week after week of fighting during visitation switches is emotionally damaging.

11. Teach your children that they have two parents who love them very much. Reinforce the fact that even though you are no longer married, Mommy will always be Mommy and Daddy will always be Daddy.

12. Develop a common set of disciplinary rules and actions. If there are two different sets of rules, your children will manipulate the two parents so that they are always on the side of the one who will give them less structure, and that will cause them to grow up undisciplined. Again, if you have trouble accomplishing this, get a trained professional to help you.

# THE CUSTODIAL PARENT
# USUALLY GETS THE GRIEF

Whenever there are behavioral problems, it is usually the custodial parent who complains that the children are misbehaving. That's because the custodial parent has more day-to-day contact and is responsible for setting down the majority of the disciplinary rules and regulations. It is common for children to go through periods where they complain and ask to move in with the noncustodial parent, especially when the custodial parent is restricting them from doing what they want. Just about the worst thing that the custodial parent can do is say, "OK, if you want to live with your father [or mother], pack your things right now. I'll get on the phone and you will be out of here within an hour."

Never let your children feel as if they have control over or responsibility for choosing where to live. That is implying that they know what's best for them better than you do.

If the child is genuinely unhappy and old enough (at least eleven in most cases) to participate in some of the decision making, you can tell her you will consider her feelings, talk to your ex-spouse, and see if there are some changes that will make her happier. Of course, there are times and situations where this isn't even a remote possibility. Sometimes there is only one custodial possibility, and if that is the case it should be explained to the child as simply and directly as possible. Changes in custody can be very complicated emotionally, financially, and legally and should certainly never be made during the heat of an argument.

## "I WANT TO BE WITH DADDY!"

Visitation changes were always very hard on six-year-old Mitch. He was Daddy's most special person in the whole world. Though father and son were close, Mom had custody because that is what was decided. Visitation was liberal, and the relationship between Mom and Dad was cool but businesslike. Lately after visitation, Mitch would go into his room and cry. He was irritable and upset. "I don't want to leave my daddy. I want to live with him. I hate it here. I don't want to live here." The words cut through his mom like knives. She couldn't understand why Mitch was so upset. She had no behavior problems with him. For the most part he was an easy child. On most days he seemed perfectly happy and content, but when he came home from his dad's there were often fits and crying. What should she do? Mitch's mom knew that her husband would love to have custody, but she just didn't feel that was the solution. Mitch's dad worked long days and was often away on business.

Talking to Mitch when he was in one of these moods was useless. The more she tried to reason with him, the louder he wailed. She also had a difficult time controlling some of the feelings she had when Mitch got like this. She felt betrayed and unappreciated.

She spoke to a counselor, who explained that it wasn't that Mitch didn't want to live with her. What Mitch wanted was what many kids who are going through a divorce want. He wanted his family back. The fact is that Mitch relied on his mom as much as he relied on his dad, even more so at times, since Mom had always been the primary caregiver. It's just that Mitch loved his father and missed him when he wasn't around.

The solution to this problem was twofold: Mitch joined a group called the Banana Splits run by a social worker at Mitch's school. In the group he met a lot of other kids who were going through divorces, and they all talked and shared their feelings. It was a positive experience. Mitch and his dad also started spending a little more time together. Mitch's mom and dad arranged for more visitation, and that made him even happier.

Mitch seemed happier and better adjusted to the new situation, and the difficult times eventually ended.

## SHOULD I ALLOW MY CHILDREN TO INTERACT WITH PEOPLE I DATE?

Generally, no. I always recommend that parents keep their children as far away from their social lives as they can. There are a number of reasons for this.

First, children feel tremendous loyalty to parents. Being around someone you are dating can make your child feel uncomfortable with or disloyal to your ex-spouse. Children sometimes resolve this conflict by becoming a conduit for information about the people you are dating to your ex-spouse, and this can create additional problems.

Second, if your child becomes attached to a boyfriend or girlfriend and the relationship doesn't work out, your child will experience the loss from this relationship and reexperience the loss from the original divorce. It's not hard to see the danger in children's concluding that relationships are always tentative, temporary, and disappointing.

There is no need to inform your child about whom you are dating or what you do on your dates. Children will sometimes ask, and your reply should be "That is private information. If there's anything I think you should know about, I will tell you when the time is right."

> *There is no need to inform your child about whom you are dating or what you do on your dates.*

If you begin to get serious with someone, you will eventually want your child to meet the person, especially if there is a chance that you will be remarrying. This situation is much different from letting your children be around people you are dating. If marriage is a possibility, you should give your child at least six months to get used to the person you are marrying.

I know there are times when it is very tempting to believe it is a good thing to have your children around someone you care for. It is even more tempting when that person has children who are around your children's ages and you can all do things together. It has been my experience that the risks far outweigh the benefits. In the beginning things look rosy, but all relationships have a honeymoon phase, and before you know it things become difficult and complicated. The best advice I can give in this situation is to take it slowly.

## WHEN YOU AND YOUR CHILD ARE ON YOUR OWN

Unfortunately there are many cases when your child and you are completely on your own. You are a working single parent with little or no support, and the stress of just making ends meet is unbearable. Your child may find herself being a latchkey kid at a young age. What can you do to cut down on some of the stress these circumstances bring?

First, it is absolutely essential to gather available resources. Sometimes parents are too proud to ask for help, and while this is understandable, it is neither in your best interest nor in your child's. If there are people in your family who are willing to help out, let them. If there are neighbors or friends who are willing to help out, let them.

Second, take some time to get to know some of the local mothers or parents of your children's classmates. Given the statistics, you are most assured of finding someone who is in a similar predicament. Compare schedules. There may be days when you can watch the children and the other parent can get some shopping or housework done. Utilize carpools for school and sports events. Finally, be sure to program some decompression time into every week. You must allow yourself to do things that are enjoyable, even selfish. If you devote your life only to going to work and managing your children, you will come to resent both, and that will only increase your stress. In the end you will be a less effective parent. You are working hard in a difficult situation. You deserve to look forward to a few simple pleasures to make your week worth going through.

> *Don't ignore your own needs. It's important to set aside time to relax and unwind every week.*

## QUICK REVIEW

1. Parents who are divorced should strive for (at least) a cordial and businesslike relationship with each another. Children always benefit from the input of two parents who love and care for them.

2. Proper guidelines for managing children after divorce include refraining from fighting during switchovers, being conscientious about pickup and drop-off times, being sensitive when children are ill and can't make a visit, avoiding interrogating children before, during, or after a visit, and refraining from "trashing" the other parent to the children.

3. Divorced parents need to agree on basic principles of discipline to prevent a child from taking advantage of or manipulating the situation.

4. The custodial parent usually gets the most grief and difficult time by virtue of spending more time with the children. If a change in custody becomes a possibility, children's opinions should be heard, but it is not their choice. The best choice is what adults agree is best for the child.

5. It is generally not a good idea to have your children interact with the people you date, even if they have children who are around the same age as yours.

6. If you are a single parent with little or no support or contact with your ex-spouse, please take advantage of whatever support is available to you in terms of money, carpooling, or opportunities to gain some precious relaxation or enjoyment on your own. It might be true that most of the time you have to do it all, but there are always avenues for support. Use them!

## EXERCISES FOR PARENTS

### DIVORCED PARENTS' INFORMATION KIT

Sometimes parents have difficulty speaking to each other, but that doesn't mean they can't communicate. Speaking directly with a person is usually the best way to get across information, but when this is impossible, make up a few sheets that have "fill-in-the-blank" responses to mail to your ex-spouse. Do not allow your children to be couriers for information like this. Here are some examples:

> Billy has a sports event scheduled for ___/___/___. He will be
> at _____ (place of event) at _____
> (time of event). You may contact his coach at _____
> (telephone number) if you need more information.

The same note can be modified for school events.
Here is another example:

> Billy has a doctor's appointment with Dr. _____
> at _____ (place of appointment)
> on ___/___/___ (date of appointment) at _____
> (time of appointment). The nature of the appointment is
> _____ . If you have any questions, you can contact
> Dr. _____ at (___) ___-_____ (telephone number).

Other examples:
- Important medical information (when to take medication)
- Vacation itineraries with times the child is available to talk on the phone.
- Notification of special family events that might require a change in the visitation schedule. This notification should be given at least three weeks in advance when possible.

# EPILOGUE: YIKES! MY BABY BECAME A TEENAGER WHEN I WASN'T LOOKING

One of parenting's little "surprises" happens just about the time when you think you've got things under control. It's referred to as *adolescence* by some and *parenting hell* by others. First, the good news. I know it sounds as if I am making it up, but research indicates that most adolescents actually believe their parents are thoughtful, loving caregivers and wouldn't want them to change in any way. The *I Am a Teenager* handbook that is given to all kids on their thirteenth birthday, however, expressly forbids them to talk about this fact openly, unless it is a prelude to asking for a ridiculously high-priced item of teenage paraphernalia or the keys to the family car.

Prepare yourself for incredible feats of logic and reasoning, something I often refer to as "teenage pretzel logic," like "Ma, I hate it when you treat me like a baby. I am grown-up and want my independence. I should be able to decide what I want to do by myself. Now, can you please drive me and my friends to the mall?" Prepare, also, for the most tender and bittersweet moments of pride and love you will ever have as you watch your rapidly developing young adult chasing her dreams with a passion that is available only to youth.

Experience the mood swings and hormonally induced personality changes while you envy the child's ability to consume and evaporate seven-thousand-calorie diets without gaining an ounce. As I always tell parents, thank goodness the teenage phase of life lasts for only seven years.

The essentials of good parenting shift during the teenage years, so much so that I have devoted another *SmartParenting* book entirely to helping you assist your teen in conquering the problems encountered— with you, with friends, with school and career choices, and much more. (At the very least it will give you something to read while you sit up at two o'clock in the morning waiting for your teen to come in from a night out!)

I hope we meet again during your child's teen years, but for now, thanks for spending the time with me. Bye-bye.

# THE TOP TEN PRINCIPLES
# OF SMARTPARENTING

◀

**1. Fire the district attorney.** Don't ask your child questions about situations and events that you already know about. Act on what you see. **TIP:** Your child's teacher tells you your son had a bad day in school. Don't approach your son by saying, "How was your day in school?" or "Did anything happen in school that I should know about?" Instead, say, "I hear you had a difficult day in school. Tell me about it."

**2. Concentrate on the positive rather than the negative.** To build self-esteem and encourage listening, be sure to give your child three positive comments for every negative comment or criticism. Always work on the positive side of the behavior. **TIP:** Praise effort over performance or outcome. Focus on cooperating and having a good attitude.

**3. KISS: Keep In Synch with Your Spouse.** Coordinate your child management strategies with your spouse; the two of you must both work with the same set of rules. **TIP:** Teach your kids that all requests are likely to generate no's when both parents aren't made aware of the situation.

**4. Spanking is no solution.** Hitting your children will only teach them that violence is an acceptable way of handling conflict. They will be more likely to hit others, too.

**TIP:** Whenever you feel like hitting your child, walk away, count to ten, or shout "stop!" to yourself.

**5. Hugs can be as good as toys.** You don't always have to reward good behavior with material things such as toys or money. Praise, smiles, and affection are all powerful motivators of behavior.

**TIP:** Keep your praise specific. Instead of saying, "You're a good girl," say, "Thank you for cleaning off your plate. That's really helpful."

**6. Aim for the sky.** Keep your expectations for behavior and performance high, but help your children reach those goals by praising performance, avoiding negative criticism, and teaching them how to learn from their mistakes.

**TIP:** Never take a positive situation, when your child has done 95 percent of a good thing, and turn it into a bad one by concentrating on the 5 percent that wasn't successful.

**7. Teach your child "smart risks"**—when to challenge the norm, try something different, stand out in a crowd.

**TIP:** Be a good role model for this behavior.

**8. Be a strong advocate.** Do not allow teachers, coaches, baby-sitters, or other caregivers to damage your child's self-esteem.

**TIP:** Keep your eyes open. Stay in contact with your child's teachers. Make sure they recognize you by name and face. Offer assistance when you can (but don't be annoying).

**9. Make an impression while you can.** Teach lessons about drugs, alcohol, and cigarettes early. Have your conversations about drugs, AIDS, alcohol, and cigarettes as soon as your child is capable of understanding about these things (age three or four). As children get older, peers have more influence than family.

**TIP:** Role-play situations, starting when your kids are very young. Make these role-playing games a routine.

**10. Make every day a learning experience.** Encourage curiosity, experimentation, "everyday science."
**TIP:** Go on as many field trips with your kids as you can when they are young. Learn something about the weather, the environment, and the kinds of plants and animals that live near your home.

# INDEX

# Smart Parenting™

## FREE OFFER!

## JUST FILL OUT THE CARD BELOW

You will receive a **FREE** issue of *SmartParenting*™ *Digest*—a newsletter filled with the most up-to-date information you need for effective parenting:

* new ways to motivate your kids
* techniques for teaching responsibility
* bedtime stress reducers
* handling concerns about TV
* improving schoolwork
* single parenting issues

As a registered SmartParenting Family member, you'll receive **special discounts** on:

* cassette and video products
* parenting books and guides
* local and national seminars
* games and teaching aids

Direct access to SmartParenting through

* our Parent Advice Helpline
* the Internet

**SPECIAL OFFER!** The *SmartParenting* audio series of six hour-long tapes *plus* a 32-page workbook, regularly priced at $59.95, is a great way to have easy access to *SmartParenting* while you travel. Take advantage of the special 20% member's discount and order today for only $47.95. Just fill in the card below.

---

Name (Mr/Mrs/Ms/Dr): _____

Address: _____

Home phone: _____ I am ❑ married ❑ single ❑ divorced ❑ widowed

Age: ❑ 18–24 ❑ 25–34 ❑ 35–49 ❑ 50+

Number of children: _____

Child's name: _____ Birthday __/__/__ ❑ Boy ❑ Girl

Child's name: _____ Birthday __/__/__ ❑ Boy ❑ Girl

Child's name: _____ Birthday __/__/__ ❑ Boy ❑ Girl

What influenced you to buy *SmartParenting*?
❑ In-store display ❑ TV/radio guest appearance ❑ Infomercial
❑ School/teacher ❑ Magazine/news review ❑ Recommended by family/friend

Do you own a computer? ❑ IBM/compatible ❑ Macintosh ❑ Other

❑ Yes, I am interested in purchasing the *SmartParenting* audio series of six hour-long cassettes at the special discounted price of $47.95 plus $4.50 shipping and handling. NY, FL, CO add state sales tax.
❑ My check or money order is enclosed.
❑ Charge my credit card: ❑ MasterCard ❑ Visa ❑ American Express ❑ Discover
Account number _____ Expiration date _____
Signature _____

Thank you! Your order will be on its way to you within 4 weeks.

## IF THE CARD BELOW HAS ALREADY BEEN SENT, YOU CAN STILL REGISTER WITH SMARTPARENTING!

**Just call or FAX 1-800-286-5869 today**
to join the SmartParenting Family
and receive our special offers listed
on the previous page!
Or write us at the following address
(please include your name and home address):

SmartParenting™ Inc.
Dept. CT/1
P.O. Box 116
Roslyn Heights, New York 11577-0116

INTERNET INFORMATION
Dr. Favaro's E-Mail address is drf@smartparenting.com
Visit us on the World Wide Web:
http://WWW.smartparenting.com/parents